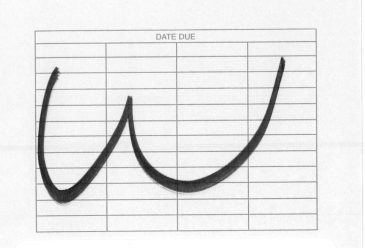

# THE BATTLE IN SEATTLE
## THE STORY BEHIND AND BEYOND THE WTO DEMONSTRATIONS

### JANET THOMAS

FULCRUM PUBLISHING

GOLDEN, COLORADO

*To Thomas, Nicole, and Michael and to Josh, Molly, and Emily—*
*who are at the very beginning of their lives.*
*May we not let them down.*

Library of Congress Cataloging-in-Publication Data

Thomas, Janet, 1944-
   The battle in Seattle : the story behind and beyond the WTO demonstrations /
Janet Thomas.
         p.    cm.
Includes bibliographical references and index.
   ISBN 1-55591-108-0 (pbk.)
1. World Trade Organization. 2. Demonstrations—Washington (State)—
Seattle. 3. International business enterprises. 4. Free trade—Environmental
aspects. 5. Free trade—Social aspects. 6. Foreign trade and employment.
7. Child labor. 8. International economic relations. 9. Developing countries—
Foreign economic relations. 10. Globalization. I. Title.
   HF1385.T48 2000
   303.6'1'09797772—dc21                          00-010867

Printed in Canada
0  9  8  7  6  5  4  3  2  1

Editorial: Marlene Blessing, Kris Fulsaas
Cover design and interior design: Kate Thompson
Formatting: Constance Bollen, cb graphics
Front cover photograph: Alli Starr, activist, organizer from Art and Revolution
San Francisco protesting the WTO in Seattle, 1999. Photograph by Dana
Schuerholz, Impact Visuals.

Printed on recycled paper.

Fulcrum Publishing
16100 Table Mountain Parkway, Suite 300
Golden, Colorado 80403
(800) 992-2908 • (303) 277-1623
www.fulcrum-books.com

# contents

# TIMETABLE
WTO* Protest Events in Seattle, November 26, 1999 (N26)
to December 6, 1999 (D6)


**N26, N27:** International Forum on Globalization (IFG) Teach-In with scholars and policy makers representing civil society from around the world. All events are sold out. The WTO Ministers come to town.

**N28:** Forum: The WTO and the Global War System; Jubilee 2000 Prayer Service at St. James Cathedral.

**N29:** Forum: The impacts of the WTO on Health and the Environment, with national and international speakers; demonstrations begin downtown; college students from around the country and civil society from around the world converge upon Seattle; there are excited TV interviews with trade leaders and economists; thousands pack an interfaith service for economic justice; at the Seattle Center the People's Gala unfolds with the likes of Tom Hayden, Jello Biafra, and documentarist Mike Moore dancing in the aisles.

**N30:** Thousands of students rally at the University of Washington, Seattle Central Community College, and other locations around the city and march to downtown Seattle; thousands of environmentalists, feminists, farmers, and human rights activists rally and march to downtown—all in protest of the policies of the WTO; inter-sections are occupied by turtles; students sit down in the streets, in front of hotels, and around the Convention Center; tear gassing begins; the Forum on Labor Rights/Standard of Living/Human Rights takes place at the United Methodist Church; the big international Labor Rally takes place at Memorial Stadium and 30,000 more people march downtown; KING-TV news announcers proudly point out that they will not be interviewing any protestors.

The tear gas escalates and rubber bullets fly; many arrests; Paul Hawken is gassed and outraged; Madeleine Albright is stuck in her hotel room; Seattle Mayor Paul Schell gets calls from D.C.; labor leaders can't get to the head of their parade; the

WTO can't get to their opening ceremonies; nor can they get to their private meetings in hotel rooms; the police can't move quickly in their battle gear. Violence increases and people are hurt by tear gas, pepper spray, rubber bullets, and truncheons; some windows get broken; the no-go zone is announced—people can't get to buses, taxis, or their cars; people are herded by the police out of the downtown no-go area and up into the nearby neighborhoods of Capital Hill where residents are arrested for going to, or coming from the corner store. Police violence continues into the night; hundreds are arrested.

The same video loops of violence—the broken window at Starbucks and the dumpster fire in Seattle—are shown repeatedly on television around the world. Hundreds are arrested, no media asks why, none of the WTO ministers ask why, the mayor doesn't ask why, the police chief doesn't ask why. The fire department does ask why they should hose people, noting that it hurts, then refusing to do so.

**D1:** Forum on Women/Democracy/Sovereignty/Development at United Methodist Church; more arrests, rallies, marches, demonstrations, tear gas, pepper spray, and rubber bullets. Labor takes a stand and the steelworkers lead a parade.

**D2:** Forum on Food, Agriculture and Biotechnology: Food Safety and Security at United Methodist Church; more arrests, rallies, marches, demonstrations, tear gas, pepper spray and rubber bullets. Citizens surround the jail in a support vigil for those arrested.

**D3:** The people of the Northwest get fed up and take to the streets en masse for democracy and civil rights. There are negotiations with the police and the long vigil at the jail continues. The dissension at the WTO escalates. It's announced that charges will be dropped and people released.

**D4:** The front page headline in the The Seattle Times is "Talks collapse; meeting ends." The WTO ministers go home.

**D5:** Continued vigil at the jail.

**D6:** Last person out of jail, free buses and free parking downtown for Christmas shoppers.

*The WTO is a global governing body consisting of trade ministers from countries around the world. They are appointed to the WTO by government leaders and typically represent the corporate sector. The WTO has its own hierarchy and subsequent conflicts. Decisions are made behind closed doors that can challenge the sovereignty of local, state and national laws if such laws are considered by the WTO as deterrents to international trade.

# INTRODUCTION

"Tell me, what is it you plan to do
with your one wild and precious life?"
—Mary Oliver, Pulitzer Prize–winning poet,
    in "The Summer Day" from *House of Light*

On Thanksgiving Day 1999, my son, Colin, and I took an afternoon stroll along the edge of Ballard, a Seattle neighborhood fondly referred to as the Scandinavian capital of the country. We'd driven down from San Juan Island earlier in the day to share the traditional holiday meal with friends who live on Ballard's west side. It was bright and sunny; the waters of Puget Sound were clear and quiet, as were the streets we walked.

We got down near the Hiram M. Chittenden Locks, which link the saltwater excitement of Puget Sound with the freshwater harbor of Lake Union, and noticed that a small grocery store was open. Colin wanted a bottle of water, so we went in. Still it was quiet. We'd seen no one else out walking on the streets and very few cars, and there was no one in the store but the clerk. We wished him a happy Thanksgiving. He was soft-spoken and shyly attentive. I recall being quite struck by his gentleness, and, like the ferry workers earlier in the morning, he seemed extra kind on this holiday when everyone else was off with everyone else.

As we walked toward the counter, I was telling Colin that I was planning to go home to the island early the next morning because on the following Monday, I was thinking of coming back to Seattle to participate in WTO week. We got to the counter and the gentle fellow said, "Just a minute, please," and disappeared. When he returned he was happy and animated as he handed each of us a bright green bumper sticker that read: "WTO. If it doesn't work for working families, it doesn't work." In small letters at the bottom it read "AFL-CIO." The gentle man, who had overheard our WTO talk, was no longer shy. "Yes, you go, you go," he said with a surprising fervor. And so I went. The rest, as they say, is history.

✿   ✿   ✿   ✿   ✿

WTO week in Seattle was a global tailspin at the end of the century, a fly in the face of the new millennium, an elephant in the ointment. It was an unruly uprising of the masses, a divine intervention, a traffic nightmare, a human rights activist's dream. The cab drivers didn't drive; the longshoremen closed down the ports on the entire West Coast; the peasant farmers came to town; the students spoke up and sat down; good people taught; and the people reigned. Many voices, in many languages, were all saying the same thing at once: "Down with Corporate Colonialism. Up with Global Economic Justice for Everybody Right Now Everywhere."

Yet the issues are rife with a quieter complexity. The economic imperative behind the things in our lives links us all together— sometimes in wealth, sometimes in poverty. Often in a gray shaded area where we are unaware of the impact of our decisions, our choices, our yearnings. When we yearn for more, more, more while so many others yearn for just enough, our own spirits as well as the health of our human family members suffer. How did this happen? How did we get into this frenzy of acquisition in which stuff has come to equate with spirit, consumerism with patriotism and human worth with human wealth? Money has never bought happiness and it never will. Yet we continue to behave as though sometime, somehow, it will happen, and finally, after all is said and bought, we'll be happy. Is it this fragile hope that has driven the corporate ethic to such obsessive profit-making? And is anybody out there happy yet?

It's a corporate illness that pervades our culture, and we're all part of the equation. We have been taken in by our own mythology—the mythology of materialism. Money has become the ultimate meaning and there can never be enough. Yet those at the "top," whose worth is measured by numbers, can be as destitute as those at the "bottom," who are struggling to meet their most basic needs. Who's to say who is poverty stricken? Spiritual poverty, too, causes hunger, dis-ease, and death. Why the obsession with money?

I've never had much of the stuff, so it's an easy question for me to ask. But I have had a job that took me to places I couldn't afford to go, so I have lived in the lap of luxury for days at a time. As editor of *SPA* magazine, I would leave the messy, pencil-driven world of publishing behind and go off on a "business" trip to experience luxury. It was nice. I liked it. I spent a week in a big fluffy robe at a spa in Florida and got pampered beyond recognition. I wallowed in Roman baths in Rome. I even got to go to a private spa in Hawaii with Fabio, which would have cost a mere mortal more than $20,000—even without Fabio (who is a very lovely man behind that lovely face and in spite of that lovely hair). Sometimes I'd wonder what it would be like to live in that realm, where money really does talk its way through your life. I think I would be very afraid of what it would say.

Money cannot live our lives for us, but the corporate illness that defines value in numbers of dollars and amount of stuff is trying to convince us that it can. That it's what makes life worth living. But *life* is what makes life worth living. Money can come between us and our lives. It can actually keep us from being happy, from being human, just as a terrible lack of it can deprive us of what we need to be human.

A few years before I fell into the world of high living through publishing, I had a job cooking at a Buddhist retreat center where money really was no object. Fifteen people were in silent retreat for a year. Not only was there no money floating around, nobody could talk about it either. And for some, there was no touching it. One visiting teacher, Ajaan Pabakaro, came out of the Buddhist forest tradition of Thailand, in which money cannot be touched, nothing can be asked for, cars cannot be driven, and the one meal of the day is to be eaten before noon. Ajaan Pabakaro is a tall, handsome (imagine Fabio with a shaved head) American who first went to Thailand on R&R from the Vietnam War, where he was a fighter pilot. The Thai forest tradition caught his heart and his mind, and he returned there after the war and trained in the Buddhist path based on *Vinaya,* the Buddha's strict monastic code. Out of the jet fighter and into the fire. During his New Year's teaching weekend at the retreat center, Ajaan Pabakaro was accompanied by an assistant who handled his money and mediated his life with the world in which he traveled. Being in his presence was like hanging out with the real Santa Claus, the one who fits down the chimney into our hearts and gives us what we really need, undivided and loving attention. He could see right to the core of our yearning. He was happy, funny, and utterly penniless. What does money have to do with anything? And why does it have to do with everything?

These are the questions underlying the questions that were raised during WTO week in Seattle. And they are questions for us all—whether we are highly paid corporate execs or highly busy peasant farmers. Our lives are formed by our attitudes about money and what it means to us. How having it or not having it serves our quality of life, and life itself. WTO week was ripe with the meaning of money, yet it was issues and individuals that enlivened the streets and took hold in the hearts and minds of those of us who were there. The confluence of people on the streets was nothing short of stunning. The international nature of the crowd—farmers from South America, union groups from Canada, activists from India, Africa, Asia, and Europe, indigenous peoples from the Northwest and around the world—was a rising tide of inspiration. There were moms with kids, students with stamina, and labor leaders with big bellies. It was a great ruckus, a carnival of cause. It had all the grace and grandeur of a global family reunion—complete with teenagers and turtles, misfits and ministers. It was a parade, and everybody came.

> **"Some may remember the final days of the old century, when the World Trade Organization was in town, as dark days in Seattle. I won't. I'll remember those glimpses of a renewed and restored human community."**
>
> —The Reverend Tom Quigley, president-director, Church Council of Greater Seattle

But you had to be there. If you weren't, it was a week of shame, a shocking example of violence and mayhem, a blight on Seattle's shining reputation, a disgrace.

The discrepancy between being in the experience and then seeing it portrayed in the press was like cuddling up with your teddy bear and waking up with a crocodile in your bed. It was a bad dream. A repetitive bad dream. Over and over and over, the rest of the world was exposed to the same loop of burning trash cans, black-masked marauders, and broken windowpanes. It seemed as though every coffee bean in the city was on fire, every dot-com in jeopardy, every shopping opportunity destroyed. It was a desecration of Christmas. It was a bad joke.

What really wasn't funny was what *wasn't* shown on TV. The extensive police violence against nonviolent people, the systemic economic violence against much of humanity, the unrelenting violence perpetrated against individuals fighting for human rights and freedoms all over the world, the ever-increasing rate of hunger, disease, and illiteracy among so many people, whose countries' resources are serving the profits of outside companies rather than the needs of the population. All these issues, along with the growing concern about our environment, our farmers, our labor community, our food, our young people, were why the streets of Seattle were overrun with people singing, chanting, and shouting out for change.

WTO week in Seattle was a week of scholarship. A week in which concerned scientists, policy makers, business visionaries, labor leaders, and savvy activists came to Seattle to speak out against economic injustice and its impact. There were familiar names in the crowd: activist icon and presidential candidate Ralph Nader, author and green businessman Paul Hawken, Body Shop founder Anita Roddick, Teamsters president Jim Hoffa Jr., Sierra Club director Carl Pope, and radio commentator Jim Hightower were just a few notables on the scene. Vandana Shiva came from India, Jose Bové came from France, Michael Moore came from Flint, Michigan; and thousands came from around the world to express their hopes for, and fears about, the future. It was a week of sustained compassion and concern expressed by the people on the planet for the people on the planet. A week in which civil society took the helm, charted the course, and steered the way toward a landscape in which life is the answer and profit-at-all-cost is in question. It was a week of global populism at large, but for far too many, it was simply portrayed as the week that Seattle was disgraced.

This book, however, is about the grace of it all. It's about the real faces in the crowd, the extraordinary ordinary people who helped to give Seattle a new and different face during WTO week, the face of a different future. They were all shapes, ages, colors, nationalities; all intent with reasons for being present. "Who are they?" I wondered, as I looked around during the big labor march on N30 (November 30, 1999—N30 in the lexicon of WTO-speak). Why were they here?

And why were they everywhere? Thousands packed the teach-ins on the weekend before N30; thousands were at the multi-faith gathering at the First United Methodist Church downtown; tens of thousands circled the now-demolished Kingdome in support of Third World debt relief; thousands sat in nonviolent protest in intersections, in front of hotels, at the Washington State Convention and Trade Center; thousands crowded into forums about genetically modified foods, logging practices, labor issues, human rights, animal rights. I ate hot dogs with steelworkers at the huge labor rally in Seattle's Memorial Stadium, and walked with Japanese rice farmers in the labor march that swelled the city streets to their very limits. I didn't get tear-gassed, pepper-sprayed, or thrown in jail. My civil rights weren't violated, my human rights weren't ignored, my community wasn't invaded. I had a good time.

Lots of people didn't. There was shocking violence perpetrated against peaceful protesters, against unwitting city residents simply doing what they do every day, against demonstrators trying to get home and ordinary citizens trying to get to work, against the unruly and the otherwise. But as far as I've been able to figure out, not one of the so-called anarchists responsible for the property damage in the city was arrested. More than 600 ordinary people were rounded up, many of them aggressively, and put in jail for simply exercising their civil rights. The police were protecting profit and property, not people. And it wasn't their fault. Like the rest of us, they, too, have lost their freedom to a preordained culture of consumerism. But, as Noam Chomsky says, "Even a real tyranny is not immune to public pressures." Researching and writing this book was like breaking through a time barrier. I was propelled through a veil of complacency into a landscape of truth where all was not well—but at last it was real. And it made all the difference. The corporate clock was stopped. What I discovered was deep time. A place where the past and the future are still alive. The place of Seven Generations.

In the tradition of many Native American cultures, life is lived with concern for not just the next generation, but the next *seven* generations. Decisions are made to honor those who have lived before us and those who will live in the future. The people whom I talked to, and those whose WTO stories are in this book, are all, in some way, living in deep time. They are bringing history into their lives and living consciously toward the future. None of them gauge their day by the split-second vagaries of the stock market, or the comings and goings of the latest dot-com catastrophe. Their lives, like most lives on the planet, are linked to that which is most personal and most timeless—time and its meaning.

Chris Peters, executive director of the Seventh Generation Fund, spoke at the Indigenous Forum when he was in Seattle during WTO week. "We need to look at a new narrative if we are going to survive in the next millennium," he said. "That new narrative has to be founded upon principles that the whole earth is sacred, all life is sacred."

The word "sovereign" resonated through the week. The sovereignty of the WTO over individual nations is the most visible threat. But we forget about the sovereignty of individuals over their own lives, and the sovereignty of indigenous peoples over their own lands. It is not only the sovereignty of governments large and small, town and country, that is at stake. It's the sovereignty of fundamental freedoms that are being sacrificed to a faceless, corporate illness that is defining our global culture.

We need a new story. And in many ways it's an old one. This is one of the deepest tragedies of our time. We are drawn more and more to the wisdom and spiritual wealth in the cultures of the First Peoples of the planet, yet we are systematically exploiting their resources to serve our material needs. We get co-opted by a materialistic lifestyle, get lost in the meaninglessness of it all, then turn to the old-wisdom cultures, which are reeling from exploitation, to help us get back on track. As WTO week unfolded and the stories rose up from the people, this was where the heart lay broken. We are desperate for the wisdom of old because we have lost our own. And now the WTO threatens the very autonomy of our indigenous peoples as well as that of our national governments. All to feed the corporate bottom line, where numbers say it all.

But the numbers on the streets of Seattle told their own story. And it was a good one. The stories in this book are of ordinary people who were there, who are creating new narratives without forgetting the old. They are not out in the forefront of global leadership, but they reflect the leadership of civil society around the globe. Their stories are uncommonly common. They could be anybody. This was the lesson of WTO week in Seattle. It could be anybody out there—and it usually is—who is making a difference, effecting change, putting the brakes on greed and material consumption.

It was a conscious decision to tell the stories of people in the Northwest, not because these are such special people (even if they are), but because they are an integral part of the place where it all happened. They reflect the local landscape that hosted the global gathering. They are citizens of the world, in the world. And they just happen to live in or near the city that lost its face and gained its soul during WTO week. No matter how much wealth washes upon these shores, there is a spirit of Seattle that is sometimes down but never out. Perhaps it's because of the man the town was named after, Chief Seattle, who said, "At night, when the streets of your cities and villages are silent and you think them deserted, they will throng with the returning hosts that once filled them and still love this beautiful land. The White Man will never be alone."

There is a lot that's not covered in this book. The media minefield would take an army to excavate. The police presence remains a mystery; some were from the City of Seattle, others from other cities, some came from the Washington State Patrol and various federal agencies. Some came from the military. Some came straight out of *Robocop*. It is too easy to vilify the behavior of the police en masse, without also taking into account who was telling them what to do, where to go, and when to eat, pee, and go home. It was a mess of "police" violence in the same sense that it was a mess of "anarchist" violence: Unless individuals can be identified, their stories can't be told.

The same is true of all the city, county, state, and federal decision-makers. They jockeyed for kudos when it was announced that the WTO was coming to town, and then they all ran for cover after civil society sent it packing. Those folks have stories, too. In spite of all the reports.

And, oh, the reports. The finger-pointing going on has a half-life longer than a rubber bullet's. There are city reports, city council reports, county reports, police reports, ACLU reports, lawyers' reports, citizens' reports, and reports on reports. Each one warrants at least one investigative reporter's life.

It's what wasn't reported that counts, the people around us and around the world who are living for the seventh generation, who are concerned not only about what they are getting out of this life, but about what they will be leaving behind. The billions of people who aren't perfect, who make mistakes, who start over every day, sometimes every hour, in an attempt to put things right.

One of the stories in this book is that of Ethiopian national Hannah Petros, who was one of the organizers of Seattle's Jubilee event to bring attention to global debt in Third World countries. When she described her experience during WTO week in Seattle, she said, "It was like a dark room without windows. We opened the door to let in some light. After WTO week was over, suddenly the dark was gone, but not the light. The light shines on as bright as ever."

# 1 TURTLE ISLAND—IN WHICH BEN WHITE TAKES A BATH AND THE TURTLES TAKE THE DAY

"My soul turns into a tree,
And an animal, and a cloud bank.
Then changed and odd it comes home
And asks me questions. What should I reply?"
—Hermann Hesse
    Translated by Robert Bly

Ben White gets most of his good ideas in the bathtub—which seems appropriate for the man responsible for the herds of turtles that strolled, roamed, and infiltrated the streets of Seattle during WTO week. The turtle people, with their big-eyed hoods and exposed undersides, seemed tender and vulnerable amid the dramas playing out all around them. Yet they captured the imagination—and media attention—around the world.

"I've come to the conclusion that strident doesn't work," said White, in our first interview. This is a startling statement coming from a fellow who's locked himself in a holding tank with whales; been arrested umpteen times for protecting dolphins, goats, elephants, and all fur-bearing beings; climbed buildings and circus ceilings to hang banners; slept 100 feet high in a tree to protect a cedar; and generally been on the front lines of animal and environmental protection for thirty years.

Ben White is my neighbor, but we've never been neighborly. I've been aware of him primarily as a parent; he's a single parent raising a young son and a teenage daughter. Our chauffeur schedules have overlapped as we drive our kids to school and our daughters to ride horses. We've occasionally tried to do the carpool thing, but it's never quite worked out. He drives a dusty old Volvo with a bumper sticker that reads "Yes on 655 for Bears and Cougars." He always looks preoccupied. I knew he was an animal-rights activist, and I heard him testify eloquently at the San Juan County Jet-Ski hearings in the mid-'90s. Jet-Skis/personal watercraft are hard on marine life not only because they pollute the habitat, but because animals can't hear their engines until it's too late for them to get out of the way.

In the fall of '99, I noticed that the roof of White's car was often loaded with cardboard when it went by my house. And when I took my routine walk with my dog, Buck, to our local beach, I noticed mountains of cardboard piling up in his yard. I had no idea that it would be transformed into street turtles for WTO week.

"Turtles are the most successful life-form on earth," White told me. "They have existed for 200 million years, sea turtles for 90 million years." He went on to talk about the creation myth in which our planet, Turtle Island, sits on a turtle, which is sitting on another turtle, which is sitting on yet another turtle, and on and on throughout the universe. "Hark again to those roots, to see our ancient solidarity, and then to the work of being together on Turtle Island," writes poet Gary Snyder, who has been White's favorite writer for decades. And now the turtles are endangered.

In the 1980s, it was discovered that each year, hundreds of thousands of sea turtles throughout the oceans of the world were drowning in shrimp nets. The solution to this mass drowning was for shrimp trawlers to use turtle exclusion devices (TEDs) in their nets. A TED, which costs $50–$400 per net, deflects trapped turtles to an escape hatch at the mouth of the long, tunnel-like nets. It does not interfere with catching shrimp. Since 1989, the TED has been mandatory on most U.S. shrimp trawlers. In that same year, under a provision of the Endangered Species Act, foreign shrimp boats that harvest in waters shared with sea turtles were required to reduce turtle deaths to U.S. levels by May 1, 1991, or they would not be able to sell shrimp in the U.S. market. This law was immediately applied to fourteen Atlantic and Caribbean countries, but the largest exporters of wild-caught shrimp to the United States (India, Indonesia, Thailand, Mexico, Malaysia, Brazil, Korea, and Japan) were not held accountable because of a shipment-by-shipment loophole that was overlooked by U.S. officials.

On June 7, 1994, with the turtle population dwindling, the Earth Island Institute, the American Society for the Prevention of Cruelty to Animals, the Humane Society of the U.S., the Sierra Club, and the Georgia Fishermen's Association filed a lawsuit against the U.S. Departments of State and Commerce for not upholding the turtle-protection law. More than 2 million U.S. citizens were represented by these groups. A year and a half later, in January 1996, Judge Thomas J. Aquilino of the

U.S. Court of International Trade ruled in favor of the lawsuit: All countries that want to sell shrimp to the United States were required to adopt sea turtle conservation measures—or face a ban on sales.

Later that year, India, Malaysia, Pakistan, and Thailand filed a complaint to the WTO claiming unfair trade practices by the United States because of its pro-turtle policies. In response, in late 1998, the WTO ruled against U.S. law and demanded the United States stop any embargo of foreign shrimp. The WTO ruling said that requiring these countries to use turtle conservation measures was arbitrary and unjustifiable discrimination. The United States could not control the shrimp sold within its borders, nor how it was caught.

> "Sea turtles have an inherent right to exist, beyond all trade and economic considerations. To measure them in economic terms is to set the framework for their extinction."
>
> —Sea Turtle Restoration Project

The treatment of turtles has taken on global proportions, and these gentle creatures have become a symbol of the dangers of WTO rulings. Why does this world body have the power to overturn the conservation laws of a country in order to serve unencumbered international trade? It's a question that's thorny with answers.

But the turtle problem resonates much closer to home as well. "There's a huge fad of having turtles for pets," said White. "We're taking them all. And now all seven species of sea turtles are endangered."

❀  ❀  ❀  ❀  ❀

White, who has been active in many movements over the years—civil rights, anti-war, anti-nuclear, pro-environment, and animal protection—was first inspired to animal activism in 1971. He'd fallen and injured himself while working as an arborist (a tree doctor) and had gone to the Big Island, Hawaii, to recuperate. "I was there by myself," said White. "I was meditating. It was *Be Here Now* time."

While on the Big Island, he went out and swam with the spinner dolphins off the Kona coast. "It sounds trite," he said, pausing a long moment as he began his story. "But swimming with dolphins changed my life."

The dolphins were out at the mouth of the bay, and he swam out to join them. "I was surprised at how big they were," he said. "One of them hit me with its sonar. It was an amazing feeling throughout my whole body. Then it turned sideways and looked at me. It regarded me."

This sense of being seen, of being regarded, had a big impact on White. "It shattered my worldview," he said. He spent a half hour with the dolphins that day, and it defined the rest of his life. "I made a vow," he said. "I swore that I would do everything I could to be their voice in the world of humankind."

In the 1970s, White educated himself about dolphins, including researching the records of the National Marine Fisheries Service, in which he came across the sad statistics about dolphin survival in captivity. "I realized what a deadly, mean business captivity is," he said. In 1981, White joined Sea Shepherd International, and eventually set up the Dolphin Rescue Brigade in 1988. The first interference with a dolphin capture happened off the Florida panhandle. The rescues were often a dive-and-release operation, usually at night, and performed without diving equipment. "The easiest way to cut them loose was to go in like a swamp monster and come in from the side of the cage," said White. Free-diving without masks and snorkels meant that there was less noise and no glare. There was, however, adrenaline. "I'm a risk junkie," said White, who quoted outdoor writer Tim Cahill on the vagaries of the subject. "But when I was climbing trees for a job, I risked my life every day." He stopped to think about it a moment, then said, "It's not a bad thing. You just have to know you're doing it."

✿　✿　✿　✿　✿

White lived inside WTO week in Seattle for at least ten months before it happened. He was at the first planning meeting. "There were about forty of us grizzled old activists," said White. "We looked at each other in amazement. 'Can you believe they are coming *here*?' we asked one another. 'They don't know what they're in for.'"

This is not a complacent part of the country. The Northwest has a long and illustrious history of activism in labor rights and environmental protection, as well as in the anti-war and anti-nuclear movements. Everyone knew that, and understood what it meant. Everyone, that is, but the organizers of the WTO ministerial meetings, who somewhat obliviously saw their hosts, Microsoft's Bill Gates and Boeing's Phil Condit, as the accurate reflection of the psyche of Seattle.

That first organizing meeting was held in early February 1999, at the King County Labor Temple in Seattle's Belltown neighborhood. "It was clear that this thing was going to be big," said White. The eclectic nature of the participants, the passion of their concerns, and the WTO link that brought them together were at once startling and invigorating.

Mike Dolan of the broad-based Washington, D.C., organization Public Citizen was instrumental in getting everyone together at that first meeting. For nearly thirty years, Ralph Nader's group has been working diligently to expose the wasteful and exploitive aspects of government and corporate policies. The WTO, organized in 1994, became an immediate Nader target. Ironically, by giving itself a name, the WTO suddenly made tangible and visible all the behind-the-scenes trade policies that had been developing over the years. In 1999, Lori Wallach and Michelle Sforza of Public Citizen's Global Trade Watch came out with the book *Whose Trade Organization? Corporate Globalization and the Erosion of Democracy*. It's a scathing exposé of the ways in which WTO policies affect our environment, the quality of our food, our public health, our economic well-being, human rights, and labor rights—all on a global scale.

Public Citizen knows how to organize well. As a national nonprofit organization with more than 150,000 members, Public Citizen has activists all over the country. One of them, Sally Soriano, lives in Seattle; she rallied the locals to those early meetings and became a driving force behind the anti-WTO momentum. Soriano, who went on to manage the campaign for universal health care in Washington State, the Health Care 2000 initiative (I-725), was on the steering committee of the *other* WTO Host Committee, People for Fair Trade. The name claiming was only part of the sleight-of-mind that contributed to the quickly seeded grassroots movement that grew into such a whopping groundswell of support. As the official WTO organizers came up with committee names, the activist organizers came up with their own. It was a chess game, and there were times when it was hard to tell who the players were. As quickly as a website was opened by the official WTO, an unofficial one would surface with a similar name. But it was a game with repercussions, most of them in-house.

"There were bumps along the way," said Ben White. "For one thing, what do we call ourselves?" The organizing group had representatives from all over the activist spectrum. Earth First!ers, organic farmers, labor representatives, academicians, university students, puppet makers, gay and lesbian activists, peace workers, and, yes, anarchists—from *Seattle;* the list went on and on. So did the controversy over the name. White's favorite was the "WTO Welcome Wagon." Somebody even came up with a logo—a wagon carrying a prostrate, tied-up corporate muck-a-muck Gulliver who was being scrambled over by a horde of Lilliputians with big intentions. "But the women involved with labor unions took great umbrage," said White. "They said this was serious business." The "WTO Welcome Wagon" moniker was shelved.

Then there was the monthlong argument about whether the slogan should be "No to WTO." "'Do we really want to kill it?' was the question," said White. "Or do we want to change it?" Eventually the answer was "No, this thing's gotta go. It can't be amended." The battle lines were being drawn through the messy process of democracy. "We weathered the divisiveness," said White. "But people got tired. We started to lose zip."

The antidote came in the form of Dr. Michael Fox, senior scholar in bioethics at the Humane Society of the United States, who flew in from Washington, D.C., in July 1999. At one of the meetings, Ben White had approached Sally Soriano about focusing on animal activism. This was another contentious issue. "Animal protection is the illegitimate child of the activist world," said White. But thanks to Lisa Wathne of the Seattle Humane Society, who brought out the troops to hear Fox, a couple hundred people showed up at the meeting. "It was a pivotal moment," said White, who considers Wathne an unsung hero on the WTO front.

> "Old hippies don't die, they just lie low until the laughter stops and their time comes around again."
>
> —Joseph Gallivan in *The Sun—A Magazine of Ideas*, January 1999

Fox, author of *Superpigs and Wondercorn* and *Eating with Conscience: The Bioethics of Food*, addressed the issues of genetically modified foods, biotechnology, and animal research. He spoke about the need to "apply global bioethics to transform global capitalism into a more enlightened and caring enterprise." He spoke about the dangers of patented seeds, the engineering and cloning of animals, "the holocaust of the animal kingdom and the annihilation of the natural world." He spoke about the spiritual, moral, and ethical dimensions of sustainable and ecological agriculture: real food, real farmers, a real economy. Fox's presentation riveted the audience. "Food linked it all together," said White. "Food linked *us* all together." Suddenly environmental rights, human rights, and animal rights were all in the same corner, and there was no looking back. "There was such a buzz, such excitement," said White. "Such a feeling of 'gotta get those bastards.'"

✿   ✿   ✿   ✿   ✿

Sometime soon after, White climbed back into his bathtub. "I don't like meetings," he said. "It was time to do something." The link between the WTO and the plight of sea turtles inspired his thinking. "It was such a bad decision," he said of the WTO shrimp trade ruling. "Here the WTO was saying, 'Yes, [turtle conservation] works. There are good reasons to require the TEDs—and, no, you can't do it.'"

The turtles themselves inspired his street theater instincts. He described the ancient animals' placid demeanor and their great patience. The way they would most likely turn and gaze at an aggressor, as if to say, "Go ahead, hurt me. You're really just hurting yourself." And then live on for another million years. They were the perfect image—gentle, stalwart, and true. But how, exactly, were they to be reproduced for street action?

One day illustrator Bryn Barnard, White's friend and collaborator, took a piece of paper, made a few folds, cut a few curves—and there was a mini-turtle, ready to be replicated on a big scale. White scoured the neighborhood and found a ready supply of cardboard at a local freight company. "I asked the guy what kind of beer he drank," said White.

---

## The Biotech Agenda

Some 130 biotechnology activists from twenty countries all over the world met in Seattle on November 29, 1999, and agreed to the following actions:

■ To keep biotechnology out of the WTO Ministerial Declaration and out of its future activities

■ To emphasize that the Biosafety Protocol is the correct forum to assess, regulate, and monitor the transfer of genetically modified organisms (GMOs) and products thereof

■ To support the African proposal to ban patents of living organisms and their parts

■ To institute a global ban on all genetically engineered processes, foods, crops, and animals

■ To require complete labeling of all substances and processes, including GMOs and pesticides

■ To criminalize biopiracy and stealing of indigenous genes and knowledge of farmers, peasants, and indigenous peoples

■ To establish strict corporate liability for all economic loss and personal injury resulting from genetically engineered crops and food

■ To intensify global campaigns for organic agriculture and other forms of ecological farming

—Reported by Dr. Michael Fox in *Acres U.S.A.*, March 2000

"When he said 'Bud,' I thought 'Oh, no.' I wouldn't buy it because it's owned by Anheuser Busch, which owns Sea World." The fellow's second choice was Miller, yet another eyebrow raiser. But White swallowed his politics and delivered a twelve-pack of Miller every time he arrived to load cardboard onto the top of his car.

White cut out the patterns and delivered them to Seattle, where turtle-making parties took over. "We did them cheaply and by hand," he said. "Everybody loved them."

Some of the first turtles were put together at the home of Nancy Pennington, a longtime animal activist who lives in West Seattle. For the past three years, she has been working to free a capuchin monkey that's been in a small cage in a Seattle dentist's office for twenty-three years. Periodically, to get attention paid to the monkey's plight, Pennington gets into a cage herself in front of the downtown dental office where the monkey is held. "There are advantages to being sixty-two years old," she said. "The media shows up." Pennington was also a turtle for WTO week and had her picture in *Newsweek*, which was seen by her son who lives in Barcelona. "It was a wonderful experience," she said.

The turtles were stored in a cold, damp warehouse on Rainier Avenue in south Seattle, where the last of them were completed just hours before WTO week. White credits David Solnit, a carpenter from San Francisco and a member of Art and Revolution, for helping with some critical details: forget duct tape, it's ugly; use cloth for the shoulder straps and try stapling them; and for painting the shells, use exterior latex.

White, who'd had the turtle idea in the first place, was attending to such details in the last place. "I had to stay focused. I had to do this one thing," he said. But he was focusing on turtle tactics as well. For the planned and permitted march on Monday, November 29, 1999, he wanted to have the turtles make a resounding and traffic-stopping statement at four of the busy intersections around the Washington State Convention and Trade Center, site of the WTO ministerial meetings. He figured that 240 turtles would do it.

✿  ✿  ✿  ✿  ✿

The convention center sprawls over a couple of city blocks very close to the heart of downtown Seattle. As with a lot of development in the city over the years, where to put the convention center was almost as controversial as whether or not it should even be built in the first place. There was a creative compromise. By building it utilizing the air space over the freeway, it lessened the impact on the limited land available downtown.

For a touch of green, the convention center was linked to Freeway Park, an oasis of gardens and waterfalls created years ago on a lid over the interstate. Tendrils of ivy cascade down the freeway walls from the roof garden; the high glass walls of the convention center rise up above. The freeway slices along underneath, effectively blocking access to the convention center from the east.

Approximately a half mile to the west, the waters of Elliott Bay are another effective boundary. Both the freeway and the bay became defining points of a demarcation zone during WTO week, but during normal life they serve to keep downtown Seattle contained and vertical, and the nearby residential areas residential. The convention center itself is bordered by Pike Street, Union Street, Seventh Avenue, and, rather irregularly, the freeway.

Just to the northeast of the convention center, on the other side of the freeway, is Capitol Hill, a neighborhood loaded with apartments, condos, and both fine and funky old houses. At the top of the hill is Broadway, where the street scene is gay-friendly, youth-friendly, and radical-chic. This area is also home to Volunteer Park, where

> "What of the ethics of labeling all genetically engineered products and processes? Consumers surely have a right to know."
>
> —Dr. Michael Fox at the Seattle Round Agriculture Committee press briefing, November 30, 1999

'60s activists gathered in regular protest against the Vietnam War.

Within blocks of the convention center, to the west, are all the major hotels, including the Sheraton and the Westin—where the WTO ministers stayed during their visit. This area is also Seattle's retail core, which was gearing up for the biggest shopping week of the year. Which in 1999 just happened to be WTO week.

The lay of the land, the sea, the neighborhoods, the convention center and the freeway running through it, combined with the WTO in town, holiday shoppers, city workers, fair-trade activists, environmentalists, and every shape, size, and color of human rights activist, made for a carnival of opportunity. Those organizing in opposition to WTO policies could use everything from geography to geopolitics to map out a strategy that would flatten the tires of the official WTO Welcome Wagon. And they did.

On Tuesday, November 30, 1999—N30—opening day of the WTO meetings, Ben White's goal was to lead a smaller herd of turtles in civil disobedience to block delegate access to the WTO meetings scheduled for the convention center. On Monday, however, it was a big party.

The buildup to WTO week in Seattle was already ringing in triumph by the time the turtles gathered for that first Monday foray into the streets. The weekend teach-ins, organized by the International Forum on Globalization, had been an astonishing success, with turn-away crowds at all the venues, some of which required tickets from Ticketmaster. At Benaroya Hall, the fancy new home of the Seattle Symphony just five blocks from the convention center, Friday night's "The Impacts of Economic Globalization" was the hottest ticket in town. The same was true on Saturday, when the topic branched out to include forests, rivers, and oceans as well as labor rights, biotechnology, global finance, and corporate power. About a mile north of Benaroya Hall, at the King County Labor Temple, a two-day People's Tribunal played out the case of WTO and multinational crimes, complete with judge and jury.

In Tacoma, 30 miles south of Seattle, the United Steelworkers of America held a daylong conference featuring Steelworkers President George Becker, U.S. Senator Paul Wellstone (Minnesota), and Lori Wallach from Public Citizen, among others. Seattle activists were galvanized when they learned that the steelworkers had chartered several entire airplanes to get the rank-and-file to WTO week (Thanksgiving holiday flights had been filled far earlier than usual, creating a mad scramble for flights to Seattle).

A plethora of anti-WTO events were held all over Seattle on the pre-WTO weekend. "Alternatives to Corporate Globalization" drew speakers from around the world, as did the International Women Workers Forum and "The Need to Advance the People's Resistance Against Imperialist Globalization." The global representation at all the events was a powerful and poignant reminder to everyone of how deeply the people of the planet are connected. A great spirit of celebration was growing, and the weekend culminated Sunday evening in music, dancing, and a Jubilee 2000 Prayer Service at St. James Cathedral, just a few blocks southeast of the convention center. It was a prelude to the "Break the Circle of Debt" Jubilee 2000 event scheduled for the following evening.

Monday, N29, was designated as Environment and Human Health Day. The Plenary Session, held at the First United Methodist Church at Fifth and Marion (a few blocks southwest of the convention center and hotels), was "The Human Face of Trade: Health and the Environment." It was to be followed by a march and rally—all prearranged and with necessary permits—at noon. The rallying cry was: "Make Trade Clean, Green, and Fair!"

Ben White knew that 120 turtles had signed up ahead of time for N29, and he was hoping that the momentum from the teach-ins would help fill in the ranks. On Monday morning, he loaded the turtle suits into the "Cows with Guns" bus (a black-and-white getaway vehicle used for cows on the run from the slaughterhouse) and headed off to the church to hand them out. The place was packed. "We turned away at least 100 people," said White, shaking his head in amazement. "What is so compelling about being a turtle?" he asked.

What indeed? None of the teach-in events had focused on animal rights, and this pissed White off. After all, Dr. Michael Fox from the Humane Society was the one who had nailed the final spike of commitment that had coalesced the anti-WTO planning committee. But animal protection wasn't high on the list of priorities. Even trees seemed easier to support. Yet it was the WTO decision against the big and benign sea turtle that had garnered so much attention. It made a clear picture of one policy within a WTO soup of policies that were often all too easily hidden by jargon and complexity. Turtles have survived a long time as a species, and they live a long time as individuals. And, after all, it's always the turtle that's supposed to win the race. What happens if there isn't one around to lumber across the finish line?

Two hundred and forty people went in one door of the church and came out another, all turtled up and ready to go. They were environmentalists, steelworkers, church members, college students, feminists, animal activists, and people working for the right to eat, have decent shelter, and enjoy good health. The herd gathered outside in front of the church to wait for instructions. White tapped into turtle consciousness. He thanked everyone for coming and went over their animal obligations. "One: Not only are we nonviolent, we're anti-violence," White told the crowd. If the turtles encountered any violence, their job was to stop and surround it with peaceful turtle power. "Two: If you do anything aggressive, you will be de-turtled on the spot." This included hostile language as well as actions. "Three: Comport yourself as a turtle. Turtles are ancient repositories of wisdom. They never fight back. We're representing them. We owe it to turtles to be their voice." Number four was

"A deadly monoculture of global economism is now being created by the WTO. As with fundamentalist religionism, we must face this materialistic ideology at the beginning of the new millennium as a major threat to world peace and the integrity and future of the Earth."

—Dr. Michael Fox

housekeeping. They were all asked to return their turtle togs to the church at the end of the day so that Tuesday's turtles would be ready for a day of less turtlish activities—civil disobedience.

At noon, the "Clean, Green, and Fair" Monday march got under way for its journey of less than a mile to the convention center. The 240 turtles rallied at a meeting point with the Sierra Club, the Humane Society, and Friends of the Earth. Then, from all directions, ten thousand others—university students, union activists, street theater players, and other enthusiastic people—poured in to join them. Traffic came to a stop and there was turtle dancing in the streets. "People loved it, the cops loved it, bystanders loved it," said White. The Monday turtle brigade was the antithesis of an angry, strident protest, and the image of the lowly turtle taking on the multinational corporate consciousness surfaced in cartoons across the country. It was a triumph of turtles, and although White had not been invited to speak at the rally point, he climbed onto the huge AFL-CIO flatbed truck and came out of his shell. His first words were, "Welcome to the revolution." The crowd roared. The plight of the turtles was something that the entire crowd could respond to without struggling through the polemics of politics.

It was also the first time that Ben's thirteen-year-old daughter, Julia, had heard her dad speak to such a huge crowd. Even after all his years of activism, it was a pivotal point in their relationship. "There she was, right in the middle of an international populist movement," he said. "What a perfect thing for her." Later, when White went off to meet someone at a Starbucks, Julia shook her head in enlightened exasperation, "Geez, Dad, Starbucks?"

The midday march and rally went off without a hitch—from either police or protesters. But on the way back to the church, the march was blocked by a commotion a few blocks away. The turtles diffused and, in true turtle fashion, went back to the church and obediently left their shells behind. "We got all the costumes back," said White.

⚹   ⚹   ⚹   ⚹   ⚹

The commotion that had impeded the return march turned out to be at a downtown McDonald's at Third and Pine, where French farmer turned rabble rouser Jose Bové was holding forth about Roquefort cheese and economic justice. A broken window underscored his point, but it was broken by people in the crowd, not by Bové himself.

Bové, a farmer since 1975, actually spent most of his first seven years in Berkeley, California, where his parents studied biochemistry at the University of California. His early farming career included partici-pating in a peasant protest against the expansion of an army base in southern France. He went to prison for three weeks in 1976 for "invading" the base, the expansion of which was eventually abandoned.

Bové, who founded the Confederation Paysanno in 1987, is infamous for his attacks on McDonald's, which he sees as a symbol of industrial food production. In August 1999, he led a commando attack on a McDonald's under construction in Millau. The tactical "weapons" were crowbars, wrenches, sledgehammers, and screwdrivers. The goal was to dismantle—symbolically and otherwise. This specific attack was in reaction to the high U.S. tariff on Roquefort cheese (and other fancy French foods) that was instituted in retaliation for the European ban on U.S. hormone-treated beef. The WTO had approved the United States' retaliatory tariff, and Bové and other French farmers were mad. As were the rest of the French people. When he got out of jail from his attack on McDonald's, Bové was a hero. A few months later, he headed off to WTO week in Seattle, where he expanded his heroic status. This French flurry of Roquefort cheese activity in downtown Seattle on Monday, November 29, was one of the first events to be marred by property damage.

In other parts of the city, the peaceful, productive teach-ins were still going strong. It was a smorgasbord of WTO topics, including but not limited to "Forests, Fisheries, Toxics"; "Genetically Modified Organisms"; "Trade Related Intellectual Property Rights (TRIPS)"; "Corporations and Democracy"; "Multilateral Agreement on Investment"; and "Global Trade Unionism." Sites for the teach-ins included the Musicians' Association of Seattle Local 76 Hall, the International Brotherhood of Electrical Workers (IBEW) Hall, the King County Labor Temple, the Filipino Community Center, and Town Hall.

The evening activities also offered something for everyone. There was a People's Gala at the Seattle Center with music, dancing, and enter-tainment by Michael Moore (the social critic and documentarian from Flint, Michigan). The Gala was hosted by The Body Shop, the Citizens Trade Campaign, and the United Steelworkers of America. In Seattle's south end, there was a People's Assembly, where international solidarity was the focus. The film *The Golf War*, which depicts the plight of Filipino peasants struggling to protect their farmland from corporate interests wanting the land for golf resorts, was the evening's entertainment. And there was the Jubilee 2000 Interfaith Service at the First United Methodist Church, after which would be yet another Monday march— this time to form a human chain around the Kingdome, where the WTO ministers were gathering for an Opening Gala featuring fine food and a Michael Moore of their own, the head of the WTO. The human chain was to symbolize the struggle to "break the chains of global debt" that are crippling so many Third World countries. It was a very full evening.

Ben White stashed his turtle costumes and went off to participate in the chain around the Kingdome, then went back to the Best Western on Denny near the Seattle Center for a decent night's sleep before Tuesday, N30—the really big day.

# 2 THE WINDING PATH—IN WHICH RELIGION AND POLITICS HAVE EVERYTHING TO DO WITH ONE ANOTHER

"Oftentimes, one strips oneself of passion
In order to see the Secret of Life;
Oftentimes, one regards life with passion,
In order to see its manifest forms."
—*Tao Te Ching*

My own journey to WTO week had started in church a few months earlier, and in Maui nearly thirty years ago. The more recent impetus was a notice posted on the wall of the undercroft in tiny St. David's Episcopal Church in Friday Harbor, on San Juan Island in the northwest corner of Washington State. It announced an upcoming workshop on "Global Economic Justice" at St. Mark's Cathedral in Seattle. I took note of the date—September 30, 1999—and didn't know I was going to attend until I got there.

St. Mark's is a big place. When I arrived that Thursday evening, it was standing room only. A thousand people were packed into the cathedral. I remember my astonishment when I tried to sign up for the subsequent weekend workshops and discovered that there had been a waiting list for weeks. I hadn't seen such a crowd of activists gathered in one place in twenty-five years. And never in a church. What was going on? Bewildered by my own attendance almost as much as by the whopping turnout, I found a seat and for the next two hours was called home to a consciousness of conscience that had been too long absent. Things weren't right in the world and I was beginning to find out why.

I am not a comfortable churchgoer. Even after four years of attending St. David's, I feel awkward about my allegiance to my Sunday morning activities. I'm shy about confessing to my friends that it's important to me. I've known most of them since b.c. (before church), and suspect that several find it amusing and even a bit confusing. Especially those in my Buddhist community.

I have, in fact, been a borderline Buddhist for nearly thirty years. My first introduction came through the poetry of self-avowed Buddhist Kenneth Rexroth, whose work was my companion during a difficult year. Two years later it came politically, via two Chinese men I met in Lahaina on Maui in the summer of 1971. I had moved there with my five-year-old son for a year of teaching at a Montessori school. In those days, Lahaina was a funky little town where flavored shaved ice was the specialty and watching the sunset was the social life. There was a small mini-mall in town, and somehow I discovered Felix and Bing, who were managing a little tourist shop. As things go that are important, the details of just how we met are not remembered. That we *did* meet, however, has etched my life with meaning.

Felix and Bing (I never knew what their real names were) had escaped the Cultural Revolution in China. One of them, I remember, was a philosophy professor; the other was also an academic, but I don't remember his discipline. (The educated were the first to be rounded up and killed. The lucky ones escaped—with their lives and nothing else.) We talked about lofty things and also about the Vietnam War. I had married young and been an army wife at Fort Dix, New Jersey, from 1966 to 1968. My second son had been born there—and died shortly after birth. I then went on to volunteer at the army hospital; it was full of young men recovering from the war injuries and the tropical diseases they'd acquired in Vietnam. I was young and grief-stricken; I felt right at home.

> "The word *Buddha* comes from the root *buddh*, which means 'to wake up.' A Buddha is someone who is awake."
>
> —Thich Nhat Hanh in *Living Buddha, Living Christ*

By 1969, I was back in Seattle, divorced, studying to be a Montessori teacher and marching along the freeway in protest against the war with my son, Colin, whom I pushed along in a stroller. On Sunday afternoons, we'd go to Volunteer Park and be a very quiet but supportive part of the peace rallies taking place. When the opportunity to teach in Hawaii surfaced, I didn't think twice. In the summer of '71, we were Maui-bound.

Whenever I got the chance I'd go and sit with Felix or Bing, whoever was working that day, and chat. We'd sit outside the shop and wait for customers to stroll by, and a breeze to blow by. One day, in the middle of the conversation, Felix or Bing said, "If you do not revolt when you are young, you have not the right to grow old." The sentence entered my soul intact and stayed there.

At some point during that hot Hawaiian summer, one of them gave me a copy of *The Wisdom of Laotse*, translated by Lin Yutang. It was published in 1948. Laotse (often spelled Lao Tsu), who was born in 571 B.C., contributed Taoism to world religion, and his wisdom would be translated many times as the *Tao Te Ching*. "It is convenient to pronounce the first syllable as *dow* in dowager," began the book, which went on to explore the principles of life through eighty-one poetic proverbs. I was enthralled by its mysteries and comforted by its recognition of conundrum and contradiction. Taoism is funny, intuitive, peaceful, and filled with reverence for nature and the complexity of human nature. Laotse

"**Meanwhile, many Buddhists celebrate Jesus as a consummate bodhisattva, one who refuses to abandon this world of suffering and illusion until all sentient creatures can accompany him.**"

—Harvey Cox, professor of divinity at Harvard University

was a mystic who believed in the importance of failure but didn't reject success. He celebrated paradox: "Do nothing and everything is done." He hated war: "The slaying of multitudes should be mourned with sorrow. A victory should be celebrated with the Funeral Rite." An ancient philosophy that partnered perfectly with my feelings about the Vietnam War.

Felix and Bing and this book somehow led me closer to Buddhism. Perhaps because such books were next to each other on the shelves of libraries and bookstores. Perhaps because there were new Buddhist groups forming in Hawaii at the time; perhaps just because. I liked that Buddhism and Taoism were not deity-based; they were philosophies of mind, supporters of heart, and celebrations of soul. And they both rested deeply in nature—which was the only place where I ever deeply rested.

But after a year in Maui, the slow, somnolent seductiveness of it all seemed more appropriate for the end of a life—not the beginning. So Colin and I moved back to Seattle and settled on Bainbridge Island, a ferry ride away from downtown. In 1975, the Vietnam War finally came to an end, but I was still young enough to revolt, so when the anti-nuclear movement took hold in Kitsap County, it was natural to get involved. The Bangor Naval Base, on the pristine shores of Washington's Hood Canal, would be home to a fleet of Trident nuclear submarines, each of which is capable of overkilling any nation on earth. The Trident submarine is a first-strike weapon, which raised moral and spiritual issues far more complex than those of defense and protection.

From the mid-seventies through the mid-eighties, the anti-nuke movement was deeply rooted and widely active in the Northwest. And just as the Ruckus Society offered training in the art of civil disobedience in the months leading up to the WTO demonstrations in Seattle in 1999, twenty-five years ago the Ground Zero Center for Nonviolent Action, founded by Jim and Shelley Douglass, was doing the same to support the anti-nuke movement. Civil disobedience, which surfaced with a vengeance during WTO week, has lots of precedent in these parts.

For Ground Zero, it was faith-based. The Douglasses came to their commitment through profound belief in the deep meaning of what it means to be a Christian activist. Jim Douglass was well prepared to lead the way. In 1969 he'd torn up his draft card during a peace Mass at the University of Notre Dame, where he was teaching. In continuing protest

---

## Distracted Hearts

There is a loss of peace, and a loss of peace of mind, to the velocity of up-to-the-minute life. A feeling of powerlessness increases cynicism and a bitter resignation to continuing injustice. A feeling of vulnerability makes people reluctant to address the burdens of memory, to acknowledge and seek absolution for past wounds inflicted and received. A spiritual vacuum seems to divide us from ourselves, and we have neither the time nor the energy with which to address it.

—Jubilee 2000, Episcopal Church, Office of Peace and Justice Ministries

---

against the Vietnam War, in March 1972, he'd been arrested for pouring blood on secret files at Hickam Air Force Base in Hawaii. In his 1979 book, *Lightning East to West,* Douglass wrote about his history of civil disobedience in relationship to both his Christian faith and his marriage. It had a big impact on me.

This weaving together of faith, politics, and protest has always been provocative. Drawing the line between the action and nonaction of pacifism requires a fine discernment, a heartfelt faith, and a sense that one can indeed have an impact. This is not easily come by. Especially today, when the injustices are more subtle, less easily seen, and hidden deep within the culture. It's easier to protest a nuclear bomb than a corporate policy. You can get your hands on a nuclear bomb.

When the Buddhist monks from Japan came to Kitsap County to join in the protest against nuclear weapons, it was a mobilizing moment. They brought with them photographs and the knowledge of what had happened in Hiroshima and Nagasaki. There was an outpouring of welcome. The Suquamish tribe held a welcoming prayer ceremony for them at Chief Seattle's grave. Steve Old Coyote sang high from the sky, the monks chanted low from the earth, the Lutheran minister sang a sweet hymn from a place still young in the universe. This coming together of culture, religion, and song was deeply moving— it was a return of some sort, to a place I didn't know I was missing. All of us brought together by nuclear missiles on submarines based in our collective backyard.

**In 1994, a Gallup poll reported that 86 percent of Generation X said that religion is "important" to them.**

The monks were nonviolent, pacifist to the core. They prayed. They walked. They drummed. And they invited the community into their unique peace movement. Then Ground Zero invited them to build a peace pagoda on the land that bordered the submarine base. They started building, then someone set fire to it and it burned to the ground. When the monks resettled on Bainbridge Island, the community pitched in to help build a Buddhist temple. One summer I spent my spare time peeling the bark off a madrona tree that would brace up the roof. It was repetitive, tedious work that became peaceful and oddly reassuring. There were many mornings when meditation and chanting with the monks started my day at 5:00 A.M. They had drawn me in by their activism, but it was their silence and song that became sustaining. And remained so when we sat in silent vigil on the shores of the Klallam Reservation and witnessed the first nuclear submarine coming through the fog to its home in Hood Canal. I was learning about the utterly contradictory and compatible natures of peace and protest.

# 3 WAR AND PEACE—IN WHICH FATHER AND DAUGHTER PRESENT "INCREDIBLE FEATS OF STUPIDITY"

"I have always believed that I could help change the world, because I have been lucky to have adults around me who did."
—Marian Wright Edelman, author and president of the Children's Defense Fund

The first time I met Fred Miller, he was overseeing the installation of an espresso bar in the very downscale Seattle office of Peace Action, the largest peace and justice organization in the country. We got right into a discussion about coffee politics because he was looking for a good cup of fair-trade coffee to sell in the café. Seattle may be home to Starbucks, but it's also home to coffee-consciousness.

Miller, who's program director of Peace Action Washington, looks as if he could hold forth reading poetry in a Beat, or offbeat, coffeehouse in sixties San Francisco, or perhaps Leningrad. He took me back. With his long blond hair and blue-eyed, open gaze, he looks way too young to have an eighteen-year-old daughter. And he sounds way too old to look so young. After a quick tour of the soon-to-be Peace Café, we went upstairs to an office that was itself a throwback to the sixties. Old "Give Peace a Dance" posters, weird carpets, facts about the Trident nuclear submarine posted on the back of the bathroom door. No techno-snazz in sight.

So just what is this "Ban the Bomb" organization doing in these days of relative nuclear peace? For starters: attending to the violence on our streets and in our schools, working to eliminate land mines abroad, working to reduce the military budget and its subsequent arms trade, and lobbying to make gun manufacturers responsible for the damage caused by guns. To paraphrase Pogo: "We have met the enemy and it is still us."

None of this, of course, is a surprise to Fred Miller, who is himself a surprise. He is a man who likes to play war games to advance peace. His father was in military intelligence, and Miller doesn't hesitate to call him up to find out what's going on when he can't figure it out himself, which isn't often. He's got the inside scoop on the military mind and knows how to do military research. "Why did we give a gift of an anti-submarine rocket to a corrupt leader in landlocked Zimbabwe? And where is it now?" These are the kinds of questions that fascinate Miller. And the answers always lead somewhere.

Why does Congress give billions of dollars more to the military than it requests? Including funding a $1.5 billion B-2 Stealth bomber that the Air Force says it doesn't need.

Why has $30 billion been paid out to the biggest weapons makers in the country, with no record of what was bought?

If Boeing and Lockheed go to great lengths to convince Congress to spend $100 billion on F-22 jets because dozens of countries have advanced fighter jets, why don't they also tell Congress that all those countries bought their F-16s and F-18s from the United States in the first place?

> **"They're telling me what? This is my town. They're telling me that because we have these foreign guests that the citizens of the town are no longer allowed to express their First Amendment rights?"**
>
> —Martin Fleck, Seattle resident and director of Washington Physicians for Social Responsibility

Why is annual U.S. military spending more than $150 billion greater than the combined military budgets of Russia, China, North Korea, Iraq, Iran, Syria, Libya, and Cuba?

These are all questions on Miller's mind, and he won't be happy until they're on everybody else's mind as well. But where does the WTO fit into all of this?

According to Miller, everywhere. The military buys its stuff from "Guns and Tanks and Fighter Jets 'R Us." Some of it is bought by the U.S. military, some of it is sold abroad. All of it is produced by private corporations that are constantly out lobbying Congress to spend more on the military. This is supposed to create jobs, but many military planes are now being built overseas by foreign workers, while the money from sales, supplemented by tax subsidies, ends up in the pockets of the corporate elite. The weapons industry, nuclear and otherwise, carries a big corporate stick (see sidebar, Physicians for Safe and Sane Trade).

The WTO policies that support unregulated free trade mean that everything from wheat to weapons is sold to the highest bidder, and it doesn't seem to matter that we sell arms to our own "enemies" and end up being threatened by the very people to whom we've sold them. According to Miller, Congress spends billions to protect the United States from countries that buy their military equipment *from* the United States. This is when he raises the "Incredible Feats of Stupidity" banner and breaks out into street theater with General Warren D. Struction.

There's a movement these days toward simplicity. To cash in early, sell the big house, buy a small one in the country, live off your interest, and grow lettuce instead of money. But there are some people out on the front lines of the social justice movement who have never known anything *but* simplicity. Miller doesn't make much money, and he spends even less. And, yes, he does live off his interest—it just doesn't happen to come from principal, it comes from principle. He puts his lack of money where his mouth is.

For starters, Miller rides a bicycle everywhere, which made him very useful to Direct Action Network during WTO week. He knows

## Physicians for Safe and Sane Trade

Washington State Physicians for Social Responsibility (PSR) helped organize "WTO and the Global War System," held in downtown Seattle on November 29, 1999, at Plymouth Congregational Church. "This forum was the only actual linkage to the military-industrial complex," said Martin Fleck, director of Washington PSR. "In WTO rules, governments are not allowed to subsidize industry within their borders. However, there's one big, huge, glaring exception, and that's military work—work that can be defined as in the national interests. It's safe." This means that countries can develop weapons without coming under the jurisdiction of the WTO. It's the last bastion of industrial independence for countries unable to compete in the global marketplace.

There were four speakers at the forum in Seattle, which was moderated by Fleck and played to a packed church.

Susan George, associate director of the Transnational Institute, spoke about how the WTO moves power and money to the top. "Through globalization, we're creating a three-track society in which there will be the exploiters, the exploited, and the outcasts—the people who are not worth exploiting."

Mark Ritchie, president of the Institute for Agriculture and Trade Policy and a board member of the International Forum on Globalization, spoke about the need ➤

downtown like the inside of his bike helmet, and he knows how to get everywhere quickly. He also fed himself and his cohorts out of grocery store dumpsters—the places where bruised bananas and other cosmetically impaired fruits and vegetables end up. As Seattle has gone upscale, so has the discarded food. Miller supplied the DAN folks with some 300 pounds of designer food out of dumpsters during their stay. It was then prepared by Seeds of Peace, a roving food-prep group on a mission.

When there's a big event like the WTO coming down, "people need food and furniture," Miller told me. "A sofa, a fax machine, a microwave, and something on the walls." He rounded up all but the microwave for the People for Fair Trade office. He might have a military mind, but he's got the hospitable instincts of a Martha Stewart. After WTO was all over, Miller gathered up all the lost-and-found clothing from warehouse and crash pads, washed out the pepper spray and tear gas, and took it all to a battered women's shelter in Everett, 30 miles north of Seattle.

---

for globalized thinking and grassroots organization. "If we want peace on the planet, we mustn't ask the governments to give us peace, we must *make* peace. If we're going to have global governance, it's going to have to be the civil society of the planet that provides the legitimization of that process."

Alice Slater, a director of the Global Resource Action Center for the Environment (GRACE), talked about how corporate interests are all wrapped up with the production of nuclear weapons. "The Star Wars lobby has been led by companies like Lockheed Martin, Raytheon, Boeing, and TRW, which are dividing up billions of dollars in contracts, connected in no small part to the $23 million they spent lobbying and the $4 million in campaign contributions in 1997 and 1998."

Steven Staples, chair of the International Network on Disarmament and Globalization, addressed the ways in which corporate mergers in the weapons industry are transcending the borders of nation-states. "In this new global economy that favors the military, peace activists are losing their ability to work for peace and human rights."

At the end of June 2000, Martin Fleck went to Paris for the World Congress of International Physicians for the Prevention of Nuclear War. He was asked to lead a workshop on "Transnational Capitalism and Ethical Issues." The military-industrial machine has a lot of different parts but, whether they're nuclear warheads or corporate lobbyists, PSR has a long history of working for all-around responsibility.

"It had been a busy summer," said Miller, "so we didn't get really involved with WTO until September." Peace Action had been otherwise engaged with the test-ban treaty, the politics of the nuclear cleanup at Hanford in eastern Washington, a "MAI Day" event in protest of the Multilateral Agreement on Investment, and the annual Hiroshima Day event on August 6 at Green Lake in Seattle. On this evening every August, paper lanterns are lit with candles and floated out into the lake in memory of those who died when nuclear bombs were dropped on Hiroshima and Nagasaki. Green Lake is the city's favorite running, walking, rowing, in-line skating, personal-ad meet-for-the-first-time playground. But on August 6 each year, the sound of Japanese *taiko* drums fills the air. As a result of all this activity, Miller went to just a few WTO meetings throughout the summer "to keep my finger on the pulse" and to keep his 17,000 members in the state informed as the planning progressed. When September came, they would go into action.

✢ ✢ ✢ ✢ ✢

Peace Action has its roots in nuclear devastation. World War II, which started out "conventional" and ended up "unconventional" with the dropping of atomic bombs on Japan, forever changed the stakes for humankind. The "Ban the Bomb" movement was started soon after the war by a group of ordinary people with an ordinary concern: to preserve the future of the human race by ridding the world of nuclear weapons. In 1957, Dr. Albert Schweitzer's "Call to Conscience," published in the *Saturday Review*, brought home the dangers of nuclear radiation. Norman Cousins, editor of the magazine, and Clarence Pickett of the American Friends Service Committee then called an ad-hoc meeting to confront the fallout from nuclear testing. Poet Lenore Marshall offered her New York apartment for the meeting, and out of it came SANE—the National Committee for a Sane Nuclear Policy. Its mission was "to develop public support for boldly conceived and executed policy which will lead mankind away from war and toward peace and justice." It was the beginning of the nuclear disarmament movement, and its reach went far beyond "the bomb."

The issues involved—moral, ethical, theological—were represented by some of the early activists in SANE, including Eleanor Roosevelt, baby doctor Benjamin Spock, philosopher Bertrand Russell, theologian Paul Tillich, psychologist Erich Fromm, civil rights leader the Reverend Dr. Martin Luther King Jr., his wife Coretta Scott King, actor Harry Belafonte, and cellist Pablo Casals. It was an era of urgency; celebrities took a stand, kids practiced hiding from H-bombs under their desks, and backyard bomb shelters flourished alongside backyard barbecues.

During the 1960s and '70s, SANE's mandate was expanded to include the anti-Vietnam War movement. In 1978, SANE led the successful fight against the MX mobile missile deployment, which would have wreaked environmental mayhem in Nevada and Utah. In the early 1980s, the Nuclear Weapons Freeze campaign was born. Grassroots groups across the country worked to get initiatives on the ballot that demanded sanity in the face of nuclear insanity. In 1987, the two groups joined to become SANE/Freeze. In 1993, it changed its name to Peace Action and encompassed a much broader mission. Abolition of nuclear weapons and elimination of conventional weapons trade became the mandate, as did the development of a peace-based economy that serves human needs first over the demands of the corporate military industry.

To reinforce this emphasis on human needs, Peace Action took to the community. Which is why, in 1999, Peace Action of Washington State fed homeless teens and worked for peace in the schools as well as lobbied the U.S. Senate for ratification of the Nuclear Test Ban Treaty. Fred Miller takes gracefully to the complexity.

Nationwide, Peace Action has 70,000 members. It's a membership that in the past has risen and ebbed with the tide of fear about nuclear war.

> **"Every gun that is made, every warship launched, every rocket fired signifies, in the final sense, a theft from those who hunger and are not fed, those who are cold and not clothed. This world in arms is not spending money alone. It is spending the sweat of its laborers, the genius of its scientists, the hopes of its children."**
>
> —President Dwight D. Eisenhower

The Washington State membership was down to 5,000 in 1993, after the Gulf War, when the fear of nuclear weapons was down and the aftertaste of victory was up. In recent years, however, Peace Action has grown steadily, finding that the quest for domestic peace has a great deal in common with the need for international peace.

I spent some time with Miller, and attended a meeting with him as he went about his business as program director for Peace Action. It was a meeting of the Safe Schools Committee at the Seattle School District offices near the Seattle Center, about 5 city miles from his office. He rode his bike, I drove; he got there first.

Including Miller, there were six people at the meeting: Sally Telgrove, from Middle School Support; Lin Carlson, from Seattle Public Schools' Connections; Cynthia and Charles Jefferson, who lead a group called "Everyone Has a Song"; and Dianne Newsom, who heads up the Truancy Unit of the Seattle Police Department's Gang Unit. Newsom talked about enforcing the law: no possession of tobacco in any form on school property. Miller talked about prevention: "We're not going to break addiction, not one in ten," he said. Newsom then told the group about one of her interventions at a neighborhood fast-food place where a high school student was smoking and not in school when he was supposed to be. One of those big-hearted tough cops who's seen it all before, will again, and still cares, she has a surprisingly up-close-and-personal commitment to the kids on her watch. Miller had expressed his respect for her, and I could see why.

Her next story wasn't quite so heartwarming. A teacher had refused to identify a student who was supposedly in possession of a 45-caliber gun at school. The teacher cited reasons of confidentiality. This caused a lot of confusion. The principal sent the teacher home. The police investigation became a process of elimination, and there was the possibility of filing charges against the teacher, who, said Newsom, "doesn't appear to care about the safety of students in the school." The discussion then focused on how to support students who share information so that guns can be rounded up before they go off.

Toward the end of the meeting, almost as an aside, Miller asked the group for help. Food once again was the issue. Part of Peace Action's mandate in Washington State is to create peace in the streets, which means feeding teens who are homeless and hungry. There are a lot of them. Miller is on the board of University Street Ministries, which feeds about thirty a night at any one of the participating church kitchens in the University District north of downtown Seattle, where homeless teens tend to gather. The "Teen Feed" program is staffed by volunteers, and Miller was dealing with lots of burnout. He was looking for support for his volunteers to help them process the intensity of the evenings, during which the threat of violence was often on the menu along with the mashed potatoes and vegetables. "There's way too much speed on the streets," said Miller. He looked hopefully around the table. There was a big silence. Someone asked him if he had any money in his budget to hire a therapist to come in. His face went expressively blank and he didn't say anything. Someone else suggested that he call the psychology department at the University of Washington; maybe there were students who could help. The meeting went on to other things.

In Seattle in the seventies, there were community mental health clinics, a generous food stamp program, drop-in centers, readily available medical care, and a variety of public agencies that kept young and old from falling between the cracks in our society. Listening to Miller and Newsom talk about things made me realize how stingy we've become and how hard it is for those working on the front lines of life-beyond-Boeing, Microsoft, and Amazon.com. The safety net is no more.

❖ ❖ ❖ ❖ ❖

Both Miller and Newsom were on the streets of Seattle during WTO week, Miller because he was representing the thousands who belong to Peace Action, Newsom because she works on the other front line—riot control. The two had much more in common than a lot of protesters, even if they were on different sides.

On N30, Miller and his daughter, Erin, performed the "Incredible Feats of Stupidity" satire of Pentagon policies, and carried a banner that read: "Sure, WTO cost me my job, but at least now I can get cheap guns from China." Erin dressed up in General Warren D. Struction's coat. They passed out brochures about land mines: There are an estimated 110 million that are still active scattered throughout 68 countries around the world—and as many in storage. More than 26,000 people will be killed or maimed by a mine explosion this year, most of them after the conflict is over. During the Vietnam War, the U.S. Army estimated that 90 percent of the land mines used against U.S. troops either were made in the United States or included components made in the United States. There is an international treaty banning land-mine production, use, export, and stock-piling that has been signed by 120 countries. Four nations that refused to do so are China, Iraq, Bosnia, and the United States.

During the labor march on N30, lots of union members came up to the Millers for information about land mines. Fred and Erin stayed downtown after the official march passed through, and found their way to Sixth and Pike, near Niketown, Planet Hollywood, and the Sheraton Hotel, where the Secret Service was keeping Madeleine Albright behind closed doors. The Millers had been there for the labor march, and there was the faint smell of tear gas in the air when they took up position with their banner between them to protect the windows of Niketown and Planet Hollywood from brick-throwing anarchists. Niketown had already lost a few by the time Miller and his daughter arrived on the scene. There were groups of young people taking aim at windows, so Fred and Erin decided that this was where they would stay and do some peacekeeping.

"There was no looting on that block," said Miller, "a few broken windows and some spray paint. That was it." At one point he confronted a window-smashing kid and wrestled away a 2-foot-long piece of angle iron, which Miller then tossed up onto an awning to put it out of reach. "Planet Hollywood kept its glass because of us," he said, well aware of the irony of protesters wrestling with one another while the police were teargassing the nonviolent ones. Miller and his daughter held their ground, protecting the Nike shirts in the broken open window and the windows that were still intact. "It was an amazing moment to be a father," said Miller. "I felt tremendous pride in Erin." When I interviewed him, Erin was away in Chiapas, Mexico, working with Pastors for Peace.

The actions of media-identified anarchists during WTO week have roused a twisted controversy throughout Seattle's communities, geographic and political. The rage cuts across the board—from WTO

## The Art of Anarchy

An anarchist is as an anarchist does. There were so many forms of anarchy at large during WTO week that clustering all the meanings of the word into the phrase "Eugene anarchists" is like saying there is only one shade of green.

"Anarchist" is simply and broadly defined in the dictionary as "resistance to organized government." Which makes Nelson Mandela an anarchist, as well as Gandhi, Dr. Martin Luther King Jr., the Dalai Lama, and, some would say, Jesus, who is described by respected scholar and distinguished professor Marcus J. Borg as a man of "sociopolitical passion" who "challenged the domination system of his day."

Borg, who was asked to give a seventy-five-second description of Jesus on NBC's *Today* show on Good Friday, concluded, "Jesus was an ambiguous figure—you could experience him and conclude that he was insane, as his family did, or that he was simply eccentric or that he was a dangerous threat—or you could conclude that he was filled with the Spirit of God."

Most two-year-olds are anarchists. They want to be who they are. Anarchism strikes adolescents, too. They want to be who they are and do whatever they feel like doing. Anarchism is a natural state in the face of oppression. It's akin to passion, albeit not always "passionate." One could describe the lumbering turtles as a green horde of anarchists. They were resisting the rules of governments, which these days ➤

protesters, to downtown businesspeople who lost windows, to residents who saw only what was shown on their TVs. The truth is that very few stores were looted, and even those that were looted lost just a few things. In some cases, this was thanks to protesters like Miller, who were there, knew immediately what the impact would be on the cause, and acted quickly to contain property damage. It was quite astounding that there could be upward of 70,000 people on the streets with a few bands of marauders intent on mayhem, thousands of others intent on civil disobedience, and a phalanx of exhausted, hungry, pissed-off cops unidentifiable in riot gear and wielding tear gas, pepper spray, rubber bullets, and batons—and no one was killed.

Miller, who's both radical and rational, has his own perspective on the anarchist movement. "Their notion of building a movement is all backward of mine," he said. "Most anarchists won't get involved with the

---

are often indistinguishable from the rules of corporations, that threaten the natural integrity of life on the planet.

The turtle anarchism was sweet and slow. The anarchism that broke a few carefully targeted corporate windows was quick and testy. The anarchism that happens when regular people act to do for one another what governments, and corporations, refuse to do—feed, clothe, shelter, and provide health care, fair labor practices, and human rights—is deep, compassionate, and sustaining. One could say that these days anarchism is at the heart of civil society, which sees the acquisition of money for money's sake running roughshod over the survival needs of much of the world's population.

Anarchism has an illustrious history. The Declaration of Independence could be called an anarchist document. Labor history is rich with anarchist individuals who worked for such things as the five-day work week, the eight-hour day, and the freedom of kids to have a childhood before they grew up.

In Burma, right now, Aung San Suu Kyi is choosing to live under house arrest, rather than in freedom, to show support for the people of Burma who are suffering under a harsh dictatorial regime. She is far from her home in England, where her children live and where her husband died while she was in self-exile. The Burmese government would not allow him to visit her before he died. She was afraid to leave for fear that they wouldn't allow her back in to continue taking a stand for her people. Hers is an anarchy of heart, soul, and mind. Its silence is deafening.

political process. They don't look at revolution in the sense that I do, of building a huge base by going out and asking people what's important to them, then working on that and connecting it together. Everyone's concerned about our schools; and it's a foreign policy issue because we're sending helicopters to Colombia while our schools are falling apart."

His distress at the attention the media gave the anarchists is evident. This issue has a two-edged truth, and leaves a big question in its wake: Would the WTO protests have received as much worldwide attention if anarchists hadn't done their thing in Seattle and if the media hadn't focused on it? Would WTO now be a part of the lexicon of daily life?

To Miller, the real issues are much more dramatic. "I often encourage people who feel alienated to go out and talk to $100,000-a-year households in north Seattle, two-income families with two nice cars, and you'll find out these people have some deeply radical sentiments. They really know that the U.S. government has incredible problems. You start connecting with these folks, and they start finding out that you're working on the same things that they're wishing they had a way to work on. That's where the revolution comes from. But some see everything about the U.S. military and our consumer society as being so inherently evil that all they want to do is destroy it. They came to smash windows, to open up corporate property so that poor people could liberate goods. Unfortunately, it was others who got arrested. The anarchists exposed others to hazards that they themselves were very careful to avoid. If you want the masses on your side, then you're going to have a lot of people with college degrees and view houses. In a global sense, there aren't any poor people in America. Two thousand dollars a year in most of the world, and you're middle-class."

Miller scoffed at the idea that breaking windows was in any way revolutionary. "The cameras were looking for violence, and the police were providing it. If there hadn't been window-breaking, then maybe all the pictures of violence would have been of cops clubbing nonviolent protesters. I don't care if the media is corporate-owned; that would have been a story."

On N30, it was the billowing tear gas and concussion grenades that finally uprooted Miller and his daughter from their vigilance at Niketown, where they had stood guard for several hours. Parental protection took over at that point. "I didn't know what we were getting into," said Miller. They took cover a few blocks away at the People for Fair Trade office, where the policy-of-the-moment was: "We're a cooling-off station. This is not the place to be if you want to talk about the action out on the streets."

Miller eventually made it back to the Seattle Center, got on his bike, and rode 6 miles home. Early the next morning, December 1, he was in the Direct Action Network (DAN) communication office, where he helped people get "from here to there," helped organize radio communications for medics and legal observers from the National Lawyers Guild, and helped them respond where needed. Miller is a calm and reasonable man, but his voice went up a notch when he talked about the police abuse meted out to those who were out there to help. "[Medics and legal observers] were not protesting; they should have had the same immunity as the press," he said.

According to Miller, there was an agreement reached with the mayor's office and DAN organizers just before N30 that nonviolent protesters would not be treated violently, that legal observers, medical people, and tactical people would not be arrested, and that medical equipment would not be confiscated. "But did it get out to the cops out there?" asked Miller. At one point the medical center set up at Gethsemane Lutheran Church, four blocks north of the convention center, ran out of supplies, so Miller loaded up some from the DAN office, got on his bike, and delivered them to the church, where people were being brought in from the streets, triaged, and treated.

"It was a game of cat and mouse on December 1," said Miller. The violence that had exploded the day before had initially stunned the city; the next day there was a different kind of outpouring. It wasn't just the WTO anymore, it was the basics: freedom of speech and freedom to gather peacefully. And the freedom to be free of abuse from those who are supposed to protect us. If N30 brought out the spirit of social and economic justice in Seattle, D1 brought out the soul of the city.

The steelworkers, whose march route had been diverted the previous day, organized another labor march along Seattle's waterfront and invited students and environmentalists to take a place on the stand. Thousands joined in; hundreds of people took up residence in intersections around downtown; people in support of those arrested sat in a circle around the King County Jail; and there was yet another convergence on the convention center.

"I'm a hard person to surprise," said Miller, "and I was stunned. I know how hard it is to get a thousand people to turn out. To get tens of thousands out at the end of November is amazing. Even two weeks before, I thought that the only thing that would shut down Seattle would be a winter storm."

# 4 THE ABCS OF THE WTO—IN WHICH WE MAKE ALPHABET SOUP AND EVEN TRY TO EAT IT

"As a result of the war, corporations
have now been enthroned
and an era of corruption in high places will follow…
until all wealth is aggregated in a few hands,
and the Republic is destroyed."
—Abraham Lincoln

Who makes things happen? A simple question with endless answers—many of them abbreviated into ease-of-mouth initials. AAA keeps us on the road, AA keeps us sober, AT&T keeps us connected; ABC keeps us (somewhat) informed, and sometimes CBS does, too; NPR and PBS keep us giving and giving and giving, the UN tries to keep us globally aware, the IRS tries to keep us honest, B.C. gives us Christmas and is also British Columbia. Most of the time, we have an instant understanding of what the initials in our world stand for, what they do, and why. But we don't usually know *who*. We trust the organizations; therefore, we trust those who work there.

Which brings us to the World Trade Organization—the WTO—and its relatives, GATT, NAFTA, IMF, MAI, TNCs, and TRIPS. The brain glazes. It can make one feel like a SAP (otherwise known as a structural adjustment program). But if we are to really understand what goes on in our world—and why—we have to eat our alphabet soup. And it's good to know what's in it.

At the Mount Washington Hotel in Bretton Woods, New Hampshire, in 1944, the stage was set for our current economic system. World War II was not quite over; Hitler was still at large, but Mussolini had been overthrown. The allies had invaded Normandy, but dropping the bomb on Hiroshima and Nagasaki was more than a year away. There was, however, some future planning going on by economic leaders who assumed the war would eventually end, and that when it was over, the world would need prosperity as well as peace. So they met at Bretton Woods and created institutions that have defined and controlled our world economy ever since.

This historic meeting, held by the United Nations Monetary and Financial Conference, became known in the rarefied world of economists as simply "Bretton Woods." A folksy, woodsy way of saying that everything ever deemed important about money, development, and the worth of the world was determined here. And it was here that the World Bank and the International Monetary Fund (the IMF in the soup) were born. (Note that the "World Bank" has such a nice, round sound that it doesn't need initials.)

Although Bretton Woods set the stage, economic construction started earlier, in the 1930s, with the U.S. Council on Foreign Relations. This was when the corporate and foreign-relations experts of the day

## Railroaded

The modern corporation came to life in the hands of nine men. In *Santa Clara County vs. Southern Pacific Railroad,* an 1886 dispute over a railbed, the U.S. Supreme Court made a historic decision. It held that, under the U.S. Constitution, a private corporation was a "natural person," entitled to all the rights and privileges of a human being.

This single legal stroke changed America fundamentally. From that moment on, the country's citizens would have to think of corporations very differently. Every corporation—though it was still technically only an idea, a paper phantom—nonetheless had its own "life" now, its own "ego." Corporations could compete directly against real people and demand equal treatment under the law.

Were corporations suddenly as powerful as people? No. Because of their vast financial resources, they were now much *more* powerful. They could defend and exploit their rights and freedoms more than any individual. In real terms, the corporation was actually *more free* than any private citizen. The whole intent of the U.S. Constitution—that all citizens have one vote, and exercise an equal voice in public debates—had been undermined.

—From "Corporate Crackdown" by Kalle Lasn and Tom Liacas, in *Adbusters— Journal of the Mental Environment,* August/September 2000 gathered together to figure out how the growing global economy could be controlled by U.S. corporate interests. One key was having access to the natural resources of other countries—this would serve industrial growth. Another key was the creation of worldwide financial institutions that would stabilize currencies—this would help ease investment in foreign lands where the wealth of raw materials was abundant, but where financial help was needed to build the mines, roads, factories, et cetera, for easy access.

At the opening session of Bretton Woods, Henry Morgenthau, the U.S. Secretary of the Treasury—and the president of the conference— was the visionary-at-large. He saw "a dynamic world economy in which

## Cap the Corporations

In Boulder, Colorado, a group of 140 local independent businesses has formed the Boulder Independent Business Alliance (BIBA) to promote a citywide initiative that would put a cap on the number of chain businesses in the city. The group wants to show that small businesses are themselves victimized by corporate globalization. Their initiative, the Community Vitality Act, grows out of the national Reclaim Democracy! Group, which has a growing number of IBAs across the country.

—Website: www.reclaimdemocracy.org

the peoples of every nation will be able to realize the potentialities in peace and enjoy increasingly the fruits of material progress on an earth infinitely blessed with natural riches." But just how long can one cup runneth over?

Forever, according to the World Bank, which, after its birth at Bretton Woods, got right to work. Forever, says the International Monetary Fund, which makes sure the World Bank doesn't run out of money while it's doing its job. And so began our current way of doing worldly business. For more than fifty years, this system of lending money to Third World countries so they can pay people from First World countries to build things, know things, manufacture things, and excavate things has been the foundation of trade.

But all was not wonderful. "We're going broke paying back the interest on the debt, let alone the principal," realized Third World countries. "Tough," said the Big Lender, "so cut your social, health, and education programs."

"But, but, but. …"

This is where the SAP comes in. A *structural adjustment program* is a fancy way of saying, "We'll give you more money to get outta debt, but you gotta do it our way."

The main demand that the IMF and the World Bank make of countries to which they lend money is this: Get over self-sufficiency and sign up for an export/import lifestyle in which the Big Guys from the developed countries will invest in your natural resources, build an infra-structure to get to them all, and then export them for big bucks. This means you'll have jobs and money, but maybe not enough to pay the high price of the other things in life you need—the stuff that has to be imported because you can no longer produce it yourself. But don't worry, that keeps the other Big Guys rich so that they, too, can keep their workers working.

Coffee, that Northwest staple, is a good example. Growing corpo-rate coffee beans depletes the land, the birds, the shade, and the scenery. It also means that growing anything else—like vegetables for the family—becomes impossible. But because your country agreed to specialize in growing coffee beans for export as a condition of its World Bank loan, grow coffee beans you must. Besides, you can buy imported vegetables from the country next door—even though you can't afford to because you're being paid practically nothing for the coffee beans in the first place. It's those guys who sell it in Seattle who make all the money—and all those shareholders who love their lattes. And the nonshare-holders, too (like me), who also love to drink it at about $2 a shot—which is likely to be a day's wage on some coffee plantations.

This is, of course, a vast oversimplification. But the scenario is true; working people from all over the world are being deprived of self-sustaining lifestyles so that corporate interests can be fed. And the systems that serve these corporate interests are deeply imbedded in global economics through the actions of the World Bank and the IMF. It has become a closed system, in which the people outside the corporate architecture have no say in the goings-on that define their lives.

Yes, Bretton Woods exceeded its goals of economic expansion: International trade is booming and foreign investment is expanding at an even greater rate—but at what cost? David Korten, who has a Ph.D. from Stanford, has taught at Harvard, and has worked for both the U.S. Agency for International Development and the Ford Foundation, acknowledged this success in his keynote address at the 1994 convention of the Environmental Grantmakers Association of America (coinciden-tally held in Bretton Woods on the fiftieth anniversary of the other conference). But after doing so, he went on: "Yet, tragically, while these institutions have met their goals, they have failed in their purpose. The world has more poor people today than ever before. We have an accelerating gap between the rich and the poor. Widespread violence is tearing families and communities apart nearly everywhere. And the planet's ecosystems are deteriorating at an alarming rate." There are fatal flaws in the economic ointment.

✻   ✻   ✻   ✻   ✻

Back in the beginning, there were, of course, good intentions: Jobs at home and abroad. Food for all. A system of prosperity that would serve everyone. Lofty goals, indeed, but material progress doesn't bear fruit, it bears more material progress. Fruit can sustain itself; material progress can only deplete itself.

An example of the World Bank run amok is the dams that are being built in India. Arundhati Roy, who wrote the best-selling novel *The God of Small Things*, also wrote *The Cost of Living*, two nonfiction essays about two tragedies in India—dams and nuclear weapons. Millions of people are being displaced from self-sustaining agrarian lives to the slums of big cities because of the hundreds of dams being built throughout India. The World Bank was offering money to build the biggest, the Sardar Sarovar, before it was even determined whether it was a good idea. Why? Because dams take a long time to build, use a lot of raw materials, require a lot of heavy lifting, and rely on a lot of professional expertise—most of it from foreign experts from foreign corporations. There's lots of money to be made.

Now, because India owes more and more money to the World Bank, it has to keep borrowing to keep up its payments. Between 1993 and 1998, this impoverished country paid the World Bank $1.475 billion *more* than it received. That's a whole lot of interest. Yet the needs of the millions who go hungry and uneducated, whose lives are destroyed, appear not to be considered at all.

This is where we raise the curtain on the WTO. But before we do, let's not forget its predecessor, from which the WTO got its clout, the mighty GATT. The General Agreement on Tariffs and Trade was negotiated in 1947 as a direct result of Bretton Woods. It's loaded with trade agreements about everything from soup (alphabet and otherwise) to nuts. The most recent version, GATT 1994, was absorbed into the WTO when the latter was established in the United States on January 1, 1995, voted in by a lame-duck Congress as a harmless trade association. But there is one big difference between the WTO and its predecessors,

GATT and the North American Free Trade Agreement (NAFTA): The rulings of the WTO are binding.

And harmless this isn't.

In its few short years as a world governing body, the WTO has issued 175 rulings to settle disputes between countries. These have all favored corporate interests at the expense of the environment, labor rights, animal protection, family farms, and freedom of choice. And the decisions have been close to home. When Massachusetts passed a law forbidding the investment of state money in Burma (now Myanmar) because of its anti-democratic, anti-human-rights regime, the WTO ruled the law illegal. Yet it was because of such laws that citizens in the United States were able to contribute to the end of apartheid in South Africa and help free Nelson Mandela. If the WTO had been in place then, Mandela could still be in jail.

But the United States wields the WTO as well. Europe doesn't want to import U.S. hormone-treated beef; the WTO says it must, or sanctions will be imposed. The United States says genetically modified organisms (GMOs) are good for all; Europe says, "No way." There's a big food fight going on, and it's getting messier and messier.

---

## Democracy Unleashed

In 1998, residents of Arcata, California, voted to "ensure democratic control of all corporations conducting business within the city." Town-hall meetings brought out close to 600 people, and the debate continues: "Can we have democracy when large corporations wield so much power and wealth under law?"

—Website: www.monitor.net/democracyunlimited

---

The WTO's Article III, National Treatment, gives us an idea of how intensely the WTO protects trade. Article III makes it *unlawful* for a government to discriminate against products that are manufactured, harvested, or produced in ways that are destructive to people and/or the environment. For instance, if one country uses child labor to make toys and another country doesn't, there can be no discrimination in trade. According to WTO law, the toy made by an underage kid working long hours in an unsafe factory for low wages has every right to the market-place. Products are protected at all costs, as is their trade. Which brings us to the TNCs in the WTO alphabet soup.

A transnational corporation is like a floating company that has a national flag for every port. Its ownership crosses boundaries, so it can operate under the laws of whatever country has the best deal. The TNC approach is, "If Indonesia has cheaper child labor than India, let's manufacture our shoes (or toys, or clothes, or microchips, or whatever you need next) there." A transnational corporation then has the freedom to find the most lucrative marketplace for its goods—usually the United

---

## Unchartered Territory

Corporate charters used to be revoked on a regular basis, but for the past hundred years, the option has rarely been activated. In fact, it's been considered obsolete, and many states have removed revocation clauses from the books. But as globalization has reared its head, revocation has suddenly gained clout. In 1999 in British Columbia, in order to keep civil society in the loop, the Citizens Council on Corporate Issues lobbied the provincial government to keep the law on the books.

In 1998 in California, thirty individuals and organizations petitioned to revoke the charter of the Union Oil Corporation. The revocation team included the Rainforest Action Network, the National Lawyers Guild, and the National Organization for Women. The petition was resubmitted in 2000 with an additional 160 supporters. They claim that the company violates human rights, workers' rights, and environmental integrity. Although so far the State Attorney General has not acted to revoke the charter, he has acknowledged the right to do so. More corporate charter revocations are now in the works.

—Website: www.heed.net

---

States, Canada, Europe, or Japan, because that's where the money is. The most common story in production these days is that the workers can rarely afford to buy the products they make.

Now, it is extremely important to recognize that there is no single entity to blame. There is no big bad owner, no diabolical dictator at the helm. Nobody's name is rising to the surface. That's because we're living in the middle of a CC soup of our own—Corporate Culture. As far as I'm aware, these dastardly initials are not in the common domain, but I use them here because the Corporate Culture is not only defining what we buy, it's defining who we are. Coca Cola Consciousness, CCC (just kidding), is a collective consciousness. Even if we don't buy the stuff, we're consumed by it as much as it's consumed by us. We are branded by brands, we live in a logo-land of infinite possibility. A virtual, and nonvirtual, cornucopia of consumption is what defines our Corporate Culture. The bad guy is us. *And* it's them.

Which brings us to the ubiquitous Inc. This is where the fun really starts. What, exactly, *is* a corporation? According to the official American Business Association dictionary, the definition of "corporation" starts out with "a fictional entity." (Try telling that to anyone whose midnight ramblings take them straight to the freezer for Ben & Jerry's ice cream.) Here's the definition in its entirety: "Corporation: A fictional entity created under state statute that can act only through human agency: directors, who are elected by shareholders, and who guide its general policies and elect its officers. The officers in turn, run the day-to-day operation of the corporation and select and hire employees."

The questions this definition provokes are endless. What is "human agency"? What's a state statute? How do employees know who they are really working for? Who's in charge of a fictional entity? A quick, knee-jerk analysis is that the shareholders are the key. Whoever has invested the most money gets to pick the directors, who in turn elect officers, who run the corporation and hire employees. So who, exactly, is making the decisions? It's a slippery slope, and that appears to be precisely the intent. A corporation is a fictional entity passing for a person, a person without name, face, or fingerprints. The unaccountable. No one person in a corporation can ever be blamed for anything. No one person can be sued or held responsible. In a corporation, the power is so far behind the scenes that even the stagehands don't know who the actors are. Herein lies the twisted secret: A corporation is a fictional front for reality. The real question is: What is reality?

This is where it really gets tricky.

At one end of the corporate ladder, and easiest to make sense of, are companies that are readily identifiable with their products—The Gap (clothing), Nike (sports stuff), Starbucks (coffee products), McDonald's (hamburgers). Unless they've branched out into leather products recently, Ben & Jerry's also falls into this category.

At the other, more obscure end are the transnational corporations with such complex international holdings and interests that it's very difficult to readily identify their products—often because they make or mine the materials that go into the products made by other corporations: Dow Chemical, Monsanto, Union Carbide, Boeing (lots of weapons parts as well as 747s), Pfizer, Mitsubishi, and IBM, for example. And then, of course, there is your local financial institution, which is likely linked up with any number of international financial institutions.

Transnationals, be they visible or invisible, work in various guises in various countries, with various connections to local and international players. To complicate matters even further, corporations are merging with other corporations, banks with banks, media empires with media empires, industry with industry. And at the very tip of this megacorporate iceberg is the notably undemocratic World Trade Organization, where decisions are made to support the corporate powers sprawling just below the surface. The very people making these decisions are trade representatives from the Corporate Culture. They are appointed by the governments of Corporate Culture—and should you be enamored of our congressional democratic system as it now looks, just know that nearly all top-level elected officials come out of the Corporate Culture and go back to it when their public tour of duty is over. It never ends.

This is a hugely complex issue. Which is why more than 50,000 people—with more than 50,000 reasons—showed up on the streets of Seattle to protest the policies of the World Trade Organization. Unlike a corporation, which in its unreality can elude one's grasp so cleverly, every single person on the streets of Seattle during WTO week had the inside scoop on their very own personal reality. Whether or not they were inspired to be there because of the environment, human rights, workers' rights, women's rights, children's rights, farmers' rights, labor rights, animal rights, WTO delegate rights, anarchists' rights, or that numinous, inarticulate right to spiritual harmony, they were there for a most personal reason. The decisions trickling down from the lofty heights of the World Trade Organization have had an effect on their lives, and on the lives of those to whom they are linked. They came from all over the world to tell their stories. And the corporation, that wily, elusive, fictional entity, was at the top of the list of offenders.

# 5 ON GETTING PERSONAL AND GOING PUBLIC—IN WHICH A PERSONAL WATERCRAFT BY ANY OTHER NAME IS NOT ALLOWED

"The edge of the sea is a strange
and beautiful place."
—Rachel Carson, *The Edge of the Sea*

had my own personal run-in with a corporate power in the summer of 1994, when I was superintendent of county parks here in San Juan County. I tell this story because it is an example of big corporate bullying of small local government. And it is a circumstance that could well fall under the jurisdiction of the WTO.

One day I got a call from a staff person at one of our camping parks. It was the week before the Fourth of July weekend, and someone was asking for permission to launch Jet Ski whale-watching tours from the park. I said, "No." Seemed pretty simple. It was a small park full of campers, kayakers, and kids. The bay was tiny and the risks apparent. Besides, I didn't think the whales would like it.

Within an hour, the words "Kawasaki attorney" had been brandished at me like an invincible weapon. "Discrimination!" was the next shout of "got ya" mentality. But it didn't make any sense. Surely the folks who love the peace and quiet of the park, the kids who splash fearlessly at the water's edge, the kayakers slipping silently in and out of the tiny bay deserved not to be discriminated against by noisy, invasive, and dangerous Jet Skis. I stood my park-professional ground in "protecting the health, safety, and welfare of the park and its users." The response from my county attorney was not reassuring. "We'll just have to defend you," he said, with no small tone of frustration. I couldn't believe that such a simple, common sense decision warranted any sort of defense whatsoever.

But I quickly discovered that the "fictional entity," Kawasaki Motors Corporation, was not to be thwarted. Letters began to arrive from attorneys for the Personal Watercraft Industry Association (PWIA). One eight-page argument accused me of being "discriminatory, arbitrary, and capricious." (These are precisely the words used by the WTO when it overturned the U.S. law on turtle protection.) The word "Kawasaki" was carefully left out of the correspondence, which referred only to the PWIA. However, the first person on the cc: list was a fellow at Kawasaki in Santa Ana, California. Throughout the ensuing legal battle, there was always great care taken to keep the name of the corporation from public awareness.

There was also great care taken to defuse the words "Jet Ski." Suddenly we were not allowed to use the term because it is a registered trademark. The appropriate phrase to use, we were told, was "personal watercraft." Their battle was going for the throat—mine as well as that of the English language. The words "Jet Ski" very accurately define the object under observation: a big ski that goes fast and sounds like a jet. But what are the implications of the words "personal watercraft"? Sounds like one of those big slow things that kids pedal peacefully through the water. Kawasaki knew well what it was about. Just rouse a few guys with Jet Skis and get them to start yelling about their personal rights, and then the corporation can hide in the wings. Which is exactly what happened.

I learned very quickly how corporations work. First of all, they don't exist. Then they invest in an attorney hired to take on any poor county employee just trying to do a job. I was subpoenaed twice and grilled in a room without windows. First the attorneys would be nice, then they'd be tricky, then they'd whisper together, then they'd try being nice again, then they'd leave the room for a break. It went on for hours. But the bottom line was that I'd done my job. Period. Even if I didn't know the small-print, fine details of international marine law that they flaunted in front of me. That wasn't in my job description. Protecting the park and its users was.

Unbeknownst to me, while I was off behind closed doors, something really important was happening. Jet Skis had been seen and heard zooming about our local waters, and citizen activist Maryann Anderson was mobilizing people throughout our island county. The community reaction was instinctive and overwhelming. The Jet Ski represented an invasion of our peace and quiet that was going just too far. Anderson minced no words: "The insensitivity of the macho thrill-craft maniacs who wreak havoc and destruction on our pristine parks and waterways is truly appalling," she announced.

A lot of things happened almost at once. The San Juan County Parks Board enacted an ordinance protecting all county parks from Jet-Ski launching. The county commissioners were besieged with requests for an ordinance that would keep Jet Skis out of the county altogether.

Before long, the groundswell encompassed people from all over the world who sympathized with the cause of peace and quiet, as well as environmental groups at home and abroad that sympathized with the delicate nature of our marine life—on the shoreline, where life is fragile and vulnerable, and in the depths, where the orca whales are fragile and vulnerable. Jet Skis are dirty as well as noisy; they pollute the water and air as well as the peace and quiet.

Suddenly it was a huge collective movement made up of many independent interests and concerns. It was as though the issues at large represented a harmonic disturbance in the universe and everyone knew it—whether or not they could articulate it. The collective threshold had been met and its voice was resonating around the world. Even our county's legal department finally got the picture. Realizing there was a David-and-Goliath fight to be fought and that the whole world was watching, they jumped into the fray with a vengeance. The fight was on.

It took three years and was a battle every second of the way. Maryann Anderson's tenacious talents and unswerving faith kept the community flame alive. She networked around the world and kept the information pouring in to fight the cause. Real cream-of-the-crop attorneys from all over the country offered free legal services to our small county. The Jet-Ski industry mobilized its own vast resources, and I'm sure they weren't free. It was astonishing how successful Kawasaki was at keeping its name out of things. Yet it was desperate to win. If this small upstart county could keep Jet Skis out of its waters, what next?

The county did win. Big. County jurisdiction over local waters was supported by the courts. The arguments were many, and encompassed

> **"Who are these legal fictions that we ourselves have created? And why have we allowed them to worm their way so intimately into our lives? How did they get to be omnipotent? Who gave them personhood, limited liability, and immortality under the law? And many of the same rights and privileges that we humans have? Does a corporation have a soul? Can it love? Show remorse? Seek revenge? Do corporations serve us, or do we serve them?"**
>
> —Kalle Lasn and Tom Liacas, "Corporate Crackdown," in *Adbusters*, August/September 2000

environmental rights of marine life and ecological integrity as well as the intrinsic right to peace and quiet in these islands. By then, I suspect, the "personal watercraft" industry was wishing it had quietly tucked its Kawasaki tail between its legs and left our small county park and its users alone. But they had to have it all. And the people said, "No!"

✿ ✿ ✿ ✿ ✿

It's this same corporate illness that's at the core of the policies of the WTO. A corporation per se could be a beautiful thing. It could foster health among employees, well-being throughout the cultures it impacts, a ray of hope for our beleaguered environment. It could help to make life better. But corporations are organized in a very specific way to make a very few people very rich—the behind-the-scenes players who are so well disguised by the corporate mask, the fictional entity that does not exist.

I say this over and over because it's frightening. Corporations have become the Emperor-Without-Clothes of the planet, and the rest of us are acting as though this nonexistent, bare-assed corporate catastrophe is fully dressed for winter at the North Pole. The corporate structure starts with evasions. We are misled by savvy and slick advertising, and kept in the dark about the devouring bottom line.

The World Trade Organization, as it now exists, is structured to support the care and feeding of corporate fortunes at the expense of the democratic way, and to fill the deep pockets of a few at the expense of the no pockets of the many. The question is: Can we wake up in time? The people on the streets of Seattle during WTO week had only one thing to say: *"Yes!"*

> "The power of the West to define and determine what is good for the whole world should be challenged. If we continue to allow the WTO, World Bank, and IMF to define how trade and development should take place, sooner or later those who are in the margins will be defined out of existence."
>
> —Victoria Tauli-Corpuz, director, Indigenous Peoples' International Centre for Policy Research and Education, Baguio City, Philippines, at WTO teach-in in Seattle

Now to the hard part. What exactly do we wake up to? A corporation is easy to vilify precisely for the same reason it succeeds so well: There is no readily visible person at the helm. Nobody is accountable;

nobody is responsible. Nobody is there. When we recoil and rebel, we are recoiling and rebelling from that which appears inhuman. A corporation, let loose to do its job, will always exploit without conscience. When money is the only measure, there is no other landscape upon which to gaze. But when human beings become measurable, as they did in Seattle, suddenly there is a shift, and the geography of corporate cause and effect is shown in its rightful complexity. A complexity that encompasses us all.

Recently somebody said to me that "a corporation has all the attributes of a person." His comment took me aback because I realized that it was partly true. A corporation is as complex as each of us, but there is at least one critical thing missing: empathy. Which means that if a corporation is a person, it is a sociopath. It changes shape to please its audience, it charms and seduces, it's brilliant in rationalizing its position and in getting its way. But it has no ability to feel. And this is why it engenders so much fear and frustration, so much reaction. The potent beauty of being human and in partnership with one another, as well as with this sustaining earth, is threatened by a nameless, faceless, powerful sociopath that is out of control.

A corporation is distinct from its people. The Battle in Seattle railed against corporate greed, not against any individual involved. In fact, throughout the entire week of education and protest, I don't remember one instance of personal name-calling. No CEOs were attacked; no general managers, no board of directors were named. It was the Corporate Culture that brought people out into the streets. And the WTO exists *because* of the Corporate Culture. It exists to support the Corporate Culture. And it exists at the behest of the Corporate Culture.

The conscience on the streets of Seattle was sophisticated. Here was the WTO, meeting deep in Microsoft territory at the invitation of Bill Gates, who lives just across Lake Washington from downtown Seattle. Yet there was no vilification of Bill Gates. This seemed remarkably restrained. How easy it would have been to take the protest to his front door, to scapegoat him as a billionaire villain and his company as a monopolizing scourge of society. But the collective consciousness in Seattle that week was sensitive to something far greater than the comings and goings of Bill Gates. It was resisting a consciousness that has no reverence for life because it focuses on the pursuit of profits.

But Bill Gates exists; so does his money. So do we. Even though Gates's charitable contributions (free computers to kids, et cetera) have been self-serving, recently he's given away millions, perhaps billions by now, to causes that help infants and children survive all over the world. These charitable causes reflect a humanitarian's concern for health and education of the poorest among us. This is a good thing. And, given his resources, an easy thing. What's harder—for Bill Gates and the rest of us—is to see how our fortunes, big and little, are intricately involved with the misfortunes of others. It's easy for us to see how our habits of consumption contribute to keeping people in jobs that support poor families in poor countries. It's not so easy for us to see how we are contributing to an unsustainable system that is slowly destroying the very finite resources that could keep entire societies self-sufficient into the foreseeable future.

These might be flourishing times here in the Northwest, but the growing economic inequity between the rich and the poor worldwide is widening dramatically. The combined incomes of three of the world's richest people—Bill Gates, Paul Allen, and Warren Buffett—exceed the combined incomes of the entire populations of the forty-eight poorest nations—totaling more than 600 million people. Gates, Allen, and Buffett may not be bad people. However, if we were to trace their corporate holdings and examine the deep impact of the companies in which they are involved, we'd be likely to find that there is not justice and equality across the board. "That's just the way it goes," say some. But Allen, Buffett, and Gates are thriving in a country founded on the principles of equality and justice for all. Shouldn't these very basic values extend beyond our borders and out into the human community at large? Why should these values lose significance when applied to those who service us but don't live within our borders? And what does "equality and justice for all" mean, anyway? It's an overwhelming question—for all of us, no matter what our income.

It's all too easy to be overwhelmed and shut down, or underwhelmed and apathetic, because we are so distant from the details of things. On a morning in March (March 25, 2000, to be precise), I woke to an interview with Nigel Noble on National Public Radio. He's a filmmaker who recently completed *The Charcoal People*, about the pig-iron industry in South America. It sounded like something out of the Dark Ages, but it's going on in Brazil right now. Huge trees are dragged out of the earth, cut into suitable lengths, put into huge ovens, and slowly burned into charred wood. This charred wood is welcomed at the iron factory, where its carbon strengthens the iron, which then is incorporated into fine-quality steel. Welcome to your new sports utility vehicle.

There are seven-year-old kids in these rapidly dwindling Brazilian forests whose job it is to pat down the mud at the entrance to the kilns that char the wood. They make a dollar or two a day working in an atmosphere that's smoke-filled and primitive. At the end of the interview,

Noble was asked about the value of this work to the Charcoal People. "If we stop importing pig iron, the people will suffer," commented the interviewer. "Yes," replied Noble. He went on to speak about the conflict between preserving biodiversity and employing the people. Complexity strikes again.

It might not be an inherently bad thing to have an SUV, but it is good to know what it's made of, where the stuff comes from, and whose hands have contributed to its existence. And it's good to question how equitably the profits from steel sales are spread among those who labor and sacrifice for our pleasure and convenience.

Corporate injustice was responsible for thousands of people coming from all over the world to Seattle to protest the policies of the WTO. Policies that serve the unfettered financial well-being of the corporation over the physical, spiritual, and economic well-being of the people. The picture is complex, challenging, and layered with questions of the corporate kind. The least we can do is ask them.

> "Thirty years ago, the richest fifth of humanity received 70 percent of world income, and the poorest fifth received 2.3 percent. Today, the richest fifth receives about 85 percent, and the share for the poorest fifth has shrunk to 1.4 percent."
>
> —The Canadian Ecumenical Jubilee Initiative

# 6 SHRINK TO FIT—IN WHICH THE WTO TAKES TO THE COUCH, THE THERAPIST ANSWERS THE QUESTIONS, AND THE DAUGHTER WINS THE CONTEST

"Do you pay regular visits to yourself?"
—Rumi, thirteenth-century Persian poet and mystic,
    from *The Illuminated Rumi,* translated by Coleman Barks,
    illustrated by Michael Green

A lot of interesting things have happened in my therapist's office, but I didn't expect the WTO to be one of them. Psychotherapist Brian Moss lives and works in Seattle, I live and work on San Juan Island; these days I see him regularly but not often—which, after fourteen years, is a good thing.

Shortly after Christmas 1999, I was in his office carrying on about my WTO experience when he told me that he'd been there on N30, too. I was very surprised. It meant he'd abandoned all his clients for the day and gone off to protest. Which meant some serious planning ahead. Brian (I cannot call him "Moss") is very tall and very thoughtful. Rather reserved, too.

He pointed to a pile of books on the corner of his desk. "I read those to get prepared," he said. "Oh," I replied, realizing that I hadn't read anything at all and had better get their titles before I left his office.

We went on to other things. How was Christmas? White-knuckled but no bleeding. Was there a boyfriend? No, but I was hopeful. Was I writing? No, but I would be. Mostly we sat and liked each other, which is what happens after fourteen years of good work on both our parts.

As I was leaving, after I'd written down the names of the books by Lori Wallach, Michelle Sforza, David Korten, Steven Shrybman, Michel Chossudovsky, and a couple of others, Brian said, "Hmmm, I wonder if I can tell you this?" My hand was on the doorknob. "Of course you can," I said quickly. He never tells me anything, so I thought, "Hmmm, this must be good." It was.

Brian's twelve-year-old stepdaughter ("He has a stepdaughter?" I thought) had entered a national WTO essay contest and had won a trip to Ireland as a result (see sidebar, The World Trade Organization). Startling all around. It was early in my research into who was at the WTO and why, and this synchronicity was a harbinger of things to come. Everyone I contacted about the WTO spilled forth stories and contacts that wouldn't stop.

I e-mailed Brian some questions, and in his thoughtful way he answered some of them.

*JT:* Would you please tell me the logistical details of your participation in N30? Did you bus downtown? Drive? Walk? With others? Where did you join the march? What was your experience throughout? Did you walk with a group? How long did your day last? Et cetera.

*Brian:* Cary Birdsall, an activist from Talkeetna, Alaska, who had come to Seattle to take part in the protest, was staying at our house. A schoolteacher, he was active in his community creating discussion and awareness regarding the issues of WTO and globalization, privatization, deregulation, commercialization, concentration of media, and corporate cartels.

We woke early and walked to the nearby bus stop. Waiting for the bus was a prelude to the remainder of the day. First of all, it was inspiring to see the large number of people all headed downtown. We were packed into the bus, and my thoughts drifted to the nature of community, and the lack of a meaningful one in most of our lives; what people are capable of when they organize; and of course I thought of Montgomery, Alabama. Already, at 7:00 A.M., there was that kind of resonance in the air, that this was a defining event.

There were two factions on the bus: an articulate group that was politically aware and could tell you why they were there, and a smaller group that had "issues with authority." The informed group was unimaginably diverse: The graduate student in physics from Chicago who was covering the event for an alternative radio station. The French farmer and his American counterparts who were deeply concerned about genetically modified food and the implications of corporate farming, in which profit takes precedence over food quality or sustainability; we talked about how tomatoes tasted when we were kids (haven't we all?) and how silly it was that most stores had only one or two varieties of apples (waxed, dyed, and mealy) when there are thousands of varieties, each unique. There was a mom, determined and completely without cynicism; there were high school students whose teacher was obviously teaching beyond the book; a physician who cut her political teeth on her experiences with managed care; a man representing a nongovernmental organization promoting equitable, democratic, and ecologically sustainable development. There were young artists already having fun at this early hour, and two union leaders in jackets with their Local numbers on the back who looked like they never had any fun, which made their presence all the more meaningful. How did the media so completely miss these people?

The other faction didn't seem to know why they felt so disempowered, but they were angry about it. I thought about how easy it would be to manipulate this anger, to splinter it and project it onto an unrelated

## The Tip of Civil Society

It's estimated that at least 700 groups were represented at the WTO demonstrations in Seattle. Most of the groups represented civil society; they were not affiliated with governments, although some were agencies that were affiliated with the United Nations. A very short representative list:

AFL-CIO
Alliance for Democracy
American Corn Growers Association
American Friends Service Committee
Animal Welfare Institute
Art and Revolution
Asian Indigenous Women's Network
Canadian Labour Congress
Center for Food Policy
Center for Labor Research and
  Education
Chilean Ecological Action Network
Citizens Action Group
Council for Responsible Genetics
Council of Canadians

Direct Action Network
Earth Island Institute
Earthjustice Legal Defense Fund
European Union Trade Forum
Friends of the Earth
Global Action
Global Exchange
Greenpeace
Humane Society
Indigenous Environmental Network
Indigenous Peoples' International
  Centre for Policy Research and
  Education
Institute for Agriculture and Trade
  Policy
Institute for Consumer Responsibility
Institute for Policy Studies
Institute of Science for Society
International Brotherhood of Electrical
  Workers (IBEW)
International Brotherhood of
  Teamsters
International Center for Technology
  Assessment
International Federation of Free Trade
International Forum on Globalization

and undeserving source, a different race, for instance, or a religious group, or the "government"—you know, anyone "different" from "us." The power of the N30 protest was that there was no unified "us." In fact, it made for some awkward moments when so many groups, many historically pitted against each other, came together in a single voice of protest against the WTO (see sidebar, The Tip of Civil Society).

When we got off the bus, we headed to the First United Methodist Church in downtown Seattle, which served as the home base for much of the day's activities. After the two-day teach-in at Benaroya Hall organized by the International Forum on Globalization (IFG), the workshops and lectures continued at the Methodist church. I was unable to attend the IFG event. Without a prior ticket, thousands of us were being turned

International Longshore and Warehouse Union
International Network on Disarmament and Globalization
International Society for Ecology and Culture
Jubilee 2000
King County Labor Council
Movement for the Survival of the Ogoni People
National Family Farm Coalition
National Farmers Union
National Organization for Women
Organization of African Trade Union Unity
Peace Action
People for Fair Trade
People-Centered Development Forum
People's Assembly
Polaris Institute
Program on Corporations, Law & Democracy
Public Citizen
Raging Grannies
Rainforest Action Network
Research Organization for Science
Ruckus Society
Sea Turtle Restoration Project
Sierra Club
Students from Everywhere
Suzuki Foundation
Technology and Ecology
Third World Network
Transnational Institute
United for a Fair Economy
United Steelworkers of America
Via Campesina
Washington Association of Churches
Washington Physicians for Social Responsibility
Washington Tilth Producers
West Coast Environmental Law Association
Western Sustainable Agriculture Working Group
Women, Food & Agriculture Network
Women's International League for Peace and Freedom
World Forum of Fish Harvesters and Fishworkers

away. More than 700 groups took part in the N30 protests, and many of them were represented and networking at the teach-in and the ongoing activities at the church. In his essay "N30—Skeleton Woman in Seattle," Paul Hawken wrote, "It was an extravagant display of research, intelligence, and concern, expressed by scholars, diplomats, writers, academics, fishermen, scientists, farmers, geneticists, businesspeople, and lawyers. Prior to the teach-in, nongovernmental organizations, institutes, public-interest law firms, farmers' organizations, unions, and councils had been issuing papers, communiqués, press releases, books, and pamphlets for years. They were almost entirely ignored by the WTO." (And, I might add, by the mainstream media.)

I looked in on a lecture by an Indian woman who used the word "fascist" to describe the concentration of power in the world and the way it was being used to exploit the poor in her country. It was jarring to hear the word used in a scholarly presentation instead of being shouted on the street. On my way to find a bathroom in the basement of the church, I overheard a radio interview being prepared. The alternative radio station, broadcasting over the Internet, was crammed into a small room opposite the bathrooms.

We had planned on attending the 10:00 A.M. labor rally at Memorial Stadium, but there was so much happening around the convention center that we decided to go over there and take it all in. It was surreal. Cops in all-black uniforms, complete with black capes (rain parkas), more science fiction–looking than even the military. This wasn't the clean-cut-looking National Guard from the '60s. Undercover police and members of intelligence agencies, easily spotted by the wires in their ears, stood at strategic street corners.

Many of the protesters had a sense of humor. Some of the protesters, and most of the police, did not. The air was so charged with tension, it felt as though it would ignite if someone lit a match. We retreated to the Monorail and headed for the Seattle Center and the labor rally. This was the first time in my life I had seen the Monorail full of people, as though it were truly a form of mass transit and not a theme-park ride. Still, I was not prepared for what was ahead at the stadium.

It was standing-room only, including out on the field. Later on, I talked to a union representative who told me about the petty politics being played out in the stadium: how the various local union leaders were quarreling over who would get to sit under the limited tarp space, out of the rain and in close proximity to the free doughnuts and coffee that had initially been intended for the speakers. It is amazing that N30 happened at all.

I climbed up high to the back of the stadium near the entrance. And there it was so crowded that I decided to stay where I was. I noticed that the dignified man standing next to me was wearing a three-piece suit and appeared to be surrounded by a group of younger aides. Curious, I asked him who he was. It was Senator Carl Levin, from Michigan. First elected in 1978, he is the senior Democrat on the Senate Armed Services Committee and a member of the Small Business Committee. He also serves as the ranking member of the Government Affairs Permanent Subcommittee on Investigations, as well as of the Senate Select Committee on Intelligence. Why was the mainstream media more interested in kids breaking windows than in what this man might have to say? Did they even know he was here?

The speakers at the rally ranged from pedantic to passionate. As several spoke, I had shivers up my spine and could see the value of a truly great man or woman capable of speaking for, and leading, the people. I was wondering about our own leaders here in the United States: where they were, and how their voices have been replaced with the voices of pundits and celebrities with nothing to say.

The labor march was delayed, and restless thousands started off on their own. Eventually we joined them. As we entered the downtown core, there were protesters everywhere. What had been a well-planned march completely disintegrated and was absorbed into the sea of people surging back and forth through the canyons of downtown Seattle.

We stayed until evening and then went home. At this point, there was no way I could ride. I needed to walk.

*JT:* What was your reaction to the media coverage of N30?

*Brian:* Two books I think of repeatedly are Ben Bagdikian's *The Media Monopoly* and Herbert Schiller's *Information Inequality: The Deepening Social Crisis in America.*

The first news coverage, often live, was on television. How can I describe the television coverage? How would a sports enthusiast feel if he tuned in to see the big game, and the entire coverage was focused on the guy selling peanuts in the stands? His every move. And endless speculation regarding his motives. That is how I felt. The coverage was a veil that missed or minimized every substantive issue, diverting attention to the violence or threat of violence in the street. But isn't that what television news coverage is usually about? (I recently heard that violence on television may finally be taken seriously because research is showing that when programming becomes too violent, the resulting stress makes viewers unable to remember the commercials!) To watch the television coverage, one would think that the defining moment of the entire movement, the culmination and purpose of the N30 protest, was the throwing of a newspaper dispenser through the window of a Starbucks.

The print media was a little more sophisticated, but to the same end. Endless articles, the likes of "Why Would Anyone Be Against World Trade?" and "World Trade Creates a Strong Economy," surfaced in the daily papers. The articles misleadingly implied that 50,000 people were in the streets of Seattle protesting *trade*, which wasn't true. We were protesting unfair trade policies.

The financial press went further than discrediting the issues; they portrayed the demonstrators themselves as "irrational." This was best exemplified by *New York Times* columnist Thomas Friedman in his article "Senseless in Seattle," December 1, 1999 ["a Noah's ark of flat-earth advocates, protectionist trade unions and yuppies looking for their 1960's fix..."]. Since the dominant media is entirely a voice for corporate interests, it follows that social criticism will be directed at individuals or groups within society (including government, even though there is essentially corporate control of policy-making), while leaving corporate interests unchallenged. This tendency to point to individual weaknesses and failings reinforces a dark and mean-spirited view of human nature, further fragmenting prospects for social cooperation and human solidarity. The disturbing condition whereby the social needs of the many are thwarted by the private interests of the few remains veiled and beyond discussion. It is this condition that was challenged on the streets of Seattle and around the world. The protest movement has an Emperor's-New-Clothes way of saying what is not supposed to be said, which might account for the virulence of articles such as Friedman's.

*JT:* From a psychological perspective, how would you describe the existing structure of the WTO? The nature of the WTO protest? Is there a metaphor in psychology that describes their relationship to one another?

*Brian:* For some reason, the first thing that comes to me is the following story: Two men are walking down a road barefoot, before the invention of shoes. The road is rocky and uneven and painful to their feet. The first man says, "I have a great idea! Let's cover this road with leather so it will be easier to walk on." After thinking about it for a while, the second man replies, "Wouldn't it be easier to just cover our feet?"

*JT:* Where does greed come from?

*Brian:* Greed is the fear of not getting what we want or of not having enough. When we do get what we want and it doesn't make us happy, we want more. Instead of questioning this, we simply escalate the process. It is the pursuit of pleasure, yet rarely results in pleasure. The fruits of greed cannot make us whole. It is a paradoxical process, much like paranoia, which is the paradoxical attempt to feel safe by always reminding oneself how unsafe life is.

*JT:* Is there a new psychology of spirit that needs to surface to ensure our survival as a species on the planet?

*Brian:* The word "psychology" derives from the Greek word *psyche,* meaning "soul." Psychology was originally the study of the soul. Our culture, the culture of the WTO, and, for the most part, psychology as it is currently practiced are so thoroughly mechanistic and reductionist (the doctrine that complex systems can be completely understood in terms of their simplest parts) that we, like psychology, have lost our original purpose. This is an important insight when one realizes that the word "heal" derives from the word that means "to make whole."

To stay within the domain of psychology: The word "therapy" derives from the Greek word *therapeia,* meaning "to heal." The derivation of "heal" is from the Old English word *haelan,* meaning "whole." Integration is the process of making something whole and, sure enough, the Latin derivation of "integration" is from the same root as "heal."

To survive, we must heal in this true sense of the word: by becoming whole. There is no enemy. Those spreading violence of whatever kind, military or economic, those motivated by greed and power, are simply in greater need of healing. Shaming them does not help them heal.

I would go so far as to say that the present concentration of wealth, the unprecedented levels of commercialization and exploitation, in which even schools, medical care, and public utilities are becoming realms for corporate profit, are the direct result of this fragmentation. A new psychology of spirit is a psychology of wholeness, and not just within the individual but within the community at large. A wholeness in which we would no more exploit someone, be it for labor or profit, than we would attack one part of our body to make another part more comfortable.

I like the way you say "psychology of spirit that needs to surface," because it implies that it was always there but simply eclipsed, veiled, and in the background. Our religious institutions, instead of being avenues of enlightenment, have often contributed to this veil. Power accumulates and dogma begins to serve the privileged. There have always been the mystics and sages in every tradition who threaten the accepted doctrine even as they provided the original inspiration for it. They lived within the tension of the church or the doctrine of their day. This is where true spirit is found, a spirit that serves no one if it does not serve all.

I remember the story of the black boy walking with his father past the all-white church in the South. "Is it true that a black man has never been in that church?" he asks. "Yes, that is true," replies his father, "and neither has God."

I started talking about psychology and here I am discussing spiritual matters, which is how it should be, because one is the microcosm of the other.

## The World Trade Organization

by Alana Byrne, age 12

The idea of the World Trade Organization is good; representatives of the different countries get together to discuss world trade. Unfortunately, it didn't turn out quite like that. The representatives were not democratically elected and their definition of world trade is different than mine. WTO wants every country to be able to sell their products in every other country. This sounds great but there are problems. For example, France does not want America's beef, which has been treated with hormones so the cow could be butchered sooner. The French, who do not like cow hormones, are now not allowed to sell their cheese in America. They also have huge fines against them and are being threatened to be kicked out of the World Trade Organization.

A major problem is that countries' health, safety, and environmental laws are affected. If the WTO makes laws that have a lower standard than any country, that country will be forced to submit to WTO's laws. For instance, Guatemala, which has a high illiteracy rate, passed a law that said baby formula jars should not have pictures of fat, smiling babies. This sounds weird, but they had a good reason; babies were dying because mothers thought that if they gave their babies the formula instead of nursing them, their babies would be fat and smiling. They ➤

*JT:* How can long-term activists avoid burnout?

*Brian:* (1) By living within a spiritual context, which makes us less dependent upon (and depressed by) outcomes. A spiritual life does not relieve us of responsibility, but it can add acceptance and joy to the journey. (2) By developing community. (3) By maintaining a sense of humor.

When dealing with such urgent issues in the face of such crippling injustice, burnout is inevitable. For long-term activists, it's a cycle they learn to go through. What helps activists survive in the long term is the ability to emerge again and again. To resurrect themselves, much as in the making of charcoal—a process that provides a perhaps quieter, but hotter, fire. I am reminded of the Victor Frankl quote: "What is to give light must endure burning."

---

would take the formula home to mix with contaminated water and the babies would get very sick and eventually die. Guatemala wanted to encourage nursing to save the babies' lives. Gerber filed a complaint and the WTO would not allow this law. They said it excluded Gerber's products. The babies kept getting sick.

If you think about it, you realize that countries all over the world have incredibly different climates, populations, needs, and types of flora and fauna. No one set of rules should apply to all these different places; the Amazon rain forest needs different standards than New York City.

The WTO can and does do good things, but there is certainly room for improvement. One of the first things I think they should do is to have the WTO vote democratically on important things. That way, all countries would have an equal voice. Having the delegates elected would also help; it would be the people's voice.

The delegates didn't get a lot of work done at the current meeting in Seattle. There was much disagreement and thousands of protesters. I don't think all the protests were needed, but it was good to make a point. Many Third World countries were supportive of the protesters because the protesters were saying many of the same things the countries themselves had said.

So with all of its ups and downs, the World Trade Organization is a great idea, but revisions are necessary.

*JT:* Your stepdaughter won a WTO essay contest; how did she develop this political awareness? Do you think that there is a surfacing global consciousness developing in our young people?

*Brian:* Alana won the "Newspapers in Education" essay contest sponsored by the *Seattle Times* and *Parade* magazine. When I talked to her about it, she said that she became aware of the issues through listening to National Public Radio, discussions at school, and researching her essay. Children are eager for real information, and they pay attention, more so than we give them credit for. The question is, what will we surround them with, and what will we encourage them to pay attention to? She felt that kids today are aware of global concerns, but had nothing to compare them to.

I think any increased global awareness exists in tension with the power of advertising and the commercialization of children's experience. Children are increasingly seen as another market, and the theme throughout this WTO discussion is that the values of the marketplace are not compatible with social cooperation or increased consciousness. The advertising addressed to children is very sophisticated and based on extensive market surveys and research, yet many children would balk at the idea that they are being manipulated. Advertising is also pervasive, even entering the once-sacred space of the classroom. It is encouraging to see these tools being turned around and used to different ends. *Adbusters*, for instance, with its message that it is cool for kids to resist the commercialization and the sales pitches they are surrounded by and thetruth.com, with its website and TV and print ads designed to outwit the tobacco industry at its own game. An excellent book is Jean Kilbourne's *Deadly Persuasion: Why Women and Girls Must Fight the Addictive Power of Advertising*. I would like to see media literacy taught to children, but this quickly becomes a political issue over whose interests will be served.

# 7 SITTING IT OUT—IN WHICH THE STUDENTS LEAD THE WAY AND THE POLICE USE THE SPRAY

> "You can have multiple strategies to go after the World Trade
> Organization, but one of the key approaches is: don't let
> them take the focus off where it belongs, and it belongs
> on the human face behind the label and behind the product.
> The exploitation, the starvation wages, the armed guards,
> that's where the focus belongs."
> —Charlie Kernaghan, executive director of the National
>    Labor Committee, addressing students at the University
>    of Washington, October 3, 1999, broadcast on *Alternative Radio*

There is a great irony behind the North American and European student protest movement against the World Trade Organization: The students are protesting both the physically impoverished lives of those who are exploited in the name of profit, as well as the way in which Corporate Culture spiritually impoverishes their own lives. Critics are quick to point the finger at students who are so privileged that they have nothing better to do but bite the hand of the system that feeds them. What the critics don't understand is, that's precisely what the students are trying to do, because the system feeds them nothing but crass commercialism. And they are fed up with it.

In her book *No Logo—Taking Aim at the Brand Bullies,* Naomi Klein chronicles this rising tide of frustration and rebellion among younger people. And she includes herself: "What haunts me is not exactly the absence of literal space so much as a deep craving for metaphorical space: release, escape, some kind of open-ended freedom." This gilded age of high-tech wealth has produced a wave of youthful revolutionaries who want to get back to meaning, to mystery, to metaphor. To them, freedom means more—and less—than money. It means individual and personal experience, free of corporate definition.

To those of us who are more than a few years out of high school and college, this is not an easy reach. We already got defined—by the freedom of individuality in the '60s, by the tragedies of the Vietnam War, by the threat of nuclear war in the '70s and early '80s, and by the giddy explosion into capitalistic consumerism in the mid-'80s. We have no way of knowing the depth to which this legacy of consumerism has hollowed out experience for our young people. They were born on the cusp of consumerism, and they are finding out what's on the other side. Just as we looked over the dark edge of war, nuclear arms, and communism, they are looking over the dark edge of the advertising age into consumer-driven capitalism, and they don't like what they see, or what they feel. They are following the money to find out why. And money talks.

Klein's book is full of objective facts that go a long way toward explaining the subjective experience of our young people. In 1980, in the United States, overall corporate advertising expenditure was about $50 billion a year. In 1998, it was nearly $200 billion. Way back in 1963, when a lot of us baby boomers were growing up, it was less than $5 billion. Even that sum sounds extraordinary, but compared to today's corporately defined life, it was peanuts.

And corporate advertising doesn't stop at billboards and TV. It sponsors things. In 1985, U.S. corporate sponsorship spending was about $1 billion a year; in 1998, it was close to $7 billion a year. A 700 percent increase. Klein makes a compelling case for the damage done by the corporatization of our entire experience—from soup to spirit—and the kids are seeing through it. The corporate goal of cashing in on the buying and spending power of the younger generation is backfiring.

What's not getting lost on this rising generation is that much of the profits go not only into the pockets of a few, but into the actual *creation* of a corporate-induced value system, a lifestyle of consumption that is dependent upon the deprivation of others. "I think more and more Americans are realizing that our privilege, and our lifestyle, means that somebody else is suffering," says Seattle activist Vanessa Lee. She is right. And writer Naomi Klein, a young woman herself, has cast a big light on the dark truth: Advertising is us. In her own search for meaning, she has brilliantly exposed these meaningless times.

But the times they are a-changin'. Students across the country are becoming sweatshop savvy, and they don't need a calculator to figure out that the price of a new pair of Nike shoes far exceeds the cost of sweatshop labor. In 1999, Nike spent more than a half-billion dollars in advertising. Even at the University of Oregon, which is a big beneficiary of Nike's success via contributions from founder Phil Knight, there is rebellion. In April 1999, the students there lobbied successfully for the university to join the Worker Rights Consortium, a sweatshop watchdog group that monitors the origins of university-logo clothing and products. Knight withdrew his plans to donate to the school's new stadium expansion project. Knight and his company favor the Fair Labor Association, an industry-based monitoring program, over the Worker Rights Consortium. But students are wary of industry monitoring itself, and are rapidly organizing to advocate for workers. There are now more than 150 chapters of United Students Against Sweat-shops in colleges and universities across the country and the number is growing.

In his talk at the University of Washington on October 3, 1999, National Labor Committee executive director Charlie Kernaghan called the student movement against sweatshops "the strongest human rights and labor rights movement alive in the country today." Much of his talk, which was broadcast on *Alternative Radio*, was about El Salvador, where there are 225 free-trade-zone factories that are set up like prisons—cinder-block walls with razor wire, armed guards, locked metal gates. The factories employ 70,000 young women who get fired if they meet in groups, are allowed to go to the bathroom twice a day (with permission), work forced overtime (fired if they don't), are forced to be tested for pregnancy, and are fired if they get pregnant. If they're working in a garment factory, they are not allowed to wear makeup because they might sweat it off onto the clothing. They make 60 cents an hour.

"The same system: You raise your hand, you get a ticket, you present it to the guard at the toilet. You can use the bathroom once in the morning and once in the afternoon. In this factory, you couldn't wear any makeup. We hadn't heard that one before. Like, why can't you wear makeup? And, of course, it was because the factory was 100 degrees and Nike was afraid that the women would sweat and wipe the perspiration from their faces on the Nike garment. They patrol the aisles looking for lipstick. And if you've got it, you're out of there. You lose a day's pay."

—Charlie Kernaghan, in an address to students at the University of Washington in Seattle, October 3, 1999

The argument for such labor camps is that "it's a job and the workers' cost of living is low." Kernaghan quickly dispels this myth. When a group of students from Columbia University in New York went to El Salvador to do a wage analysis, they found the wages equaled one-third the actual cost of living. After daily expenses of 60 cents for transportation, 80 cents for a company breakfast, and $1.49 for lunch, the workers were taking home $1.82 a day. That didn't count the cost of their pregnancy tests, for which they also have to pay, or the cost of day care, which was about $1.63 a day. "Women in El Salvador are raising their children on coffee, because they can't afford milk," said Kernaghan. The Nike shirts that they are making for 20 cents' worth of labor are selling for $75. When asked about the Nike Code of Conduct, the workers said that they must wash their hands and wear plastic gloves. They had no idea that the Code of Conduct actually holds Nike accountable to its workers.

The stories that Kernaghan tells about merely finding the factories, let alone getting into them and gathering information, are hair raising. There is great danger to the workers, who get fired for "crying to the gringos," and danger also to those gringos doing the research. A recent group of students from five universities—including Yale, the University of Kentucky, and Middlebury College—were attacked and had their cameras broken and stolen when they attempted to record the conditions in an El Salvador factory that was making clothes for major labels. According to Kernaghan, from 1992 to 1998 there has been a 600 percent increase in the export of garments and shoes to the United States. The World Trade Organization is suggesting that the 60-cent hourly wage is too high and should be lowered to 36 cents an hour.

> "The women told us they were searched on their way in to the factory, to take candy away from them. This is also typical. Because Nike, you see, doesn't want the women bringing in Tootsie Rolls because God forbid they should get a little chocolate stain on the garment."
>
> —Charlie Kernaghan, in an address to students at the University of Washington in Seattle, October 3, 1999

Kernaghan went on to cite similar, but worse, scenarios in China, Haiti, and Burma. In one Chinese shoe factory alone, there are more than 50,000 workers, all between the ages of seventeen and twenty-five. Workers are no longer employed after the age of twenty-five, because they are considered worn out. In Haiti, a

Disney *101 Dalmatians* shirt costing about $20 in the United States is made for 6 cents in labor costs. In Burma, now called Myanmar, where the military dictatorship runs the factories, workers make 6 cents an hour working for multinational corporations that share their profits with the military, which uses its earnings to buy weapons from China. According to a 1997 U.S. law, there is supposed to be no new investment in Burma, but U.S. investment in that country has increased 44 percent since the law was enacted. The State of Massachusetts, which passed a law in 1996 that imposed a 10 percent penalty on goods and services provided by companies with financial interests in Burma, has been called to task by the WTO and recently had its law overturned by the U.S. Supreme Court because state laws are not supposed to be stronger than federal laws. There is no penalty, however, for those corporations routinely breaking the federal law against investment in Burma. (See also chapter 4, The ABCs of the WTO.)

The craziness is not just far outside U.S. borders. In Saipan, a U.S. territory, American corporations are not subject to immigration or labor laws. Factory recruiters bring in workers from China by promising high wages and "American" jobs. For this opportunity, each worker has to pay $5,000, which indentures him or her indefinitely. Workers are locked in factories and dorms, and are fired and deported for getting married or pregnant, criticizing the company, or practicing religion (which "drains them of energy"). They are paid $3 an hour, and because Saipan is a U.S. territory, companies such as Wal-Mart, the Gap, J. Crew, and the Limited get to label their products "Made in the U.S.A."

Within the United States proper, Wal-Mart, the largest retailer in the world, pays $6.10 an hour and often caps the work week at twenty-five hours, which means many Wal-Mart workers in the United States don't get any benefits and are eligible for food stamps. Yet Wal-Mart's annual gross sales are more than the total domestic products of 155 of the world's countries. Nike's Phil Knight is worth more than $5.8 billion; Disney's Michael Eisner earns $104,000 per hour. Corporate executives make millions, while some U.S. workers go on food stamps and sweatshop workers can earn as little as thirteen cents an hour.

Nike, Disney, Wal-Mart, Adidas, Liz Claiborne, and other companies with visible identities are relatively easy to identify. It's the corporate ethic in its less easily identifiable form that breeds the more systemic threat: the politician who rides into office on a wave of corporate experience, promotes and supports free-trade laws, and then returns to the corporate marketplace to reap the benefits when the stint of "public service" is over; the military arms sales to foreign countries that don't identify the corporations that benefit so grandly from the sales; the flowers in the marketplace that are grown abroad on corporate-owned farms that still use deadly pesticides that impact the health of poorly paid workers. Neither the guns nor the flowers have labels. Tracking down the origins of the things we buy has become a complex and confounding challenge. Even when we do know where things were made, we don't know how or at what price to the laborers. And we are addicted to our ignorance.

✿   ✿   ✿   ✿   ✿

All these issues are surfacing on college campuses across the country, and it's making for a lot of queasy corporations. "They don't know how to deal with you," Kernaghan told his student audience. "The biggest

## Not-So-Hallowed Halls

My friend and spiritual colleague Richard Wright made the trek from San Juan Island to the WTO protests in Seattle with his buddies Craig Staude, a marine biologist, and Walt VomLehn, a retired physician. Richard himself is a retired teacher, and we chatted later about his WTO experiences. "Living on an island insulates us from social justice causes," he said. "The WTO in Seattle gave me the opportunity to act upon my convictions." He researched the issues on the Internet, participated in the Jubilee circle to free debt-ridden countries, and walked in the labor march on N30. "We started out with the steelworkers," he said, "and ended up with Free Tibet."

Our WTO talk ended up in the lap of education. Wright is from a family in which "education is a genetic thing." He taught for nineteen years on the island, and before that for twelve years in middle school in East Los Angeles. Somewhere in between he attended Union Theological Seminary in New York. He is also a student of Buddhism and a teacher of tai chi. His reflections about the educational process, however, focused on our public schools.

"It's become a curriculum dictated by business," he said. "It's no longer education in the broad liberal arts sense." During his thirty years of teaching, Wright said, his flexibility in teaching the curriculum was more and more limited by the state legislature. "We used to able to teach according to our strengths," said Wright. "Now business lobbies the legislature to determine a curriculum that will focus on ➤

nightmare a multinational company has is when young people ask serious questions. The minute you start challenging them, they wet their pants."

Which is why students like recent college graduate Sarah Joy Staude, who was part of the direct action protest at WTO, is not afraid to wet her pants in protest. Staude, who was born and raised on idyllic San Juan Island, came with about a hundred other students from Lewis and Clark College in Portland up to Seattle to do civil disobedience on N30. She was part of a support group this time around, and was not one of the locked-down students who were wearing adult diapers in case their sit-in immobilized them past the point of no return. (In preparing for civil disobedience, individuals decide whether they will be "arrestable" or part of the support team. If arrestable, they literally lock themselves together and stay seated in protest.) I met with Staude and her parents for brunch one Sunday after

---

the skills that will feed the business community. The curriculum is no longer so concerned with issues of truth, justice and goodness."

Commercialism is now a big part of the nationwide education system. Companies are trying to build brand recognition at ever-younger ages through direct advertising in the schools, corporate-sponsored educational materials, product giveaways, contests, and incentive programs. The Center for Commercial-Free Public Education (www.commercialfree.org), based in Oakland, California, reports such occurrences as "sponsored educational materials" that show students how to design a McDonald's restaurant and how to apply for a job at McDonald's; a reading curriculum that teaches first-graders to start out by recognizing logos from Kmart, M & M's, Jell-O, and Target; a week of classroom time during which students learn the life cycle of a Nike shoe; an Exxon video that teaches about the Valdez oil spill as a great example of environmental protection; and a National Depression Screening Day during which representatives from Prozac talk about depression to high school assemblies.

The citizens of Seattle have been active in fighting such commercialization of education. When the school board proposed selling advertising opportunities in the schools to raise $1 million per year, the community sustained a five-month fight against the policy, which was finally rescinded by the school board.

It seems a long distance between elementary school and WTO policies, but the links are readily visible, as are the young people out fighting such "branding" of their experience. Richard Wright noticed them out on the streets of Seattle. "It gave me a little hope for the future," he said.

church, and we talked about the WTO and the time she got arrested in Portland for protesting Fidelity Investment's exploitation of the U'wa people in Colombia.

Sarah Joy Staude is not one of the so-called Oregon anarchists. She's serious, thoughtful, and independent, as is her commitment to social justice. She's the only child in a family that is close and communicative; they are all active in the faith community of the island's St. David's Episcopal Church (Sarah too, when she's home). She was just graduating from high school when I started attending church, so I have watched her grow more and more independent through four years of college. And watched her parents, Craig and Krispi (maiden name Kellogg, no relation to corn flakes), respond to their daughter's growing activism. Craig, who is a marine biologist and a manager at the University of Washington's research labs in Friday Harbor, went to the Jubilee 2000 event and the labor march and rally with two other men from the community of St. David's, but he and his daughter didn't cross paths on the streets of WTO Seattle. As is representative of the two generations, she was in the heart of the protest doing direct action; Craig was on the edge of N30 with moral, ethical, and spiritual support for fair trade and liberation politics.

As we sat around the table eating scrambled eggs and fruit salad in their quiet, TV-free log home, I could feel the peace, stability, and support that had nurtured Sarah to adulthood. She would be leaving later in the day to go back to Portland, so it was her turn to talk; I would talk to her father about his experiences later.

The students from Lewis and Clark had driven up from Portland to Seattle the night before N30, and convened at a church on the east side of Lake Washington. They met late into the night, working through a consensus process to decide who would lock down (a form of protest in which the group seals their arms so that police cannot separate them and break up the sit-in), who would be the support network, where they would position themselves, and how to solve all the logistical problems of getting 100 students to the same place at the same time (and in unison with other activists from around the country). Shortly before 6:00 A.M. the next day, after an hour of sleep, they were heading to Denny Park, near the Pink Elephant car wash on the northern edge of downtown Seattle. Direct Action Network (DAN), the grassroots coalition of groups participating in nonviolent action on N30, was giving early morning guidance at the park, as well as at two other locations around the city.

There continues to be a lot of confusion about who, exactly, was the organizer of the direct action on N30. And a whole lot of planning went into the confusion. The commitment to the issues led the way, and the issues were diverse and specific. The four-page invitation to participate in the "Festival of Resistance" direct action in Seattle listed thirteen interest areas: war, low wages, deforestation, gentrification, gridlocked cities, genetic engineering, the rich getting richer, cuts in social services, increasing poverty, meaningless jobs, global warming, more prisons, and sweatshops. The only thing missing was animal protection, which was more than well covered by Ben White and his turtles.

The goal, directly and unequivocally stated months ahead of time, was to shut down the WTO in Seattle. It was no secret. David Solnit of Art and Revolution wrote in the invitation guideline, "We are planning a large-scale, well-organized, high-visibility action to shut down the World Trade Organization on November 30. We will nonviolently and creatively block them from meeting." And hundreds of groups prepared to do just that. "We envision colorful and festive actions with large-scale street theater as a major element," the invitation continued. "We will make space and encourage mutual respect for a variety of nonviolent action styles reflecting our different groups and communities." The bywords were "educate, agitate, organize." And the guidelines were clearly stated: "(1) We will use no violence, physical or verbal, toward any person. (2) We will carry no weapons. (3) We will not bring or use any alcohol or illegal drugs. (4) We will not destroy property."

The plan was to take a stand for democracy over capitalist exploitation, and to fill the jails if necessary to get the point across. And nearly all

> **"The U'wa tribal leaders are threatening to commit mass suicide by jumping off the Cliff of Death, if Shell and Occidental move into their mountains. Mass ritual suicide is part of the U'wa tradition in protest against colonization and threats to their existence as a people. Without the strong support of other indigenous peoples and nongovernmental organizations, the violation of the basic rights of the U'wa would not have been known by the world. Unfortunately, those who give support, like my friend Ingrid Washaniwatok, had to be killed."**
>
> —Victoria Tauli-Corpuz, director, Indigenous Peoples' International Centre for Policy Research and Education

the "arrestables" were college students. "What I'm feeling is a common sentiment among people my age," said Sarah Joy. "And it's a real paradox. We are privileged enough to be studying it. The poor people who are being exploited don't have the time to think about the global situation because they're just trying to survive. We have enough money, or scholarships, or whatever, to be going to a small liberal arts school and discuss and debate and get outraged."

Staude's affinity group was prepared for jail solidarity, which would protect individuals through the strength of group action. Legal support for those arrested included legal briefings, a staffed legal support office, an experienced legal coordinator, and lawyers who would make jail visits. Only those who were willing to be arrested would be in lockdown; others would support them before, during, and after arrest. Each group would choose a spokesperson to attend the Action Spokescouncil, where she or he would communicate each group's intentions and in turn report back to the group about organizing details.

All participants were encouraged to take the nonviolent direct action training that was offered in Seattle by DAN during the week before N30 and in cities around the country in the months before. With all the groundwork done in the previous ten months by Public Citizen, the Ruckus Society, Art and Revolution, International Forum on Globalization, the Talking Turtles, Peace Action, Jubilee 2000, Global Exchange, Earth First!, and the vast network of nationwide and neighborhood groups linked to Seattle, there was a great outpouring of people ready to go the distance.

It was this network that the students from Lewis and Clark joined when they arrived at Denny Park at 6:00 A.M. on the morning of N30. Staude and her friend Erik did not plan to be arrested. They were jail support for eight "arrestables." Their organizing had been done through Portlanders Against the WTO and Art and Revolution, which had been holding regular meetings in Portland throughout the months leading up to N30. Staude and others were receiving regular e-mail updates as the plans developed and the number of affinity groups grew.

When the group got together at Denny Park on N30, Staude gathered up everyone's identification so that if arrests were made, the nonviolent activists would show solidarity through anonymity. This would help protect the locked-down demonstrators, who would be vulnerable to charges of resisting arrest, which were more serious than the charges that would be made against those who were simply holding hands or linking arms. The large group, by maintaining silence, could then impede the judicial system and negotiate for the same charges for all. Jail solidarity meant communal support throughout the entire process. Staude was the holder of the IDs, and she locked them in her car.

The Lewis and Clark students were assigned "K" in the pie of activity organized around the convention center. They called themselves Key Lime Pie, and by 7:30 A.M. they got to their intersection at Fourth and Olive. There were three affinity groups working together, nearly all students and young adults from Oregon, totaling about 200 people. The support group held hands and fanned out; the inner circle went into lockdown. The inner circle of the direct action group Staude participated in used chicken wire, duct tape, PVC piping, chains, and padlocks to secure themselves together by joining arms from shoulder to hands. They sat down and took over the intersection, surrounded by their support team. Traffic was effectively blocked in four directions.

"We sat down behind those in the inner circle and used our knees to help support their arms," said Staude. "We were there to take care of them." Milling about the affinity groups were jugglers, drummers, big puppets, the radical cheerleaders, and the Santa Clauses against the WTO. They would roam around between intersections, keeping up the spirits of those in lockdown and their supporters. It was going to be a long day for those in lockdown positions.

This was Sarah Joy Staude's first demonstration. And in spite of the intense police presence at nearby areas, the Oregon contingent had a fairly peaceful time of it at Fourth and Olive. Then they were asked by DAN organizers to move to Fourth and Pine, as things changed midmorning. First they had the prerequisite meeting to get consensus about the move. This was more difficult than usual because of the large number of people, many of whom were from different groups, and the noise and the difficulty in hearing each other. What usually took a few minutes turned into an intense twenty-minute discussion; then they decided that, yes, they would relocate.

Fourth and Pine is at Westlake Center, a playground of shops and public space. Within four blocks are hotels, including the Sheraton, where Secretary of State Madeleine Albright was stranded, and stores such as Niketown, the Gap, and Old Navy, all subjects of student scrutiny regarding their sweatshop policies. The convention center was about four blocks away. The group established themselves once again; this time the police presence was dramatic. A tractor with a scoop turned onto the street and headed toward the affinity group. "We got all the supporters in line in front of it," said Staude. "The driver claimed he was lost." It was a strategy on the group's part to protect the people in the inner circle who literally couldn't move to get out of the way.

"We were prepared to be confronted by police. We were prepared to understand that they are the authority and that we were going against authority by choosing to attempt to stop the delegates from reaching the talks. That was all understood. What we couldn't understand, and what was terrifying, was the brutality and the urgency and the value placed on these talks over the well-being of people." The students were prepared to be arrested and to go through the court system. They were following in the tradition of the anti-war protests of the sixties and seventies. They weren't prepared for the attack on passive protesters. "I grew up in the community knowing my sheriff and the deputies, and I know they were watching out for my best interests," said Staude. "I'd envisioned that the cops would be taking responsibility for their own actions."

There were thousands of students in the streets of Seattle on N30. Most of them knew the issues, did the training, and made conscious, committed decisions to participate in direct action. They were prepared for everything but having their helplessness attacked. Some police lifted the protective bandannas worn by locked-down protesters who were sitting

## It's a Ruckus

Some of the people in the streets during WTO week were part of the "Carnival Against Capital," the cause with comic relief. Giant puppets parodied the issues at large with wagging fingers, dollar-sign heads, and a variety of cartoon comments. Banners flew from very high places, like the high-rise construction crane looming over downtown, with the words "Democracy" and "Free Trade" waving in the wind, accompanied by arrows going in opposite directions. It made the heart thump in appreciation and awe of the guts it took to climb so high in the dark of night and shanghai the air space for fair trade and freedom. Other banners surfaced on the sides of downtown buildings. Music was everywhere. It was a free-for-all of activism—from those locked down in earnest in the middle of intersections to the playful celebration of spirit that danced around them in the streets.

Much of these rowdy revolutionary antics were thanks to the Ruckus Society, which came to the area in September and set up a training camp at Pragtri Farm, about 40 miles north of Seattle near Arlington. The Berkeley-based group was started by veteran environmental activist and Earth First! cofounder Mike Roselle about five years ago when some forest activists needed to develop nonviolent know-how for their cause. Ruckus aims to amuse, irritate, arouse, and educate folks about ➤

in the street and squirted pepper spray directly into their eyes. Other protesters, already immobilized by tear gas, hunched over and huddled together for protection. Their heads were pulled back by their hair and their eyes were purposefully sprayed. They could neither get away nor protect their faces with their hands. Rubber bullets bruised the backs of retreating demonstrators; cans of tear gas were thrown indiscriminately into crowds of students who had no place to go. People lost consciousness.

The Oregon students at Fourth and Pine were on the periphery of the violence and, compared to thousands of others in the streets of Seattle on N30, their day had been relatively uneventful. No one was arrested, and although the police presence was felt and the group was threatened by a tractor, they had only breathed secondhand tear gas coming up out of the vents of the city's sewer system. Sometime in late afternoon, they were told that the day's protest was over and that the WTO meetings had been effectively blocked. They were also told about the imminent 7:00 P.M. state-of-emergency curfew. Once again, the consensus process was activated. Some people didn't want to leave, but at 6:00 P.M., most of the group went back

issues they deem important, such as shutting down oil refineries, blocking logging trucks, denying access to the Nevada (nuclear) Test Site, getting U.S. auto makers on track regarding global warming—and keeping WTO ministers from making their free-trade deals in Seattle on N30. Along with their own trainers, they bring in people from such organizations as Greenpeace, Earth First!, Global Exchange, and Rainforest Action Network, which was also a co-sponsor of the WTO training camp, to educate activists in the fine art of nonviolent protest that makes its point with flair and flamboyance.

According to John Sellers, the Ruckus Society's executive director and an intrepid climber who can scale tall objects in a single night, the goal of the Ruckus Society is to teach a discrete set of tactics and strategies that can be applied to just about any campaign for social change. The training includes the basics in climbing, as well as how to support those who are willing to be arrested, which might mean everything from chanting encouragement to surrounding the arrest vehicle. They learn political theater, make up protest songs, and devise cheerleading routines. They also get crash courses in media manipulation, e-mail mischief, monitoring police radios, and using walkie-talkies, scanners, CB radios, and cell phones. They learn how to shout back effectively at a CEO as well as how to get arrested well. Protesters came from all over the country, as well as from Canada and England, to take part in the training at Pragtri Farm. The slogan for the action in Seattle, coined by Sellers, was "Globalize This!"

to Denny Park. Staude handed out everybody's identification, and they piled into cars and headed back to college. During the three-hour drive to Portland, they listened to the radio broadcast of the escalating battle in Seattle. "We were elated by the day, and terrified at what we were hearing," said Staude. "What city police forces have become is a fascist force serving and protecting business, not the people."

✿  ✿  ✿  ✿  ✿

It was at this point in our Sunday brunch that her father, Craig, spoke up. "I still have a big problem with the anarchist groups that went just to cause trouble," he said. "They're begging for more force to deal with them. I'm all for free speech and nonviolent action, but when you start getting these smaller groups that aren't willing to play by those rules, then I don't know what you do to keep peace for the general populace."

His daughter was quick to respond. "Yes, the general populace," she said. "Should corporations rule our lives? That's the big question. I was thinking about it as I was driving up here. What's happened to the local grocery store, gas station, the local diner? It's now all fast food, all in one place owned by a major oil company. The anarchists targeted big corporations that are taking over small towns and pushing out mom-and-pop stores. We need to incorporate everybody into this movement. We cannot ostracize anybody."

The WTO in Seattle was Sarah Joy Staude's first demonstration. "But not quite," said Craig. "When she was still in diapers, we took her to an anti-nuclear demonstration at Bangor Naval Base." It took Craig and Krispi two ferry rides and a couple of hours of driving to get there. Probably just a little longer than it took Sarah Joy to get from Portland to the WTO demonstrations in Seattle.

By the time we had this conversation, Sarah Joy had participated in two more demonstrations. One was a protest lockdown in the lobby of Fidelity Investment's Portland office in March 2000. It was in support of Colombia's U'wa people, who were being threatened by Occidental Petroleum's planned oil drilling on their ancestral lands. Fidelity owned 30,000 shares of Occidental, and the students wanted Fidelity to divest of its interest. The Portland protest was held in conjunction with about forty other protests at Fidelity offices across the country. This time Staude was an "arrestable." She and fourteen other students refused to leave the lobby of the office while business as usual went on around them. Nine people were locked down. Outside, about twenty radical cheerleaders loudly expressed their feelings about Fidelity's policies. Within an hour and a half,

Staude was arrested and in jail. "I was terrified," she said. "But there are 5,000 people in an indigenous tribe who are willing to commit mass suicide if the oil is drilled. To them, it's the lifeblood of Mother Earth." She was jailed for ten hours. "It was an eye-opening experience," she said.

In late March 2000, a Colombian court blocked experimental drilling in the country's biggest prospective oil field, on the grounds that an indigenous tribe was not properly consulted. Roberto Perez, president of the U'wa Traditional Authority, who met with the U.S. Congress, was pleased but wary. "The injunction speaks of the suspension of the project, not cancellation," he said. "We have taken an important step and are happy because we have advanced in our struggle, even though this has come at great sacrifice." In a conference call to Staude and other student leaders across the country, he expressed the gratitude of the U'wa people. Alberto Calderon, president of the state oil company Ecopetrol, Occidental's partner, expressed confidence that the verdict would be overturned on appeal.

A month later, on the day after her graduation from college, Staude was in the streets again, this time for the international workers' rights May Day parade in Portland. The route led to Powell's Books. It was a permitted march, and there was no direct action planned. The police, however, had plans of their own. As the parade progressed, a phalanx of officers in full riot gear charged a group of black-clad participants, dispersed the crowd, used rubber bullets, and arrested several people. Staude was roughed up with a billy club for not moving faster. "They acted as if we were cattle or criminals." The parade permit had been revoked in the middle of the march. Those involved in the march, however, were oblivious to this fact and were bewildered by the police aggression, which appeared to be arbitrary and unwarranted.

The media coverage was reminiscent of WTO in Seattle. "On the news, they showed a plastic newspaper box being thrown at a police officer," said Staude. "But it was after several arrests. After they terrorized us." In reflecting back on her six months in the activist arena, Staude said that for her, the WTO and Fidelity protests were "not horrifying." But, she said, May Day in Portland was devastating.

Staude was close to tears at times during our talk. She is a twenty-two-year-old woman at the beginning of her independent life, and she felt bewildered and betrayed by what that life held. "I've been thinking about the 'Prayers of the People,'" she said. "Form three." And she spoke the words of the *Episcopal Prayer Book* from memory: "We pray for all who govern and hold authority in the nations of the world, that there may be justice and peace on the earth." Then she continued, "But praying isn't solving the abuses of power. I'm scared for the future."

# 8 DO LOOK BACK—
# IN WHICH HISTORY CAN BE FOUND

"The Ancients knew something
which we seem to have forgotten."
—Albert Einstein

t's important, especially in this sound-bite society, to understand the historical links to the actions we take—be they civil disobedience, silent vigil, charitable support, or political support. Jim Douglass credits Dorothy Day and the Catholic Worker community with his own evolution as a nonviolent activist. In 1957, Day and her coworkers refused to take shelter in a compulsory civil defense drill.

**"If we do not act, we shall surely be dragged down the long, dark, and shameful corridors of time reserved for those who possess power without compassion, might without morality, and strength without sight."**

—The Reverend Dr. Martin Luther King Jr.

They claimed that to do so was the same as saying yes to the possibility of nuclear war. It was saying yes to the sin of preparing for nuclear war. Instead, they went to jail. Dorothy Day's actions were a topic of Douglass's freshman English class at the University of Santa Clara. At first he argued that they were wrong to disobey. But then Douglass experienced a "sudden, burning awareness of two-sided reality." He realized that humanity was living at an "end time," and that from then on he would live a life based on conscience.

An end time. The nuclear arms race was an imminent threat to existence. In the mid-seventies, the Douglasses bought an old house on a few acres adjacent to the Trident submarine base at Bangor and started a ten-year-long nonviolent protest that included weekly leafleting to workers at the base, frequent peace walks, and regular vigils at the entrance to the naval base. Soon, people around the world were gathering in protest and collectively speaking out in a miracle of mobilization. Private citizens went from the United States to the Soviet Union and established personal relationships directly with the people, effectively sidestepping the paralyzed political system. Change happened. The demonization broke down and common ground took over. The nuclear alarm clock was set back. The end time was over.

But the beginning of this new millennium feels like the beginning of yet another end time. Our earthly resources are being depleted, our oceans polluted, our cultures decimated. The natural tides of our existence are assaulted by the unnatural—a landscape of technology, genetically modified foods and futures, and a woefully inadequate response to the needs of other human beings. Yet, once again, like the threat of nuclear war, this end time is resulting in mobilization. What happened in Seattle during WTO week was nothing short of another miracle of mobilization. Thousands of people came from around the world and took to the streets; thousands exercised their right to gather, speak out, and perform acts of civil disobedience. And it worked. The meetings were shut down. But not without violence. And the difference between police action in the '70s and '80s and in Seattle at the end of the millennium raises disturbing questions.

On Bainbridge Island, in the '80s, we showed solidarity for the vigils at Bangor by meeting the Wednesday-evening Seattle-Winslow ferries in a peaceful, silent, candlelight vigil of our own. "Peace" was the byword, the watchword, the password of the movement. Yet there were many dramatic direct action events taking place. Sit-down protests in front of the "White Train," which transported nuclear warheads, were a regular event, with regular arrests. Many people went to jail. And there were long, costly trials with loud, boisterous demonstrators. But given the intensity of those years and the repeated encounters with the police and the judicial system, it was a remarkably peaceful time.

> "When scientific power outruns moral power, we end up with guided missiles and misguided men. A nation that continues year after year to spend more money on military defense than on programs of social uplift is approaching spiritual death."
>
> —The Reverend Dr. Martin Luther King Jr.

# The Land of the Free and the Home of the Anarchists

This anonymously written e-mail circled the country in the days just before July 4, 2000.

Of the fifty-six men who signed the Declaration of Independence:

- Five were captured by the British as traitors and tortured before they died.
- Twelve had their homes ransacked and burned.
- Two lost their sons serving in the Revolutionary Army; another had two sons captured.
- Nine fought and died from wounds or hardships of the Revolutionary War.
- Twenty-four were lawyers and jurists, eleven were merchants, nine were farmers and large plantation owners—men of means, well educated. But they signed the Declaration of Independence knowing full well that the penalty would be death if they were captured.
- Carter Braxton of Virginia, a wealthy planter and trader, saw his ships swept from the seas by the British Navy. He sold his home and properties to pay his debts, and died in rags.
- Thomas McKeam was so hounded by the British that he was forced to move his family almost constantly. He served in the Congress without pay, and his family was kept in hiding. His possessions were taken from him, and poverty was his reward.
- Vandals or soldiers looted the properties of Dillery, Hall, Clymer, Walton, Gwinnett, Heyward, Ruttledge, and Middleton.
- At the battle of Yorktown, Thomas Nelson Jr. noted that British General Cornwallis had taken over the Nelson home for his headquarters. He quietly urged General George Washington to open fire. The home was destroyed, and Nelson died bankrupt.
- Francis Lewis had his home and properties destroyed. The enemy jailed his wife, and she died within a few months.
- John Hart was driven from his wife's bedside as she was dying. Their three children fled for their lives. His fields and his gristmill were laid to waste. For more than a year he lived in forests and caves, returning home to find his wife dead and his children vanished. A few weeks later he died from exhaustion and a broken heart.
- Norris and Livingston suffered similar fates.

Such were the stories and sacrifices of the American Revolution. These were not wild-eyed, rabble-rousing ruffians. They were soft-spoken men of means and education. They had security, but they valued liberty more. ➤

In all the years of anti-nuke protesting in the Northwest, I don't recall one incident of police violence—unlike at the WTO protests in Seattle, where the police, depersonalized behind Darth Vader masks, were quick to use pepper spray and tear gas on the people in the streets. Yes, in the anti-nuke decade, people were dragged and carted away. But they weren't assaulted. During WTO week in Seattle, more than 600 people got arrested, and many of them were battered by the police in the process. More than 600 of the cases were dismissed, which might seem like a victory. But in reality, the mass dismissals effectively short-circuited the possibility of public scrutiny. Going to trial can be powerfully effective.

In Kitsap County, on February 22, 1985, one missile-bearing White Train was met by protesters carrying white roses. The flowers were held in honor of the same day forty-two years earlier, when Sophie Scholl and her brother Hans were beheaded in Germany for their acts

**"Our government is now beginning a $6 billion upgrade of four submarines at Naval Submarine Base Bangor to the larger D-5 (Trident II) missile. No one in our government or the military can explain why."**

—Stephen Kobasa and Glen Milner, in the *Seattle Times,* January 14, 2000

Standing tall, straight, and unwavering, they pledged: "For the support of this declaration, with firm reliance on the protection of divine providence, we mutually pledge to each other our lives, our fortunes, and our sacred honor."

The history books never told you a lot about what happened in the Revolutionary War. We didn't just fight the British. We were British subjects at that time and we fought our own government! Some of us take these liberties so much for granted, but we shouldn't. So take a few minutes while enjoying your Fourth of July holiday and silently thank these patriots. It's not much to ask for the price they paid.

Remember: Freedom is never free!

I hope you will show your support by sending this to as many people as you can. It's time we get the word out that patriotism is *not* a sin, and the Fourth of July has more to it than beer, picnics, and baseball games.

of Nazi resistance. They were part of the "White Rose" resistance group. Their crime was to write and distribute leaflets urging the German people to resist the inhumane acts being asked of them by Hitler and his regime. Karol Schulkin, a nun and a core member of Ground Zero, named the February 22 train "Sophie's Train." Schulkin, along with eighteen others, was arrested for sitting and praying on the tracks and stopping the train on its way to the base. All were charged with criminal trespass and conspiracy to commit trespass. Four months later, after lengthy preparation and a long trial, they were found innocent of all charges. It was the first such verdict in nearly a decade of court cases. Yet it took all those earlier trials to get there.

I remember Jim Douglass saying over and over and over: "The power is in love and nonviolence. Nonviolence and love." Over and over and over. "It's about trust"—over and over and over. In those days I was fueled by anger and righteous indignation—even as I meditated with the monks and stood in silent vigil. The waves of rage—at the police, at the military, at the civilian workers on the base—were nonstop. Everyone seemed complicit. Yet the core group at Ground Zero knew better. They loved the military personnel, they loved the police, and they prayed for them. They also kept at bay the many protesters who wanted to join Ground Zero for less altruistic reasons. As someone who didn't feel at home with either extreme, I stuck with the Buddhist monks. We couldn't discuss the hot and heavy issues because of the language barrier; we could share chanting, meditation, work, play, and a drumming presence in marches and at rallies.

> "Nothing could be worse than the fear that one had given up too soon and left one unexpended effort that might have saved the world."
>
> —Jane Addams, born in 1860, founder of the Women's International League for Peace and Freedom

It took me a decade to understand that the process is the solution. And the process is messy, confusing, contradictory, legal, illegal, and fundamentally, deeply democratic. As Douglass says in his book *Lightning East to West*, "You can't keep anyone out of the parade." The anti-nuke parade included grandmothers camping out in Greenham Common in England, Buddhist monks from Japan, nuns in Kitsap County, infiltrators on Bainbridge Island, barefoot hippies from California, and educated theologians from the South. It involved judges and juries, attorneys and lawbreakers, international experts in nuclear weapons, and the woman who brought food and water to hungry people keeping vigil on train tracks and at seashores. The peace, freedom, and justice parade is a big one, and it's always going on somewhere. In November 1999 it surfaced in Seattle during WTO week, and its size, complexity, and worldwide representation was ready evidence of its collective underground strength, rock-bottom resilience, and historical underpinnings.

**"Once a thing is known, it can never be unknown. It can only be forgotten."**

—British novelist Anita Brookner, *Look at Me*

# 9 A CIRCLE OF JUBILEE—IN WHICH WE ALL GET WET AND CANCEL THE DEBT

"There's no compassion,
there's money going on."
—Hannah Petros, founder and director of Ustawi

I n the Biblical tradition, a Jubilee year is the fiftieth year, the year when slaves are set free and debts are canceled. Jubilee 2000 is a worldwide movement to lift the burden of debt from Third World countries, enabling them to use their resources to serve the basic health and education needs of their people. It was started in England three years ago by Anne Pettifor, a "lapsed Anglican," as she calls herself, who sat down with friends at her kitchen table and said, "Something must be done." Pettifor roused the interest of the Anglican Church in England, and now Prime Minister Tony Blair is calling for cancellation of debts owed the United Kingdom. In the United States it's also been a faith-based movement, but it goes beyond institutional religion, as do the organizers who laid the foundation for the whopping turnout in Seattle on the eve of N30.

The Reverend Dr. Peter Strimer is an unlikely priest with an unending passion. Unlikely because he bypasses altogether any typical priestly image; he's direct and irreverent, and seems almost impatient with the idea of being a priest. An unending passion because he has a cause that's perhaps even greater than God—social justice. It can be easy to work for God. It's never easy to work for justice.

Pete Strimer has been a priest since 1980. He also trained as a social worker with a focus on community organizing, and has been an activist since he was a kid. "I was involved with the first Earth Day commemoration in my school, and got kicked out for putting up unauthorized posters," said Strimer in an interview at St. Mark's Cathedral a few months after WTO week. "From the time I was in college, I knew I was going to be someone in the ministry whose commitment was to working in the community."

He credits his early inspiration to his membership in a youth group, from 1968 through 1972, that was led by college students who were engaged in the issues of the day. "We talked about civil rights and the Vietnam War, and we also did very meaningful community service. We worked at the Ohio School for the Blind, an adult sheltered workshop for mentally retarded folks. But what helped frame me for a critical consciousness was my church." It was a Methodist church in a college town in Ohio. "By the time I was a religion major at Duke, I was on my way to being trained to do community change. My role models were the Berrigan brothers, Dorothy Day, Cesar Chavez, and Martin Luther King Jr., folks who were working for change." And folks who based their radical activism for social justice on the deep principles of their Christian faith.

> **"International debt is something that is stifling human freedom, and has disastrous consequences for our global family. The debilitating reality of nations trapped in the consequences of debt creates, in my opinion, another form of slavery. Again, it seems, the poor are providing for the rich. Indeed, the awesome burden of international debt causes, at the most extreme level, a loss of dignity and hope."**
>
> —Archbishop Njongonkulu Ndungane of Cape Town, South Africa

After college, Strimer lived in Columbus, Ohio, where he did community work in inner-city churches and for three years worked full-time lobbying around hunger issues. Then he started his own church. "The Third Avenue Community Church was, from day one, committed to social change and community service," said Strimer. "We did AIDS work and theater work, youth work and parish nursing. All in the spirit of radical social transformation."

Then he got the call from St. Mark's Cathedral and was invited out to be their "urban worker" in Seattle. "Now it's called canon missioner," said Strimer. "They've made me much more churchy."

Even so, St. Mark's, which recently appointed the Very Reverend Robert V. Taylor, a radical activist (and openly gay) priest from South Africa as its sixth dean, has a well-established reputation as a place where action speaks louder than liturgy. Nobel Laureate Desmond Tutu,

Archbishop Emeritus of Capetown, came for the installation of the new dean. Tutu chaired the Committee for Truth and Reconciliation, which helped in healing the wounded soul of South Africa. He used Christianity as a base for understanding that which cannot be understood, forgiving that which cannot be forgiven.

His successor in Capetown, Archbishop Njongonkulu Ndungane, one of the leading forces behind Jubilee 2000 worldwide, visited St. Mark's not long after WTO week to further educate Episcopalians and business and civic leaders about a different kind of forgiveness—world debt. There is a vast activism going on out there, and it's being fueled by faith. And, like Pete Strimer himself, that faith is muscular, intense, and very down-to-earth.

✿　✿　✿　✿　✿

The idea for a Jubilee event at WTO first started in April 1999 when Hannah Petros, founder and director of Ustawi (a Northwest organization, whose name is Swahili for "balance," that is dedicated to helping women in Africa get an economic toehold in life), called him and said, "Pete, we have to do something about the global debt situation." She'd heard about Jubilee 2000 and decided that something needed to get started in the Northwest. "So we convened a few folks," said Strimer. "The usual suspects—Catholic Workers, the Women's International League for Peace and Freedom, the Church Council of Greater Seattle, the Washington Association of Churches. And we began to look at global debt."

I met with Petros a few months after WTO week and we talked in an alcove at Seattle Children's Hospital, where her son was recuperating from an infection in his foot. We'd had a hard time getting together. Petros is in big demand as a speaker, is directing Ustawi, and, first and last, is a mother. It was this last role that was causing her the most distress. This was not the first time something had happened to her son just as she was scheduled to travel somewhere to speak. "It's his way of saying, 'I need you, Mom,'" she said, with her big trademark laugh. "It's time to pay attention to him."

Petros, who was desperately trying to find a new director for Ustawi, had had to cancel a keynote speech at the "End Corporate Dominance" conference in Portland when her son's injury took a turn for the worse. She'd then spent the weekend sleeping in his room in the hospital. Earlier that morning, when I got to her house for our interview, it was her brother, who was caring for her young daughter, who called Petros at the hospital to remind her of our meeting. It was our only opportunity to speak, so I tracked her down at Children's.

When she addressed the crowd at the Jubilee 2000 Interfaith Gathering, her passion for economic justice permeated the church. Then she brought her two small children up onto the stage with her, and told us that they were why she was there. She wore her traditional Ethiopian clothing, including a turban, and exuded a powerful energy. When we met, though, she seemed vulnerable, slight, and sleep-deprived.

Petros started Ustawi in 1995 as a response to the image of Africa as nothing but a war-torn continent full of starving people. "The media approach to Africa is not right," she said, "but it's more than that. What do you do when an African country—Nigeria, I think—pays back $700 in debt service for every dollar it received? Yet all the resources that have come out of that country have never been measured. There are wars because of the gold and the diamonds, but the riches of the country never get to the people. For me, the picture did not look right." Petros soon found herself plunged into the complexities of global economics. "I found out that the resources in Africa have always been controlled by outside forces," she said.

Petros started Ustawi to educate the public. "It came from the painful experience of watching what's happening to your own country. Hunger, war, and AIDS. But people in the West are as much in the dark as people in Africa in terms of knowing the truth about what is going on. It's all controlled information. Why does the media always talk about all the aid given to African countries, but it never says anything about the millions in repayment? And that Mozambique pays $1.4 million a week in debt service?"

Petros came to the United States from Ethiopia in 1979 to go to college in Minnesota, where she eventually got her master's degree in public health and met her husband, Tim Overlund, now a Lutheran minister. "What I try to do is put human faces to these global issues. Stock is nothing but paper going up and down," she said. "But global debt is manipulated and results in human suffering. The West is consciously ignoring, not examining itself to see how it is accumulating wealth. And I'm part of it too. But it's very difficult for me to see the system that is manipulating me, doing everything in my name, for me, for my interests."

Petros, who received a United Nations Local Chapter Human Rights Award in 1996 for her work with Ustawi, worked nonstop to get the Jubilee event organized in Seattle. "As I walked that night, I thought about the evil empire that we must hold up and look at and say, 'This is our global economic system.' I can't breathe, it is so oppressive. I lived under the communist regime in Ethiopia, and this is as oppressive, if not more.

"There are times when I say, 'I quit.' But how can you quit when you know the prices are paid by children who have never voted and elected this system, the children who are not getting food, who are not getting education, who do not see their first birthday?"

Although the Jubilee movement started in the faith-based community, Petros has a big problem with the institutional church. "Christianity is a big corporation," she said. "The Western church will always protect its own interests over the core value of their own faith."

I asked her what her minister husband thought of her views. First she laughed. "I've never been the good wife," she said. "I respect his values and his faith, and I think there is good value in raising children in the routine of going to church, but it is my responsibility to struggle with my children and their spiritual values."

Petros grew up in the Christian church. "But I must qualify that," she said. "There is a big difference between the church here and the church in Africa. Here they are they afraid to ask the question, 'How do we accumulate wealth?' Why? Why is it easy for them to send a missionary out to talk to the poor; why can't they talk to the rich? I hold the church responsible for the fear of speaking the truth." Hannah Petros and Pete Strimer were the perfect duo to put the Jubilee event together.

✿ ✿ ✿ ✿ ✿

In the post–WWII economy, it was useful for big industrial countries to have ways of beefing up their economies by going out and building roads and buildings, digging mines and canals, constructing big dams in Third World countries. The only problem was that the latter didn't have the money to pay for these services. That's where the World Bank and the IMF stepped in. They lent huge sums of money to these countries so that they could pay for imported industrial services and supplies. A significant amount of this money found its way into the deep private pockets of the corrupt public leaders of these countries. A significant amount was used to exploit the rich natural resources of the countries. Some of it did find its way into the local economy through the workers who were hired and the services that were rendered, but most of it became very useful as a debt. A very big debt growing steadily bigger because of interest.

Many decades later, these countries are still paying back these debts and their escalating interest, instead of developing a social infrastructure to support their people with the basics of food, education, and health care. The cycle of poverty is being reinforced minute by minute, and millions of people are suffering to pay back a debt that they neither incurred nor are even aware of. By forgiving global debt, the wealthy industrial nations can help liberate these countries and their people from the helplessness of systemic poverty.

This is why the Jubilee movement planned a circle of solidarity around the WTO opening-night festivities on N29.

Less than two months after they first started meeting in Seattle, the "usual suspects" sent Hannah Petros to Köln, Germany, to join the Jubilee movement at the Group of Seven Nations meeting, where a human chain was to be formed around the gathering site of the trade ministers from Canada, the United States, France, United Kingdom, Germany, Japan, and Italy. Petros called it "a beautiful event," and at that meeting the Group of Seven, a trade organization of major nations with European interests, actually approved a call for $97 billion of debt relief.

"The movement of Jubilee 2000, represented by the human chains in Birmingham, England, and then in Köln, Germany, was finally getting the global debt situation on the agenda," said Strimer.

When Petros came back from Köln, the Northwest group started to connect to WTO week. "Those are the very same trade ministers who run the IMF and the World Bank," said Strimer. "So we decided to do a human chain in Seattle. There were about a dozen people involved at that time, and we had about $200 between us." The usual suspects had the usual reservations. "We all looked at each other and said, 'Can we really do this?' But we'd begun to sense there was going to be this kind of convergence, so as a leap of faith we declared that we were going to host a 10,000-person human chain on Monday night, November 29, 1999, and encircle the opening ceremony of the WTO. A nice, idealistic, naive goal that resulted in 20,000 people showing up."

The organizing group changed week in and week out as new allies came on board and other WTO demonstrations and activities surfaced. "We received a huge boost by connecting with Rosalinda Aguirre, the staff person with Jobs with Justice," said Strimer. Jobs with Justice is sponsored by the AFL-CIO, which also connected the Jubilee group to the Reverend James Orange, a longtime black Baptist organizer from the Southern Christian Leadership Conference. Orange was with Martin Luther King Jr. in Memphis, Tennessee, when King was assassinated. He came to Seattle for the month before the Jubilee event and went to work to get the Jubilee message out into the black churches. This was a complicated task, in part because educator Constance Rice, wife of Seattle's former (and first African American) mayor Norm Rice, was helping to educate students about the WTO, from the perspective of the

WTO. The split in the black community about who and what to support was never fully resolved. But Orange was very instrumental in bringing together union people, Jubilee 2000 organizers, and black church involvement, said Strimer. "Then we met Jim Wallis at a lunch."

Jim Wallis is the editor-in-chief of *Sojourners,* a magazine that analyzes and reports the ways in which faith, politics, and culture are linked together. Founded in 1971, the magazine has a readership of about 80,000 people. A popular columnist and the author of several books, Wallis also convened the Call to Renewal, a new national federation of churches and faith-based organizations working to fight poverty and revitalize American politics. He, too, got caught up in the WTO momentum. "We decided to have a Christian call for Jubilee at St. James Cathedral, the night before the human chain," said Strimer, "where we would intentionally invite all these ecumenical Christian groups and have a service to call for cancellation of the debt." Jim Wallis was signed up to preach at the Sunday-night gathering at St. James Cathedral.

"In Mozambique, the per capita debt is $223, while the annual average income is $80. Life expectancy is 47 years old; 15 of every 100 children die before their first birthday. Sixty percent of the adults are illiterate, and more than a third of the people do not have access to safe drinking water. Mozambique's government spends roughly twice as much on debt payments as on education, and four times as much as on health."

—Jubilee 2000, Episcopal Church, Office of Peace and Justice Ministries

The Monday-evening events started with an interfaith gathering at the First United Methodist Church, where feed-ins, teach-ins, and turtles had been happening all day long. Close to 3,000 people crammed into the church; many others were turned away. There was singing by Sweet Honey in the Rock, flute playing by Esther Little Dove John, and moving invocations from many religious traditions: Native American, Jewish, Unitarian, Muslim, Buddhist, Baha'i, Hindu, and Christian. A young Chinese woman, the Reverend Angela Ying, was the voice of the Christian tradition. She combined the passion of a black Baptist preacher with the allure of youthful faith and innocence. John Sweeney, president of the AFL-CIO, spoke of faith and solidarity; Maxine Waters, congresswoman from California, offered optimism about the governments that were beginning to act on behalf of Third World debt forgiveness. And Hannah Petros gave us what for.

When we went outside after the service, thousands of people were gathered in the streets waiting for us to start the march in support of canceling the debt. It was a dark and stormy night—cold, windy, and raining without end—and there was a great and soggy spirit among us. As we got to the Kingdome area, we divided into two lines and circled out as far as could be seen. We stood with our arms linked, swaying in the rain, and the chant became "We're Here. We're Wet. Cancel the Debt."

In organizing the march and the circle around the WTO dignitaries at the Kingdome, the committee had faced a massive array of logistics regarding permits, promotion, and networking. "The biggest hurdle was the permit," said Pete Strimer. The Jubilee group wanted to circle as close as possible to the new Exhibition Hall, where the WTO opening ceremony was actually taking place, but the permit had to come from the police, who had to get approval from the Secret Service, who kept saying "No, you can't get that close." It got frustrating. "We finally said to the police, 'Okay, here's a map, you tell us the closest circle you would allow.'"

The Jubilee group worked closely with the police in making their plans, as did nearly all of the organizations that sponsored events and protests during WTO week. This is really one of the more astonishing aspects of what happened in Seattle. Seattle's mayor, city council, and police department were all involved with the planning. Permits had to be acquired for everything that was planned on N29 and N30. I remember my own astonishment at hearing that the big labor rally and march was planned to coincide with the opening ceremonies of the WTO. Having been involved with city, county, and state government over the years, I knew that these things did not happen without bureaucratic support.

It was Captain Pugell of the Seattle Police Department whom Strimer's group coordinated with during the planning stages. "We finally came to the agreement that the human chain could circle the entire Kingdome area," said Strimer, "but for the last 150 yards on either side of the Exhibition Hall we could only have fourteen individuals who would walk in and symbolically close the chain." The fourteen leaders who spread out across the protected 150 yards included John Sweeney, Maxine Waters, Bishop Vincent Warner, Hannah Petros, and others.

✿　✿　✿　✿　✿

In May 2000, I met with Bishop Warner, who talked to me about his experience on N29. Bishop Vincent Warner is, above all in this earthly life, a Virginia gentleman. He is eminently gracious. Perhaps this comes with his bishopness and was part of his training, but when combined with a natural grace and a Southern drawl, it is quite something to bask in. We met at 11:00 A.M. at the Diocese of Olympia offices, next door to St. Mark's Cathedral. He greeted me in the lobby, which was ornate with maroon velvet furnishings and carvings of crests and lilies set into the wood-paneled walls. On the way to his office, Bishop Warner stopped to ask someone to begin a meeting for him at 12:30 P.M. so he would have time during lunch to visit the wife of a colleague who was in the hospital. We went into his spacious office, where from his window there is a view southwest overlooking Lake Union and the edge of downtown Seattle.

## Two Sides to Slavery

Although physical slavery officially ended in the United States in the 1860s, its effects continue to ripple through our culture. Nobody wants to deal with slaves, and we would prefer to think that in this modern world the problem of slavery no longer exists. Black Americans may be free from slavery, but are still subjected to daily acts of racism from individuals, companies, and organizations. Black males in this nation face a disproportionately high rate of incarceration and early death—much of it perpetuated by racism. Institutionalized racism limits the life options of millions of Americans and perpetuates a sense of there being two Americas—a land of opportunity for those of the correct skin color, education, and bank balance, and a land of grim struggle for everyone else.

—Jubilee 2000, Episcopal Church, Office of Peace and Justice Ministries

Warner's exposure to the world debt situation had started in 1998, before the beginning of the three-week-long Bishops' Conference in Lambeth, England. Two weeks before the beginning of that gathering, Warner was invited by the Church of England to represent the Episcopal Church of the United States at a conference of primarily African bishops and to listen to their stories. "There were bishops there from Rwanda, Burundi, and the Congo," said Warner. "They personalized what the debt was doing to them. The reality of always having to pay all of that interest and not be able to take care of starving people. It was something that not only disturbed them profoundly but also caused anger at the West and at the United States. By the time I got to Lambeth, I was very clear that I was supportive of trying to find ways to deal with the international debt." Then, for three more weeks at the Lambeth conference, Warner was once again in close daily contact with bishops from Africa.

The Archbishop of Canterbury had invited the president of the International Monetary Fund to come to Lambeth and address the Bishops' Conference. "He flew over on a Concorde," said Warner, with a bit of a laugh. "It was not inexpensive."

The IMF president showed a film presentation of what the IMF was doing in Africa to help cancel the debt. Then he spoke; then he was questioned. "In the questioning, he became very defensive and angry because he had expected to be treated with great respect," said Warner. "But there was such anger at the IMF that not only the African bishops but many of the other bishops just erupted." For three weeks at Lambeth, Warner learned a lot more from the contingent from Africa.

"When I found out that the WTO was coming [to Seattle], it was interesting. A bishop friend of mine called and said he was a friend of the president of the WTO, Mike Moore, and that he was a very nice man and that I should be in touch with him. 'Mike would like to hear from you,' he said to me, 'Don't believe all the things you hear about the WTO.' I said to him, 'I'm afraid that I'll probably be in a different position from the one you'd like me to be in.' I planned at that time to be part of any opportunity that we might have to make a statement that we were for canceling the debt. This was an international movement and suddenly we had an opportunity to join in."

Warner came to the ministry from a career in business and advertising. On the day of the Reverend Dr. Martin Luther King Jr.'s funeral in 1968, Warner was in Washington, D.C., on business. "Fourteenth Street was burning," he said. "There were National Guard troops all over the city, and I was unable to keep my appointment in Georgetown. I somehow ended up being drawn to Fourteenth Street, where I was one of the few white faces around listening to the funeral and seeing the rage of the African American population. I came back from that, and then several months later Robert Kennedy was assassinated."

Warner, who was in upper management of a multi-faceted industry and had been written up as one of the fastest-rising young people in business, went in to the president of the company and said he was leaving. "He told me I was crazy. I told him that I had to move away from the profit-and-loss sheet and deal with the issues of peace and justice that were going on. So I went to seminary."

Warner attended Virginia Theological Seminary, just outside Washington, D.C., where everything was going on. "My entry into all of this was through civil rights and justice issues. I remember walking near the wonderful monument for Abraham Lincoln and having the police wield their sticks at me and at others as we were protesting for civil rights," recalled Warner. "On the night we were marching for the cancellation of the debt, it was pouring down rain and suddenly Maxine Waters, John Sweeney, myself, and a number of others started singing 'We Shall Overcome.' We looked at each other and said it was bringing back all the memories of why we were doing what we were doing.

"As we marched, the closer we got to the Exhibition Hall, the more police presence there was. When we took the ribbon and started through the blockade, we had to leave the marchers behind; they had screened just a few of us. I was trying to get the Roman Catholic representative in, Sister Joyce Cox, but they wouldn't let her in because she had not been cleared and didn't have photo ID. When we got through the barricade, there were motorcycle police, mounted police, all sorts of other police, and Secret Service all around the Exhibition Hall. There were about twenty motorcycle police for every one of us. It was like being in the Gaza Strip or Israel or Russia, where the police presence is so dominant, where you see the Uzis and you're aware that you can't make a move."

When Warner and the others arranged for clearance to symbolically close the circle, they had to have their photographs taken with a police officer, who acknowledged to Warner that the Jubilee organizers had worked hard to make it a nonviolent event. But he also told Warner that there was a small group of people determined to make it into something else. And that he knew they would be there.

After crossing the barricade, the members of the small group lost contact with one another. "I was alone," said Warner, who pulled a yellow ribbon through with him. "I remember getting up by the Exhibition Hall and seeing [Mayor] Paul Schell, and others I recognized, inside the hall with all this food, mounds of food, and well protected, and we couldn't get close." The group reconnected near the entrance to the Exhibition Hall. "Our plan was to in some way have several of the WTO representatives come out while we symbolically tied together the ribbon and cut it, to cut the chains of debt. All we wanted to do was simply say, 'Here's what we're standing for—for the people of the world that are burdened by this debt.' I had no question that there were people in that hall who believe in the same thing. The reality was that nobody acknowledged us in any way at all. Except for the police. It was as if we weren't there."

When the WTO representatives started to leave the hall, the police herded the Jubilee group away to another spot. "There was just a handful of us," said Warner, "but they didn't want us to have any contact." Then the Secret Service didn't want them at the new spot, and the police had to step in to negotiate. "We were really isolated. We stood together, we prayed together, and we cut the ribbon. It was powerful for us. But it was so profoundly disappointing that nobody in the hall was willing to acknowledge us or was aware of our presence. The word was to go back to the whole community that the chain had been cut, but we had no way of knowing if the word got back."

Where I was standing, it didn't. After singing in the rain and swaying arm in arm for about a half hour, people slowly unlinked arms and began leaving. Some went off to Elliott Bay Book Company, where Paul Hawken was speaking; some went off to the People's Gala at the Seattle Center, where sixties activist and later California State Senator Tom Hayden was speaking, and there was dancing in the aisles; some, like Pete Strimer, went home.

"I remember the sense of relief," he said. "All the worries and tensions of whether it would remain nonviolent, or how frustrated people would be because the police set up their riot fences so far away from the building, and logistically whether it would all work."

The Jubilee events, the ecumenical Christian service, the interfaith service, and the secular human chain around the WTO festivities set the spiritual stage for WTO week. It was an all-souls gathering that cast the widest possible net and drew in everyone, from the outright devout to the downright unbelieving. It reminded me of the little ad for St. David's that's in our local island paper each week: "Skeptics, Doubters, Searchers, and Believers Are All Welcome."

Of the impressive number of people who braved lousy weather and lots of traffic to show up in support of Jubilee 2000, Pete Strimer was characteristically modest. "It wasn't anything that we did, except to put in the bare-bones structure of it and to work our networks as best as possible," he said. "Our Jubilee group was probably responsible for about 5,000 people; the other 15,000 came from unions, from spontaneous demonstrators, and from people who heard about it in the community. I just came out to Seattle and am doing the same things I've always done— finding ways in which the church can advocate for justice—but I try to do it out of a spirit of imagination and joy and possibility, more than confrontation. The human chain was such a beautiful example of that, and that's why it was so disappointing to see that example of Jubilee get lost in the smoke of the tear gas and the police riot." When Strimer went home for a good night's sleep, he was looking forward to the next day, N30, when he could finally relax and join in someone else's parade.

# 10 THE THIN PLACE— IN WHICH THE QUESTIONS ARE THE ANSWER

"Love is the final end of the world's history;
the amen of the universe."
—Novalis, eighteenth-century German poet

During the years when Buddhism took greater hold in my life, I read Thich Nhat Hanh and Thomas Merton. One was a Vietnamese Buddhist monk who wrote about Christianity, the other an American Catholic monk who wrote about Buddhism. Their lives and experiences overlapped in love. It was that simple, and that complicated.

But how do we mere mortals get there? If I shout at my kids, how can I go out and shout about peace and justice? If I don't honor my own spiritual being, how can I honor that of another? If I forget what a privilege it is to eat every day and have shelter for my family and have water to drink and health to preserve, how can I be in touch with those on this planet who don't have such simple, essential things?

It's hard to be grateful; I find that it is much easier to measure the things I don't have. And in this strangely convoluted time, when people are growing money like a crop, I never seem to have enough of it. There is always someone or something that needs fixing, that needs buying, that needs fuel, food, new shoes, or a trip to the movies.

When I stop long enough to look around and really feel grateful for my life, the tears flood. There is such grief in gratitude. It takes us to the edge, to a place the Celtic Christians call "the thin place," where the veil between us, between our perceived reality and a greater reality, is lifted and the beauty of it all, the possibility of grace, brings us to our knees, literally and otherwise.

But these moments of possibility and transformation are elusive. So how do we put them to work in our lives?

Just asking that question is the first answer. Then more questions take shape, and then, as in the spirited Battle in Seattle, they get a chance to take form and demand answers. The content is already intact behind them, which is why the questions raised at such events hold so much power. N30 was an opportunity for that which already existed to surface, to be seen, heard, and felt.

We forget how powerful we are. Primarily because the media, which is owned by a very few and is responsible for informing so many, tells us about so little. It doesn't tell us about *us,* it tells us about *them.* Never have I seen such a whopping number of journalists in one place at one time do such a lousy job of reporting reality. The disparity between my experience on the streets and the experience reflected in the media was shocking, as it was to everyone I've talked to who was there. I wondered, "Why?"

> **"Love and compassion predominate in the world. And this is why unpleasant events are 'news'; compassionate activities are so much a part of daily life that they are taken for granted and, therefore, largely ignored."**
>
> —The Dalai Lama

One answer rings close to home. For three and a half years, as editor of a magazine—which was my job at WTO time—I wrote regularly about people and places. When I walked into Memorial Stadium on N30 to join the labor rally, I was instantly overwhelmed by the significance of the event. And I was frustrated because I hadn't brought my camera, or even a piece of paper and a pencil. My inner journalist knew I was in the middle of a very big story. For the first hour, all I saw were missed opportunities for great shots and great stories.

Finally I had to let that all go and just be there. And everything changed. I became part of a huge tide of international friendship. Yes, there were speakers representing workers from around the world, and yes, the situations were painful to hear, but we were all hearing *together;* in this, there was a tremendous feeling of strength, possibility, and partnership.

Later on, when I walked in the march, there were journalists on every street corner, but by then I was one of "us." The distance between participant and observer, though palpable, could not be measured. It was as if we were in parallel lives. The air was different over there. And I knew that if I were over "there," I, too, would be an observer. Which means I would have been outside the experience. Perhaps it was simply much easier to accept being an outsider to the ensuing police violence and to write about that than to be an outsider to the solidarity on the streets. Perhaps it's just too hard to write about hope in these sadly one-sided and cynical times.

In the early seventies, when I experienced my first Tibetan Buddhist teacher, Chogyam Trungpa, founder of the Naropa Institute, he sipped wine as he spoke and got funnier and funnier. Laughter enlightened, not in spite of, but along with, the tragedy of those war-torn times. Trungpa, who first brought the spirit of Tibet into our Western hearts and minds in the 1960s, had us rolling in glee at the absurdity of it all; then he cut through to the serious heart of what it means to be a warrior in the world. To fight the war. He was merciless. It all begins at home, he said. Not exactly music to our self-righteous ears. "If you want to solve the world's problems, you have to put your own household, your own individual life, in order first," he wrote in *Shambhala—The Sacred Path of a Warrior*. How we put our own lives in order—morally, ethically, responsibly—whether we're journalists or judges, housekeepers or peacekeepers, really does mean something. We're all part of the picture.

For many years, Tibetan Buddhism and its gentle, gracious teachers taught me of the mind and its wonders—and its wanderings. I learned about the psychology of consciousness, the oneness of doing and not-doing, of speaking in silence, of letting it all go and gaining ever more back. I heard the Dalai Lama speak of the laws of karma. "Perhaps," he said, "if we Tibetans had been more generous with our spiritual knowledge, if we'd gone out into the world instead of isolating ourselves from the world, we would still have our country." Now the Tibetans, who have lost their homeland, culture, and too many people to Chinese invasion, are homeless pilgrims, teaching us much about the power of compassion and nonviolence.

A few years ago, I heard the words of the Dalai Lama when he encouraged a return to one's spiritual roots in search of a path up the mountain. As a result, and thanks to an enlightened Episcopal priest whose faith has no boundaries, I found my way to St. David's, to the closest link to my long-ago and very difficult experience with the Anglican Church. And to that small notice inviting me to St. Mark's Cathedral and an evening dedicated to global economic justice.

# 11 MR. PRESIDENT, THERE'S A FLY IN MY ALPHABET SOUP— IN WHICH CITIZEN SORIANO SPEAKS UP AND ACTS OUT

"If enough people think of a thing
and work hard enough at it,
I guess it's pretty nearly bound to happen,
wind and weather permitting."
—Laura Ingalls Wilder

There was a whole lot of leadership at work behind WTO week in Seattle, but it wasn't top-down; it was lateral. Anyone who wanted to could be a leader, from Seattleite Carol Jackson, who baked big cookies, iced them with the words "Eat the WTO," and sold them to raise money for the cause (then spent four days in jail during WTO week), to activist icon Ralph Nader, who has fought for the health, safety, and power of ordinary people for more than thirty years. Then there's fair-trade activist Sally Soriano.

As I was interviewing people for this book, Soriano's name kept coming up over and over as someone who had been there from the beginning. It was difficult to reach her because immediately after WTO week, she'd started coordinating the Washington State Health Care 2000 Initiative. She was working to get affordable health care for all state residents on the ballot in November, which meant working with statewide volunteers who were out collecting the required 200,000 signatures. It took weeks to get an appointment with her, and when we finally did arrange a time to meet, it was for 8:30 P.M.—after phone bank hours were over.

Soriano is a Seattleite, a bicoastal activist, a global citizen, and a connoisseur of alphabet soup. She has had them all on her plate— NAFTA, GATT, MAI, WTO, and Fast Track, too. She's digested them inside out, knows all their dirty little secrets, and isn't afraid to tell. Over the past seven years, she's been on the front lines battling the trade treaties in all their manifestations, often as the point person for Nader's organization, Public Citizen.

Soriano started her political involvement as an anti-war activist in the '70s and went on to teach in the department of community education at the University of Wisconsin at Milwaukee. The department faculty was made up of both civil rights and anti-war activists and had a social and economic justice curriculum. In addition to coordinating the Health Care 2000 campaign, she manages People's Video/Audio, a company that distributes the books and tapes of author and political analyst Michael Parenti, whose work addresses corporate power, U.S. overseas intervention, and the biases of the news media.

Born and raised in Seattle, where her family has firmly established roots, Soriano had an uncle who was the pitcher, and then general manager, of the city's first baseball team, the Seattle Rainiers, who played in Sick's Stadium on Rainier Avenue South, a couple of miles south of downtown. In the '40s and '50s, it was the place to go. Soriano's mother was active in community and education politics. "I remember her vividly," said Soriano. "She was always talking with neighbors about the importance of strong public schools." Her father worked as a longshoreman and a ship pilot, so she grew up with the stories about dynamic labor leader Harry Bridges, president of the International Longshore and Warehouse Union (ILWU). Her parents are devoted Democrats. "Growing up, we knew that if we left the Democratic Party, we'd probably get excommunicated from the family," Soriano told me.

> **"Over the past twenty-three years, [Al] Gore has solicited and accepted campaign cash from arms companies, the nuclear industry, bond traders, runaway firms to Mexico like Mattel, and exploiters of child labor. Occidental, in which the Gore family has a stake now worth over half a million dollars, is trying to drill in the Colombian rain forest on land belonging to the U'wa Indians, who are being murdered by Colombian soldiers now reportedly about to receive another billion, courtesy of the Clinton–Gore administration."**
>
> —Syndicated columnist Alexander Cockburn, in the *Seattle Times*, July 20, 2000

This Democratic fervor has lessened in recent years. "When President Clinton began promoting the pro-corporate-trade agreements, I had to make my parents understand that it was Clinton who was leading the party away from its roots. I reminded them of talk-show host Jim Hightower's satirical comment that we are in the nineteenth year of the Reagan Administration," she said.

Soriano lives in a quiet neighborhood in north Seattle. There are 8-foot-high rhododendron bushes around the edge of her small front lawn, and bits of Puget Sound are visible in the distance. It's an understatedly genteel neighborhood, and Soriano herself shares that quality. She's of a certain age (one of those sixties activists who never went inactive), yet she neither looks it nor acts it. Her unabated and youthful enthusiasm for all things political could transfer just as easily to all things playful.

She came to the politics of the trade game after a decade of work with the Rainbow Coalition, both nationally and locally. She was an alternate delegate for presidential candidate the Reverend Jesse Jackson in 1988. In 1993, she worked to get Larry Gossett, a Seattle Black Panther leader in the sixties, elected to the King County Council. After the election, Soriano was asked by the Rainbow Coalition to attend a meeting about NAFTA, which the coalition, along with the AFL-CIO, was opposing.

✷    ✷    ✷    ✷    ✷

The North American Free Trade Agreement, which was approved in 1992, lifted all governmental control over foreign investment in Canada, Mexico, and the United States. National and regional interests—be they cultural, economic, or environmental—now are subservient to corporate profit. As an example, Chapter 11 of NAFTA enables a corporation to sue the governments of Canada, Mexico, and the United States if their laws interfere with the profit-making potential of business. The rationale was that if it was good for business, it was good for everybody. Ultimately, NAFTA enabled many corporations to move their operations to Mexico, where labor is cheap and environmental laws are not enforced, thereby eliminating production and employment in the U.S. and Canada, and exploiting Mexican workers and their environment. Labor, in both Canada and the U.S., understood what was happening and went to war.

So did Soriano. "I walked into that meeting, took a look at the NAFTA material, and said, 'This will knock out our nation's laws.' I couldn't believe it." Soriano immediately called up the newly elected Gossett, who is also an attorney, and alerted him. "I was furious," said Soriano. "I'd just worked [to get a progressive person elected], and here comes this trade agreement, written by the International Fortune 500 corporations, that can challenge anything he does to protect the environment and to help people." This ability to quickly connect corporate-based decision-making with its effect on local government enabled Soriano to bring to light the ways in which corporate power was taking over government jurisdiction. She quickly got the picture. And because she was an educator, from then on, her mission was to make sure that everyone else got it, too.

Soriano immediately activated the Rainbow Coalition phone bank to lobby the state politicos in D.C., and tried to rouse editorial attention to NAFTA in the Seattle daily papers. The editors declined, saying that they had nobody quotable who was in opposition to the agreement. Soriano tapped Jesse Jackson and Ralph Nader, got their letters to the papers, and they still declined. "I'd call them every day and yell at them," said Soriano.

"The weekend before the vote, it was a 50–50 split in the House of Representatives," said Soriano. "Fifty-seven percent of the American people were opposing NAFTA and the unions were solid against it. But practically the entire Hispanic Caucus had been bought off by President Clinton and U.S. Trade Representative Mickey Kantor." She followed the last week before the final vote minute by minute, vote by vote, and was devastated when NAFTA passed. "We heard that Clinton had bought several members of the Congressional Black Caucus." The CBC had been the "conscience of Congress" throughout the Reagan era, said Soriano. "But somehow in November 1992, Clinton and Kantor convinced them that they were on to better things."

It had been a bitter fight, but it put Soriano in the trade ring and she never left. "I'd been around all these people who had been fighting against NAFTA for at least a year, and people were down on the mat," said Soriano. "They were stunned and sick. Particularly with Clinton. He had come into office saying he was opposing NAFTA, that it didn't have environmental and workers' safeguards, and then he completely switched and pushed the thing through. And he promised millions of dollars to the members of Congress who voted for it."

✿　✿　✿　✿　✿

In January 1993, not long after NAFTA went into effect, Public Citizen in Washington, D.C., asked Soriano to organize the Washington State opposition to the Uruguay round of GATT—the General Agreement on Tariffs and Trade. GATT had been around for a while, but unlike NAFTA, which was a free-trade treaty that involved only 3 countries, GATT involved 120 countries. The Uruguay round of discussion would greatly expand corporate powers over those of governments, and Public Citizen was mobilizing against it.

"It was a very lonely year," said Soriano of her GATT fight in 1994. "I went around telling people, 'You thought NAFTA was bad, well, GATT is a hundred times worse.' People just didn't want to talk to me." Even labor was tired of trade. They'd expended their money and exhausted their membership fighting NAFTA, had lost, and were demoralized. "Labor was hardly there," said Soriano. Neither was the Washington State congressional delegation. "It was like talking to the wall. Except for Congresswoman Jolene Unsoeld, who was the only member of the delegation to eventually vote against GATT when, in 1995, it was passed and reborn as the WTO.

"When they held the Senate vote," said Soriano, "there were only two prominent national figures who were opposing it—Lawrence Tribe, a constitutional law professor from Harvard who was worried about the loss of sovereignty, and Ralph Nader. Two days before the vote in the Senate, they bought off Lawrence Tribe. Vice President Gore cut a deal with the anti-GATT forces promising that if our country lost two laws, we could leave the WTO in six months. So Lawrence Tribe withdrew his opposition and that got them the vote. Ralph Nader was the only person standing there and opposing this in the United States."

Soriano had cause to remind Nader of this when she was driving him around Seattle during WTO week. "When he was thanking me, I reminded him, 'Look, I remember 1995, when it was only you. Only you.'"

When the formation of the WTO passed, "there was hardly a blip" in the media. "It went on the talk shows for about two weeks before the vote," said Soriano. "Even my mother said it was unbelievable that something with such far-reaching implications was on such a fast and greasy track. In the editorials in the New York Times, they always said that Nader was crazy and that we wouldn't lose our laws. Clinton was assuring people, [then U.S. Trade Representative] Mickey Kantor was assuring people, and especially Al Gore was assuring people that 'No, we'll never lose one law to the WTO.'"

Not long after the birth of the WTO, Soriano took a break from Public Citizen. The organization wanted to block most-favored-nation status (MFN) with China because of its prison abuses. She, along with some of the other Public Citizen organizers, thought it was hypocritical to deny China MFN status when other countries had records as bad or worse, including the United States. "The question should be," said Soriano, "why do we allow our corporations to exploit Chinese workers or any other workers?"

✿  ✿  ✿  ✿  ✿

Then, about a year later, she got a call from Public Citizen's Margrete Strand-Ragnes, who asked her to go to work in the fight against "Fast Track," which would renew presidential authority to quickly sign trade treaties free of congressional scrutiny or amendments. Although Fast Track had been available to presidents since Gerald Ford's administration, support for it in the public arena had waned as trade treaties grew more complex and far-reaching. Congress no longer automatically voted it into effect.

Soriano was impressed with the work done by Public Citizen in getting the NAFTA facts out to Congress in the 1995 fight against Fast Track, when Lori Wallach had written and distributed materials to members of the House and Senate that documented the disparity between the pre-NAFTA promises and the post-NAFTA reality. The "protective law" under NAFTA was particularly disturbing. It gave corporations the right to sue a foreign country's government if its law resulted in a loss of corporate profit. At the time that Fast Track was on the table, there was a lawsuit pending against Canada, which had banned the fuel additive MMT, produced by the U.S.-based Ethyl Corporation. MMT, a dangerous neurotoxin that can cause nerve damage, memory loss, psychosis, and sometimes death, had already been banned in most countries of the world. But Canada just happened to ban it *after* NAFTA was instituted. The Ethyl Corporation was suing the Canadian government for $250 million because of "expropriation" of its losses. (The Canadian government eventually had to pay $13 million to the Ethyl Corporation.)

Other surfacing NAFTA problems centered around the environment, health, and food safety. After the trade regulations between Canada, Mexico, and the United States were eliminated, Congress was lax in allocating sufficient funds for border food inspection. "Illegal pesticide-ridden agribusiness food imports were coming into the United States with only 1 percent of the trucks inspected," said Soriano. The incidence of disease linked to environmental contamination and crowded conditions along the U.S.-Mexico border also increased.

The four-year NAFTA record was raising alarms. Increased hepatitis A in communities along the Texas-Mexico border, pesticides on imported food, air and water pollution, factories moving south to Mexico, job loss in Canada and the United States—all of this was carefully recorded in Wallach's reports to Congress. Encouraged, Soriano signed on for the 1997 fight against Fast Track.

And finally, recovered from its NAFTA battle, the AFL-CIO joined in the fight as well. During one C-SPAN debate, a trade unionist from Oklahoma called in and dazzled the pundits with "numbers, facts, and the whole structural picture." Soriano, who taught educational sociology for ten years, was fascinated by the effective way in which the union rank and file had been educated. She tracked the curriculum materials to United for a Fair Economy, a Boston-based group connected to the widely respected magazine *Dollars and Sense*, long a leading voice for a fair economy.

During the weeks before the final vote on Fast Track in the House of Representatives, the phone calls were flying. "There were four or five of us [with Public Citizen] in Seattle calling all the secretaries and finding out what was going on," said Soriano. "One fellow was calling into the coatroom of the House. He was getting information and giving it to me, I'd give it to Public Citizen, and they'd get it to Lori Wallach, who was working with the United Steelworkers of America on this."

Public Citizen was meticulously tracking every move and mood as the Fast Track bill moved through Congress. "There were trade organizers in practically every state calling all the time," said Soriano. If one little congressional pocket started to stray, the response was immediate. "Quick, call all their offices, pull them back in" was the mantra. "And then we beat them. Clinton couldn't call for a vote. We were in complete disbelief."

By documenting the NAFTA record—a kind of "It's the facts, stupid" approach—they got Fast Track sidetracked. It was a pivotal moment in the movement. Later, when Steven Shrybman, executive director of the West Coast Environmental Law Association and author of *World Trade Organization—A Citizen's Guide*, came to Seattle to join in the early stages of WTO planning, he said that he'd never thought any of these trade agreements could be turned around until Fast Track was defeated.

"It showed that we could do it," said Soriano.

(In 1999, Fast Track backers tried to give the policy different names, such as "presidential negotiating authority" or "traditional negotiating authority." So far, it has not been renewed under any of its monikers.)

❄ ❄ ❄ ❄ ❄

Right after the successful Fast Track fight in 1997, Soriano geared up for the fight against the Multilateral Agreement on Investment. MAI is an up-close-and-personal extension of Chapter 11 of NAFTA, the provision allowing corporations to sue the federal governments of Canada, the United States, and Mexico if their laws interfere with corporate profits. But MAI went much further; it gave corporations the right to sue *any* government—all the way down to town and county governments—for any loss of profits incurred because of local laws. MAI was described as "NAFTA on steroids."

It had a few other interesting points: MAI would grant most-favored-nation status to *corporations and investors* from all countries that signed on; the clause "National Treatment" would prevent governments large and small from "discriminating" against multinational corporations in favor of domestic companies; governments—from the local to the national level—would not have any discretionary power when it came to choosing with whom they did business based on human rights records, environmental policies, labor issues, or even arms control; and no local, state, or federal government would be allowed to require performance standards from a corporation doing business in its front or backyard. In other words, if local laws were broken by corporations going about their profit-making business, nothing could be done.

> "Inasmuch as most good things are produced by labor, it follows that all such good things ought to belong to those whose labor has produced them. But it has happened in all ages of the world that some have labored, and others, without labor, have enjoyed a large proportion of the fruits. This is wrong, and should not continue. To secure to each laborer the whole product of his labor as nearly as possible is a worthy object of any good government."
>
> —Abraham Lincoln

The MAI would set strongly enforced global rules limiting our elected governments' rights and ability to regulate foreign investors and corporations. Foreign corporations can sue for "loss of profits" if a government enacts a law to protect the environment, public health, consumer protection, or local community development standards. But isn't this what government is supposed to do, make laws for the public and the environment that serve the public interest? Yet provisions in the MAI state that corporations can sue government for any policies that could reduce their future corporate profits. For example, if a local government passed a law restricting toxic emissions from a plant owned by a foreign investor, the foreign company could claim that this environmental policy would cost them "future loss of profit" under the MAI and sue for compensation.

The Canadians acted quickly in the Northwest. A group of British Columbia activists who were getting anti-MAI resolutions passed throughout the province came to Soriano for a mini-conference in her living room with about twenty-five people from around Seattle. "The Canadians laid it out," said Soriano, "and after about half an hour, all of a sudden the whole room fell silent." Then this voice came out of the crowd: "How far back in history would we go if this MAI is implemented?" Soriano remembers, "Someone answered, 'About 700 years.'"

In February 1998, Public Citizen sponsored an informational debate about MAI at Seattle Central Community College. The MAI evening had a big impact on a group from Olympia, Washington State's capital, about 60 miles south of Seattle. When the group, led by Michael McSems, got back home, they went with materials in hand straight to the Olympia City Council. "The council took one look at it and went through the ceiling," said Soriano. "They were in complete disbelief that this thing had been designed and written and that the United States was negotiating it at the OECD in Paris. They immediately signed a resolution in opposition."

In Seattle, the anti-MAI leadership was quickly taken up by Republican Brian Derdowski, then a member of the King County Council, and by Nick Licata on the Seattle City Council. In April 1998, a coalition of anti-MAI forces held a press conference, but only one reporter showed up—Arthur Grolick from the *Seattle Post-Intelligencer*, who wrote a small piece in the paper.

The planning for the MAI press conference, however, laid some important groundwork and also pointed out a missing link. In rounding up letters of support for the cause, labor was noticeably missing. All the major environmental organizations had come through with letters, but nothing had come in from the AFL-CIO. "So we went knocking at Rick Bender's [president of the Washington State Labor Council] door," said Soriano. After due consideration, the Labor Council approved a statement opposing MAI. (Five months later, the AFL-CIO came out against MAI.)

On the King County Council, Brian Derdowski, Maggi Fimia, Kent Pullen, and Larry Gossett were lobbying other members like mad to oppose MAI. It wasn't easy going. "I hit this point in August when I was very depressed," said Soriano. "I knew this was not going to move if I didn't put blinders on to everything in my life and make it happen. I had no idea how it would happen. And it had to happen." So she cleared the decks.

In September 1998, the King County Council met with the King County Labor Council to discuss two items: unionizing day-care centers and the MAI. Ron Judd, head of the county Labor Council, told everyone to get beyond acronym apathy. "These acronyms are meant to make your eyes glaze over," Judd told them. "And it works." He encouraged them to really look at the text of the MAI and pay attention to what it said. "The whole room went, 'Whoa,'" reported Soriano.

By the time the final vote came up in November, even the over-my-dead-body Boeing supporters on the King County Council were saying that if the MAI went into effect, passing laws could bankrupt the council. The MAI could go after everything. The final vote—on a council of primarily Republicans—was unanimous, 13–0. And with a passion. Derdowski said that "opposing the MAI should be the litmus test of every elected public official."

There was a big ripple effect in the Northwest. After the King County Council voted, it took the MAI issue to the Washington State Association of Counties, which also joined the battle. Snohomish County, just north of Seattle, quickly voted to oppose the MAI as well. After the Olympia City Council took action, it presented its MAI resolution to the Association of Washington Cities, which did the same. The city attorney for San Francisco came up to a meeting of the National Association of Counties in Portland and filled them in on MAI. It, too, passed a resolution in opposition.

As in the Northwest, local governments around the world were passing resolutions in opposition to the MAI, including Houston, Vancouver, B.C., San Francisco, Toronto, and Oakland. The protests hit home in Paris. The MAI negotiations were stalled, and France, the host country, pulled out altogether. The French government was worried about the impact on the integrity of French culture. According to Canadian activist Maude Barlow, "The French government was the first to pull out of the MAI, and the minister responsible said the reason was that civil society had done such a strong job convincing them of its flaws."

The link between Seattle and the Paris talks was no accident. Activists around the world had mobilized to fight MAI. The agreement's behind-closed-doors, fundamental, and blatant support of corporate interests over civil society roused international outrage. In October 1997, two months after France's decision to withdraw, the Organization for Economic Cooperation and Development, responding to international pressure, formally announced suspension of the MAI talks. But even though the OECD announced the MAI suspension, the activist community was well aware that, though MAI might appear dormant, it wasn't dead. The activism continued locally and internationally, as it was considered quite likely that the resurrection of MAI would be attempted at the WTO ministerial meeting in Seattle. So in the Northwest, Soriano's group continued to apply pressure on all fronts.

# 12 IT'S A BEAUTIFUL DAY IN THE NEIGHBORHOOD— IN WHICH GRASS ROOTS ARE ALWAYS GREENER

"Try not. Do or do not.
There is no try."
—Yoda, *The Empire Strikes Back*

In January 1999, the City of Seattle cheerfully announced that the WTO was coming to town. Yet oddly enough, in April 1999, the Seattle City Council voted 8-0 to oppose the Multilateral Agreement on Investment. In some quarters, the eyes-glaze-over effect was still working. Otherwise, surely the relationship between the two acronymic realities would have been noticed by someone.

There is a lot of subterfuge surrounding these burgeoning trade agreements. They change shape and initials, duck behind other initials, or parcel themselves out in tidy pieces to already existing agreements. If one fails to take hold, there's another one with different words but the same intention already on the boards. The only thing cannier is the network of activists keeping each other informed about what's going on. In an article by Tracy Rysavy in *YES! A Journal of Positive Futures*, Council of Canadians activist Maude Barlow said, "We are in constant contact with our allies in other countries. If a negotiator says something to someone over a glass of wine, we'll have it on the Internet within an hour, all over the world." The hills are alive with the sound of e-mail (see sidebar, Net Worth).

✿ ✿ ✿ ✿ ✿

When it was announced that the next WTO round would be in Seattle in November 1999, the free-trade fanciers danced in the streets. And the battle-weary alphabet-fighters started e-mobilizing once again. Soriano was still fighting the MAI that wouldn't die, but she looked up long enough to browse through the information packets she was receiving from Public Citizen and scoped out the next big battle brewing on the horizon. In late January 1999, Mike Dolan, who was on leave from Public Citizen to work for Citizens Trade Campaign, called for the first WTO protest meeting in Seattle from his office in Washington, D.C. The word went out to about a hundred people in and around the city. The meeting was scheduled for late February 1999.

Citizens Trade Campaign (CTC) is a broad-based coalition of labor groups, consumer groups, farm groups, environmental groups, and faith-based groups concerned about trade agreements that favor corporate interests over those of producer and consumer. More than 700 international groups, from the United Auto Workers to the Friends of the Earth, had joined the CTC to fight the MAI. During WTO week in Seattle, the media made a big deal of the turtle/Teamster connection, but the partnership was already well established.

When Dolan flew in for that first meeting in Seattle, he brought packages of information with him and handed them out all around. He talked the topic nonstop. As Soriano read through the material, she noticed that all of the WTO decisions had favored corporate interests over the interests of the environment and the people. When that first WTO meeting was over, Soriano and Michael McSems of Olympia, a veteran of the MAI fight, walked out together. Both were worried that Dolan hadn't allowed other activists in the room to talk enough, thereby limiting group process and momentum. Their own resolve, however, was clear: "The WTO is coming down. It's not good, and we're going to do something about it."

After that first "heads-up" meeting about the WTO, which drew about eighty people, Soriano called Dan Seligman, the trade tracker at the Sierra Club in Washington, D.C., and asked him about the track record of the WTO. He confirmed Soriano's suspicions, saying that in all of the WTO's decisions, "they'd never once gone with the people."

✿ ✿ ✿ ✿ ✿

The third meeting in Seattle was on a warm and sunny day in March 1999. "It was like Acapulco or something," said Soriano, "but still fifty people showed up." King County Labor Council leader Ron Judd gave the lunchtime talk. Known as one of the finest orators in the Northwest, Judd had only days earlier attended a conference at the University of Washington about the Seattle General Strike on its eightieth anniversary. He was flush with the historical fight for workers' rights as well as with the recent victory against MAI, in which he'd been extremely active. He told the group that protesting the WTO was "the most important event that any of us in this room will have in our lifetimes. We are going to shut down Seattle." Later in that meeting, Brian Derdowski of the King County Council told the group that "this was a fight for the soul of Seattle."

The meetings in Seattle continued, weekly for the steering committee, which was open to anybody at any time, and monthly for the large "event" meetings that included educational speakers and presentations and were advertised throughout the community. One of the first speakers was lawyer/activist/writer Steven Shrybman, who came down from Vancouver, B.C. Soriano credits Shrybman with fueling the fire of WTO coalition-building that was still in its formative stages in those early months of 1999. He had just written his comprehensive *A Citizen's Guide to the World Trade Organization,* but his message to the group was simple—just add "not" at the end of every sentence of the WTO manifesto. His perspective was that it couldn't be saved.

Remembering the impact that Public Citizen's Lori Wallach had had with the Fast Track materials, and taking the advice of writer and progressive thinker Michael Parenti, Soriano went for the "just the facts, ma'am" approach. She put together a packet of information that was headlined "No to WTO, Yes to Democracy!" The packet included an article from *Dollars and Sense* by Daniel Kraker and Kristin Dawkins titled "The Continuing Threat from Trade Negotiations," a piece from *In These Times* titled "Taking Care of Business" by Joel Bleifuss, and "USA: Banana Republic" by Russell Mokhiber and Robert Weissman from the *Multinational Monitor.* This was notable, said Soriano, because at that time they were the only magazine pieces about the WTO that she could find in the progressive press.

The packet went on to invite the reader to "join progressive people from around the world to protest, strategize, and educate on how the global economy affects all of us and the environment." It included a Resolution to Demand Democratic Accountability of the WTO, a succinct presentation of the record that indicated the ways in which "corporate power has been elevated above the power of all nation-states." The *whereases* cited just 4 of the 100 decisions made in favor of corporate interests in the first four years of the WTO: (1) the decision that gutted the business of local banana growers in the Caribbean in favor of Chiquita, Dole, and Del Monte; (2) the decision that challenged the State of Massachusetts law enforcing sanctions against the undemocratic government of Burma; (3) the ruling against the provision in the

U.S. Endangered Species Act that protected sea turtles; and (4) the ruling that forced the European Union to import U.S. hormone-treated beef. The *be it resolved* section said that "we, the members of international civil society, oppose any effort to expand the powers of the World Trade Organization."

When the "No to WTO" packet was sent back East for sign-off at Citizens Trade Campaign and Public Citizen, the response was a resounding "no way." The AFL-CIO had not taken an official position in unilateral opposition to WTO; it was intent on working for change from the inside. Even Public Citizen's Lori Wallach, whose life was defined by the fight against the WTO, did not want the group to come out publicly in favor of dismantling the organization. The battle before the battle was on. For two months the weekly steering committee fought about who they were and what they were about. "People were yelling at each other," said Soriano. "We had to figure out our name."

She was about to go and launch her own "Network Opposed to the WTO" campaign when she talked to two key people: David Korten, an author and anti-corporate warrior who attended some of the meetings and was a guiding light behind the scenes, and Sara McElroy, a soft-spoken and effective activist in the group who, for two years, had been convening small groups of different people every week to talk about globalization. Both told Soriano that they couldn't get behind the "total opposition" position when speaking out in the public arena. They felt it could undermine the cause by polarizing the positions, which would limit discussion about the many issues. Soriano, whose respect for them and their work overcame her rebellion, took a breath and reassessed the meaning of coalition-building.

In the end, it was a high-tech compromise that laid the groundwork for cooperation inside the coalition. At a meeting in May, Ian Murray, a Federal Express driver in his day job and an economics expert and the group's Web librarian guru in the rest of his life, laughed and told them that with desktop publishing, everything was possible, so why not be two groups? One side of the office could be "Network Opposed to the WTO"; the other could be something else; and technology could easily accommodate the differences. In this way, the radicals and the moderates could share the same office but be free to express their different views via custom-printed materials. Computer technology at its most egalitarian.

The attention then focused on what to call the other group. According to Soriano, it was a woman from the Women's International League for Peace and Freedom who insisted that they have a name that stood *for* something, and came up with People for Fair Trade. And to lay claim to the power of hospitality, the words "WTO Host Committee" were added, just for fun. It was as messy a democratic process as it was sublime. The phone number was 1-877-STOPWTO; the website was peopleforfairtrade.org. "There were no restrictions put on anybody. Everybody could think boldly about what they wanted," said Soriano. "The most important thing was that everybody could leave that room and go talk to people."

The contingent from Olympia that had been so effective fighting MAI was outraged at the compromise, and walked out of the May meeting; they continued to organize themselves under the unadulterated version of "No to WTO." The consensus of everyone else was to go with both. By May and June, the group was leveling out at about 150 people. "But it was the same 150 people," said Soriano. They wanted more, and different, faces in the crowd. Filipino activist Ace Saturay, an organizer with the People's Assembly, a coalition of civil society activists from around the world who oppose the globalized exploitation of agriculture, labor, and the environment, told the group that they should start going to the neighborhoods. Then he went off to the Philippines to further plan for WTO week with Filipino farmers.

❉    ❉    ❉    ❉    ❉

So she could get a paycheck, Soriano got officially hired in July to do what she was already doing. In preparation for the July meeting, she worked with Mike Gottfried, an architecture student; Tony Leahy, a law student; and Ian Murray, the Fed Ex economist, to map out the neighborhoods. Dr. Michael Fox from the Humane Society was due to fly in from D.C. for the meeting; also scheduled on the agenda was time to organize the groups that would work the WTO issue in the neighborhoods.

Up until the July meeting, it was the issue-oriented folks who were in regular attendance—the forest activists, organic farmers, university students fighting the sweatshops, workers' rights and Jobs with Justice people, academicians concerned about the threat to democracy, those who had fought against NAFTA and MAI. The July meeting, however, added to the mix people who love pets. Lisa Wathne of the Seattle Humane Society brought out the troops to hear Dr. Michael Fox, a veterinarian and bioethics scholar, talk about genetic engineering. Suddenly, all the past discussion about the technicalities of trade law was given heart and soul. The face of survival was the issue; the integrity of nature's most fundamental principles were at stake. Fox told the gathering that terminator genes, which keep crops from naturally reproducing, could result in terminal humanity. The WTO supported the corporate right to "own" the genes of creation, and this was wrong.

"It was like going to church or something," said Soriano. "This is the ultimate line in life, of our existence." The audience was riveted, and the seeds of solidarity took firm root between "No to WTO" and People for Fair Trade. After Fox's presentation, the group, inspired and unified, got busy and broke down into twenty-four geographically based groups for strategic discussions about neighborhood activity.

The ripple effect outside the Michael Fox meeting was dramatic. The next day, the mother of someone who had been there called Soriano and said, "I heard what happened at the meeting. I want to do something."

Seattle is a town that cherishes the integrity, individuality, and power of its neighborhoods, each with its own community councils, needs, goals, and even block watches. Neighborhoods fight hard before the city council for what they want—whether it's a new landscaped traffic circle to slow cars, a new park for kids, or an old building preserved for posterity. Some, like Montlake, have members who volunteer their skills with hammer, plunger, and lawn mower to help others in need. Other

## Net Worth

The international community of organizers working to rein in the power of the WTO, stop the homogenization of culture, and curtail the globalization of free trade used the Internet to a stunning advantage.

In an article in the *Los Angeles Times* (December 2, 1999), Public Citizen's Mike Dolan is quoted as saying, "The Internet has become the latest, greatest arrow in our quiver of social activism. It benefits us more than the corporate and government elites we're fighting."

The Internet links up activists who might have different causes, yet who are civic soul mates. There are no geographic hurdles to cross, no long-distance charges, and no limit to the amount of information that can be exchanged. The WTO was the common foe; the Internet paved the way for global populism to ride into battle. E-mail list-serves, Websites, downloaded artwork, accommodations, work parties, pirated policies, schedules of events, and the round-the-world message to get to Seattle on time rode the Internet wave as it circled, and recircled, the globe.

neighborhoods join forces to fight drugs and gang violence. When a contingent of neighbors shows up at City Hall, it means something. When the word got out about WTO, it meant something.

Seattle is not a town with a history of falling for personalities over character, for celebrity over authenticity. Up until very recently, people settled here to get away from style over substance; and even though its trendy high-tech chic dazzles the stock-market set these days, there's a deeper ethic at work in the Northwest. It's an ethic shaped by nature, by the mountain wilderness out both the back door and the front door, by the lonely and untamed Pacific coast and waters of Puget Sound. It's an ethic in which the landscape still reigns over the local multimillionaire-at-large. And it's the people rooted in an ethics-based quality of life who persevere and make things happen.

By the August 1999 meeting, the lateral leadership for WTO week had expanded dramatically. People showed up with flyers that they had made, then passed them around for others to take, copy, and distribute. "I was amazed," said Soriano. "Everyone was saying, 'Look at this, look at this.'" It occurred to her for the first time that people were getting it. "Everyone took it on, everyone went to the Web for more and more information. It took off on its own. Everybody was organizing." In August, Dennis Brutus, activist poet from South Africa, and state senator Byron Rushing, who pushed through the Massachusetts law limiting investment in Burma, came to Seattle to talk WTO. The standing-room-only event, which was emceed by King County Councilmember Larry Gossett, brought home the impact of the infamous banana ruling on the livelihoods of hundreds of thousands of people.

It was also in August that People for Fair Trade opened its store-front office downtown at Fourth and Stewart, within blocks of the convention center and Seattle's big hotels. The rent was paid by Citizens Trade Campaign; Mike Dolan made one of his high-energy visits to town to make sure the fired-up factor was still intact. He found that it was way beyond him.

Late in the month, People for Fair Trade, represented by Soriano and Ron Judd, convinced the Republican-weighted King County Council to call for a resolution not to welcome the WTO to Seattle. It was poised to pass 7-5, but was so contested that it was quickly tabled for further discussion. The pending vote sent shock waves through the mainstream press and politicos. The *Post-Intelligencer* reporter could hardly believe that the council was considering rolling up the WTO welcome mat, and wrote so in a front-page article of the paper. It was dramatic enough to inspire phone calls from President Clinton to King

County Executive Ron Sims, chair of the King County Council. "Clinton really wanted that resolution to be voted down," said Soriano, who heard all about the controversy at the annual King County Labor Council Labor Day picnic. The following week, Soriano and Judd went to work to save the resolution. But Clinton had clout. Eight council members voted to put out the WTO welcome mat. In the end, five members stayed the course.

By September, the attendance at the monthly anti-WTO organizing meetings had grown so large that they had to move from the Labor Temple in downtown Seattle to Kane Hall at the University of Washington. In October, more than 500 people showed up to hear Father Thomas Kocherry, a priest, fisherman, and renowned labor organizer from India. There were also five-minute updates from each of the groups that were independently organizing themselves for WTO week.

Throughout September, October, and November, it was debate season in Seattle. Soriano debated the WTO at Democratic Party legislative districts, before gatherings of Seattle's teachers, at churches, at community colleges, and wherever else the fair-traders could find a venue. The response was pretty unanimous. By the end of each debate, people from the audience would start attacking the position of the free-traders. "They just couldn't stand up to the record of the WTO," said Soriano. "The students at Seattle Central Community College were so angry about the WTO decision against the Caribbean banana growers that they started swearing at the free-trade people, and the president of the college felt he had to apologize for them."

It was a lot different from the national scene in 1995, when GATT was giving birth to WTO and the powers-that-be were slipping the trade bill through Congress. "They'd never debate us," said Soriano. "Mickey Kantor would never debate Ralph Nader on *The MacNeil-Lehrer Report.* Or they would lie. That was Mickey Kantor's ploy all the time." But debating in civil Seattle was different. "In Seattle, you don't lie," said Soriano. "That's pretty much a D.C. phenomenon. So the free-traders could never win out West."

The Clinton administration sent out Carol Browner of the EPA and former EPA administrator William Ruckelshaus (who is now chairman of the board of Browning-Ferris Industries, Inc.) for a Town Hall debate with Washington State Representative Velma Veloria, who was co-chair of the state House Trade Committee, and Patti Goldman from the Earthjustice Legal Defense Fund. It was Goldman who had represented the endangered Endangered Species Act before the U.S. Court of International

Trade, which resulted in a preliminary ruling in April 1999 that found in favor of national environmental law. In the debate with Browner, who was hand-picked by President Clinton to represent the WTO cause, Veloria and Goldman went for the facts, quoted from the record, and "really took them on," according to Soriano. The hometown fair-traders won hands down, and Veloria and Goldman got a standing ovation.

Goldman went on to debate the head of the WTO, Michael Moore, at the University of Washington. "She doesn't raise her voice," said Soriano. "She just has all the facts and all the words. Michael Moore couldn't stand up to her. She creamed him," a reality that was lost to at least one member of the press. At the debate, Soriano was sitting behind *Seattle Post-Intelligencer* business reporter Bruce Ramsey. "He was writing, writing, writing," she said. But the next morning in the *P-I*, his piece made it sound as though Moore had refuted everybody. "Completely distorted," said Soriano. "But at least they had it on cable television, and it was shown repeatedly, especially during WTO week."

The popularity of these debates helped to lay the groundwork for the whopping attendance at the big teach-in held over the weekend before N30. Organized by the International Forum on Globalization, which brought in bigwig scholars and grassroots organizers from around the world, it was a cornucopia of global conscience and consciousness. It stunned those who were just climbing aboard the learning curve.

✿ ✿ ✿ ✿ ✿

Although these debates, teach-ins, and monthly meetings were extremely effective ways of educating people about the WTO, the education curve was not without its rough spots. In late summer, the possibility of "terrorist" protesters in Seattle started surfacing in the press. Articles about anthrax terrorism appeared on the front page of the daily papers; the U.S. Department of Health and Human Services sent out people to advise hospital staff about the possibility of biological warfare. Police were expecting the worst. The publicity had an immediate effect. "All of a sudden, our audiences were paralyzed," said Soriano. "We had to fight through the fear to get the WTO issues out." She also had a fight with her own fear.

In mid-November, Soriano was driving back from a talk she had given at Western Washington University in Bellingham, a two-hour drive north of Seattle, when she was pulled over by the State Patrol. She was driving her sister's car (hers had a bad tire) and wasn't used to the way the lights worked. Consequently, when she'd entered the freeway from an on-ramp, she didn't immediately have the lights on. What she did have on was her "No to WTO" button. The patrolman noticed immediately. After mentioning her lights, he quickly asked, "And what are you doing protesting the WTO?" She introduced herself as a former teacher and asked him how much he knew about the WTO, then proceeded to educate him. After a twenty-minute conversation, he confessed that he hadn't known much about it at all, but that the police had heard that they were going to be killed. When Soriano got back to Seattle, she immediately called her union friends and told them to get WTO materials to the police unions fast.

There was an impact on her personal life as well. A friend, whose husband worked at a local hospital, expressed concern when the possibility of terrorism surfaced in the press. "Her husband had been briefed by the U.S. government about anthrax at the WTO protest," said Soriano. After eight months of a massive education campaign that had stuck firm with the facts and the record, the fair-trade movement was suddenly becoming unstuck by fear and paranoia.

But the WTO protest momentum was bigger than anyone realized. The student movement had grown steadily; the faith-based community had expanded throughout churches up and down the West Coast; hundreds of nongovernmental organizations with unique goals and common threads were mobilizing their members. Even Soriano, who had dedicated nine months to gestating the WTO protest, had no idea it would be as big as it turned out to be, as complex, as encompassing.

When it was all over, she asked her local Kinko's operator if he'd expected the protest to be so big. In Seattle, Kinko's is the copy center of choice. They're everywhere, and many are open twenty-four hours a day. Throughout the months of planning, Soriano was making copies of materials at all hours of the night. The manager said that around the first of November, when every other person who came in was doing something on WTO, then he knew.

The final monthly meeting before N30 was a rally on Sunday, November 14, at 6:00 P.M. It was the last chance for the coalition to get together under the same roof to plan the "un-welcome" for the World Trade Organization. The leadership was still moving outward in its trademark egalitarian fashion: "Come and tell us what you are planning" read the flyer. The groups that were already on the agenda to share their plans and enlist help included the Washington Association of Churches, King County Labor Council, Sierra Club, Earthjustice Legal Defense Fund, Humane Society, Northwest Labor and Employment Law Office, People's Assembly, Direct Action Network, and the old-timers, the two sides of the same coin: People for Fair Trade and Network Opposed to the WTO. The hall was also crowded with individuals who were planning to bring groups of their own representing neighborhoods, schools and colleges, women's issues, indigenous peoples' rights, and a vast array of unions.

In the middle of November, Soriano was still scouting around for last-minute housing for hundreds of visiting protesters when something happened that stunned even her. On the Wednesday before Thanksgiving, 10,000 copies of the morning paper, the *Seattle Post-Intelligencer*, were revisited in their coin dispensers in the early morning hours, where they became the *Seattle Post-Intelligence*. It took just one quarter to open each box; then the front and back pages of their main sections were replaced with identical-looking pages of new and revised copy.

In the look-alike trademark banner across the top of the *Seattle Post-Intelligence*, it read: "Congress Scraps One F22. Decides to build 20,000 schools instead; Mumia Freed. Tens of thousands celebrate in the streets; Jordan Gives Nike the Boot." The lead feature, "Boeing to move overseas," by a news correspondent assuming the name of Joe Hill (anarchist, songwriter, Wobbly activist, and martyr), started off with a bang. "In a tense press conference late last evening, the nation's premier manufacturer of airplanes announced that after 63 years in Seattle, it will be taking wing—for Indonesia." It went on to say why. Archbishop Oscar Romero was the name taken by the economic correspondent who wrote "Economists fear global epidemic of underpollution." Buried in the article was a quote from a Dr. Util: "What many people don't understand is that breathable air and drinkable water are a luxury." Dolly Bah, the science correspondent, wrote the "Monsanto patents food chain" article. Emma Goldman, anarchist born again as a political correspondent, wrote about a "WTO Director power grab." And Dorothy Day, Catholic anarchist cum labor correspondent, penned "Steelworker locked out." There were letters to the editor from S. Biko, Flipper, and R. Ghandi; there was a guest editorial from "one of those Hearst papers."

> "One of the charms of democracy—and one of its exasperations—is that each town council, each committee, each city government, is an ego unto itself; this ego is the sum of many individual egos, prejudices, beliefs, and even torpors."
>
> —Emmett Watson, longtime Seattle reporter-about-town, in his book *Digressions of a Native Son*

It was a brilliant piece of anarchism that was at once very funny and very provocative. The facts about issues were presented within the context of parody, but it was a painful parody that sidestepped satire for something closer to home. And the pages were so visually accurate and the articles written with such a journalistic flair that it was easy to get drawn in before you knew what was going on. There was a lot of guffawing at Thanksgiving dinner tables in and around Seattle. Nobody has taken credit for the page-swapping, so far. At least, not in public.

Blame it on the Canadians. In the new and vital partnership between U.S. and Canadian trade-game activists that has surfaced in recent years, the Canadians advised their buddies south of the border to "get to comedy. Make people laugh." In Saskatchewan, when a public utility was threatened by privatization, the mischief-makers decided they would sell the offending party's house; they would "publicize" it, and they offered sales slips to anyone interested. It made a lot of people laugh, and got quite a bit of media coverage along the way.

The *Post-Intelligence* Thanksgiving-eve prank was a good way to end the week. On the Friday after the phony *P-I*, Soriano's phone rang off the hook with people volunteering housing.

Soriano had five or six people staying at her house. She laughed as she described reading the *Seattle Times* on N29. On page two, the big story was the WTO schedule for the following day. It started with "7:00 A.M.—Shut Down the WTO—The Mass Nonviolent Direct Action. Meet at Victor Steinbrueck Park north of Pike Place Market, or at Seattle Central Community College." There was no specific schedule listed for the ministerial meetings themselves.

The next morning, the folks at her house had lots of options. Those who got up early could join the group to "shut down the WTO"; those who slept in could go to the big labor rally and march; others could wear green and meet up with the environmentalists at Denny Playfield near Seattle Central Community College (at Pine and Broadway on Capitol Hill, just blocks east of the convention center); members of the National Organization for Women could meet at a local women's shelter; the Art Bell (UFO talk-show host) metaphysical people could wear daisies and meet at the foot of the Space Needle. They would all converge in one way or another upon the World Trade Organization. N30 was born. All Soriano had to do was remember to go and pick up Ralph Nader at the airport and take him places. It was a piece of cake after the previous nine months—and many years—in the political soup.

# 13 NO ISLAND IS AN ISLAND— IN WHICH THE STREETS ARE FILLED WITH YEARNING

"It seems to me we can never give up longing
and wishing while we are thoroughly alive.
There are certain things we feel to be beautiful
and good, and we must hunger after them."
—George Eliot, *The Mill on the Floss* (1860)

Between New York and San Juan Island is the rest of the country, a fact perhaps easily overlooked by both. Between the two places, if one were to go the long way around, is the rest of the world. Another fact that is all too easy to overlook: My island's insularity breeds both compassion and contempt. When locals are in trouble—a house fire, an illness, an accident—the community response is immediate and generous. Yet when my friend Agnes Vadas tried to get the use of the community theater for a fund-raiser for Amnesty International, she was told, "No, the theater only does fund-raising for local organizations." Her request was considered "beneath notice," a definition of the word "contempt," which itself sounds harsh and unforgiving, and is a hard word to use. But it reflects an attitude, an isolationism, an assumption that we are not connected "out there" because, perhaps, "out there" doesn't matter. Agi, as we fondly call her, is Hungarian, a survivor of the Holocaust, a master violinist who retired from the San Francisco Opera, sold her violin, and used the proceeds to buy a bit of island land and build herself a house. She founded the local chapter of Amnesty International here shortly after she arrived. She will always be connected "out there."

New York City seems to nurture an opposite perspective. The world is invited in and welcomed; money is raised for all kinds of international causes, but it seems to be the locals, those out of luck and in need of shelter, who are "beneath notice." New York and San Juan Island might be a country apart, but both take part in the great divide.

What links the two together is the younger generation. Our kids. Shaya Mercer, who was raised on San Juan Island and now lives in New York, directed the first full-length documentary about the WTO in Seattle. *Trade Off* premiered at the Seattle International Film Festival on June 8, 2000. The Cinerama Theater downtown was packed with more than 600 people, and lots of others couldn't get in.

I rent a house from Shaya's mother, Lynne, who is also my friend. At the age of fifty-four, she left this quiet island to go to Sarah Lawrence College and get a master's degree in theater and playwriting. Earlier this year, I e-mailed Lynne and told her about this book I was writing about the WTO. She e-mailed me back that her daughter, Shaya, was scrambling to finish *Trade Off* in time for the film festival in Seattle. It was one of those small-world moments of stupendous synchronicity.

I was excited to see the film—because of its topic and because of its director. While waiting to go into the theater, I was surrounded by WTO talk, all of it from people who had been there and had stories. The fellow next to me was a Teamster, a business agent, a liaison between union member and employer. He was young and bright, and talked about being on the streets for all of WTO week and how disappointed he was that the unions didn't get out and follow through more dramatically when the police violence started. "We needed some leadership," he said. I asked him if he'd planned to be so involved during the days after the labor march. He shrugged and said, "Had to." And then told me about protecting a small woman "about 5 feet tall and 100 pounds" as she was being sprayed in the face by the police. His friend grabbed her and tried to pull her to safety, and still the policeman pursued. My companion in the movie line said he took his yellow rain poncho and tossed it over the offending policeman, and they got the woman to safety.

In his job, he works to encourage temporary workers to unionize. "But it's hard to get people to act for themselves. I work with the ones who've been there the longest, and hope they'll spread the word to the others." I asked him if he was from a union family. "Nope," he said. "I'm the first."

He was also one of the union members who disregarded the change in the labor march route; he broke through the human barrier and followed the original route, which went to the Paramount Theatre, much closer to the convention center. This decision symbolized the split-at-large in labor. Although much was made of the Teamster-turtle partnership, when it came down to the hard stuff—supporting the civil disobedience and speaking up against the police brutality—labor became splintered. I'd heard as much muttered from other activists who were there; this was the first time I heard it from the rank and file. Perhaps age, once again, has or doesn't have its say. He was about thirty; and he stayed the course.

I noticed a good number of union people lined up to go into the movie. The fellow I sat next to was a union man from Portland, where he worked as a librarian and was a shop steward for his union, the American Federation of State, County, and Municipal Employees (AFSCME). He said he'd been afraid to come up to Seattle for WTO week because he "knew something would happen." He was in town to catch a few festival movies and thought that *Trade Off* would be interesting. During the film, when the faces on the street were caught in a frieze of vulnerability and helplessness in the face of an anonymous brutality, he could not control a gasp. There were sobs in the audience as well. And, in places, rowdy, raucous laughter. When Mike Moore announced from his official WTO podium at the end of N30 in Seattle that the ministerial meetings were "doomed to succeed," the place roared. It was an audience that had been there and been overlooked. This film acknowledged everything that the media had considered beneath notice.

Mercer threaded the documentary with footage of the People's Gala. The big party was held on the eve of N30 in Key Arena at the Seattle Center, across downtown from where the WTO ministers gathered in opening-night festivities to eat salmon and other Northwest delicacies. While the Jubilee crowd circled outside the WTO gathering and chanted for forgiveness of Third World debt, the crowd at Key Arena rocked. Word artist Jello Biafra pumped up the audience with rhythm and human rights, Spearhead played funk, and Laura Love took the lid off "Amazing Grace."

Sixties radical Tom Hayden, now a Democratic state senator from California, came onstage and told the audience, "This is your future, this is everything." He talked about how the WTO threatens local laws and national sovereignty. "How can they be turning themselves into puppets?" he asked about the lawmakers across the country who seemed to be going like lambs to the corporate slaughter. Paul Wellstone, Democratic U.S. senator from Minnesota, showed up to encourage the WTO protest. He had sponsored a bill to temporarily freeze the explosion of agribusiness mergers to give the farm community a chance to get its footing. (Sadly, Democractic U.S. Senator Patty Murray of Washington State voted against it. She lost a lot of friends in the farming community. Her pro-WTO stance is seen as yet another betrayal in the Democratic landscape.) Republican Brian Derdowski, who'd only recently lost his seat on the King County Council because of his outspoken views, came to the podium and wryly recommended downsizing the entire CEO kingdom, cutting salaries of those left, and retraining the old ones in the art of making street puppets.

The other Michael Moore, the documentary filmmaker from Flint, Michigan, was disheveled and deadly funny. He told about masquerading as a business executive and getting himself into a car manufacturers' meeting in Mexico at which everyone was educated about how to get rid of their employees, reduce costs, and increase profits by moving south of the border. But not too far south. The maquiladoras, free-trade-zone assembly plants that nestle along the U.S.–Mexico border, have grown in number from 620 in 1980 to more than 2,200 today. There are more than 500,000 Mexican workers earning about $2 an hour working for such U.S. companies as Ford, General Motors, General Electric, Westinghouse, and Honeywell. The Mexican government manages all contractual arrangements and does not allow workers to form unions.

Moore talked about how, during his visits to these areas over a ten-year period, conditions have gotten worse and worse for those living there. There are no environmental standards established, so toxic waste from the plants poisons the air and the water. Birth defects are common and health problems abound. In his book *When Corporations Rule the World,* David Korten writes, "Mexican workers, including children, are heroes of the new economic order in the eyes of corporate libertarians—sacrificing their health, lives, and futures on the altar of global competition."

Throughout the People's Gala, and throughout *Trade Off,* Mike Dolan emceed with a peripatetic irreverence. He's a ham, practiced in the art of the glib pause that sometimes refreshes. Mercer caught the tragedy and the triumph at the heart of what happened in Seattle. Dolan wore a tie, tossed out the sound bites, and was cute. At the end of the film, Michael Franti and Spearhead pulled the People's Gala crowd to their exuberant feet, leaving them, and us watching the film, with a frenzied buzz of power and possibility. But the real ending, and perhaps the real beginning, was when "Amazing Grace" came over us, and overcame us, and the individual faces on the streets of Seattle filled the screen with such intimate sadness and confusion and yearning that one almost had to look away.

# 14 LOVE'S LABOR FOUND—
IN WHICH THE OILER IS A UNION GIRL

"Labor is prior to and independent of capital.
Capital is only the fruit of labor,
could never have existed if labor had not first existed.
Labor is the superior of capital,
and deserves much the higher consideration."
—Abraham Lincoln

When I talked to Joanne Calhoun, a longtime union woman who works as an engine-room oiler onboard the Washington State Ferries, she said, "I always felt that the unions in the United States made a mistake not going out to the Third World and helping them organize. If they had done that twenty years ago, we wouldn't be facing these problems now." (Not that they haven't tried. Twenty years ago unions did attempt to organize in Third World countries, but actually got used by the CIA and other U.S. agencies to identify dissidents and undermine labor rights in those places. This is a sorry chapter not well known by most labor activists.)

Calhoun lives on Vashon Island, a short ferry ride from Seattle. The day I went to meet her was crystal clear—mountains shining in the distance and the waters of Puget Sound deep blue and beautiful. I've ridden many a ferry during my years in the Northwest. They can be an oasis in the midst of a crazy day, or a nightmare of scheduling logistics. About one day every couple of weeks, back in the mid-seventies when the coffee refills were free, I would ride continuously back and forth between Seattle and Bainbridge Island, writing poetry. They don't let you do that anymore.

As I ferried over to Vashon to meet Joanne Calhoun, I realized that I didn't know what an oiler did; in fact, the entire workings of a ferryboat engine room were a complete mystery to me. Researching this book was starting to have an effect. I was now wondering where my food came from, what was in it, who stitched my clothes, where my shoes were made, and, now, how the damn ferryboat worked.

An oiler, it turns out, does a lot of things. Calhoun, who works twelve-hour shifts, a week on and a week off, helps keep the engines running and maintained. She makes a lot of rounds, checking gauges, looking in the bilge, changing oil and filters. She paints, takes on water, brings on stores. "Every day is different," she says. "That's what I like about it." And there's always an oiler in direct connection to the pilot. "If there's any trouble in the wheelhouse, we have to be ready." Calhoun also has to be ready for the men she works with, who are also always different. "You get everything: your jerks, your Romeos, every difficult kind of guy, and every easygoing kind of guy. It's like having another roommate you've got to get along with, but you didn't get to pick him." Her strategy for survival is simple. "I overlook stuff," she said. And then she laughed, loud and pleased.

Calhoun is good-natured. She's due to retire in a year, and at fifty-four she looks and seems a good decade younger. She's also forthright, and if she has any feminine wiles up her sleeve, they are well hidden. Twenty years in the bilge with the guys has left its mark. After retirement, she and husband Bob Underwood are headed off on an extended voyage in their catamaran, first up through the Inside Passage to Southeast Alaska, and then south to Mexico for the winter.

She told me about some of the ferries she works on, the smaller ones, the *Illahee*, *Klickitat*, *Quinault*, and *Nisqually*, all of which came up from San Francisco after the Golden Gate Bridge was built and they were no longer needed. They are the small ferries in the fleet. The big ones are double-deckers and carry more than 200 cars. In her twenty years, she's worked them all.

Before she became a union oiler, Calhoun was a union elementary schoolteacher; she also spent a short while in the Teamsters. Her family comes out of the union tradition; her mother was an activist Democrat who nearly ran for the state legislature; her great-uncle was a sea captain who worked the Seattle-to-Alaska run; he helped organize the Socialist Workers Party, got blackballed for his activities, and lost his job. Her brother is a shipfitter and a member of the International Brotherhood of Boilermakers. Her husband, who at the time was working at Seattle's Best Coffee (SBC), was trying to get the workers unionized; he's also in the merchant marine. Hers is a clan with the sea in its blood.

Calhoun, her husband, and her brother all went to the WTO labor rally together, as union individuals. They didn't sit with any one group. They did, however, run into lots of people they knew, including officials of the grocery clerks union, who were anxious to see SBC unionized. They figured if one coffee company could get unionized, the big one, Starbucks, wouldn't be far behind. In 1997, Starbucks closed down its Vancouver, B.C., distribution plant after the workers unionized.

(Not long after WTO week, Bob Underwood's attempt to unionize SBC was voted down. "You've got kids happy making eight or nine bucks an hour; the Vietnamese were intimidated because the company told them they'd lose benefits," said Joanne Calhoun. "SBC got a lawyer and called a bunch of meetings and fought the union big-time. After the union vote failed, they had a big barbecue. Bob will keep track of what the company promises. It will give maybe one or two things; then after about a year, the employees may be calling the union to come back. That's the pattern.")

✿  ✿  ✿  ✿  ✿

When I first walked into Memorial Stadium on the morning of November 30, I was literally shocked to a standstill. The noise, the numbers, the logistics, the organizational details—even to the point of passing out free ponchos in case of Seattle rain—were spellbinding. It was the pure unadulterated energy of working people in action. At one point I stopped and scanned the bleachers and the grounds, trying to count the number of union groups in attendance. It was impossible. I remember being struck by how many Canadian groups were there—teachers, airline pilots, and farmers as well as longshoremen and steelworkers. All the people that make the real world happen in all its complex glory. The people who grow stuff, make stuff, move stuff, fix stuff, build stuff, teach us, take us places. The people who rely on a union to preserve the values of daily life—time for the kids, for leisure, health benefits. Values that fly in the face of "virtual" reality with its fifteen-hour high-tech, high-paying workdays, and easy dismissal of the deep core issues of social justice. Not a nerd in sight, I thought, and went and stood in line for a hot dog that was likely genetically modified and bad for me. I didn't care. I was happy.

"This used to be such a strong union town," Calhoun told me. "I was shocked to find out that fewer than 30 percent of the area's workers now belong to unions." And she blames it on the unions themselves. "In the '60s and '70s, you got everything you wanted, raises every year, your medical benefits. But unions didn't come up with new goals. Now I don't identify with my union at all. It negotiates contracts and grievances, but it contributes to politics that I don't agree with. The position of wiper is a basic position that you don't need training for. You can come in off the street and get this endorsement with no background. I thought those jobs should be given to women and minorities; otherwise, there's no way for them to get into the engine room. But no, the union wanted to keep it under union control."

Calhoun is as union as they come, but her criticisms were the same ones I was hearing from the nonunion activists: exclusivity and lack of global concern. "The unions aren't in agreement on the WTO issues," she said. "Losing jobs is one thing, but there are so many issues going on, so many things being impacted."

The speakers at the labor rally came from around the world to represent their fellow workers. Their faces—Asian, South American, African—loomed huge on the big screen at the west end of the stadium. Their voices were passionate, their individual stories dramatic, but their message was the same. *"Be our voice,"* they were pleading. *"Help us."* "They were putting their lives on the line by being there, you know they were," said Calhoun.

"Everybody has the same needs and wants: to work with dignity and be able to have a living wage. They want what we want," she said. "And the WTO violates these basic rights. We shouldn't trade with countries that use slave labor. But we've weakened our labor force so much. There are sweatshops in the United States now; what's the deal with that? Indentured workers. We're turning into a Third World country."

She also agrees with a lot of activists—particularly in the student movement—that the longshoremen's union, the International Longshore and Warehouse Union, is leading the way in the right direction. When Brian McWilliams, president of the ILWU International, announced at the rally that all the ports on the West Coast were shut down in support of the WTO protest, the 30,000 unionists in the stadium went wild. His speech wrapped up all the labor issues in a blaze of clarity, his face intense on the big screen, his words thundering out of the huge speakers:

> The free-trade advocates of the WTO have come to Seattle to further their strategic takeover of the global economy. We in the ILWU want to give them the welcome they deserve, and let them know what we think of their plans. So we've closed the Port of Seattle and the other ports on the West Coast. There will be no business as usual today. In closing these ports, the ILWU is demonstrating to the corporate CEOs and their agents here in Seattle that the global economy will not

run without the consent of the workers. And we don't just mean longshore workers, but workers everywhere, in this country and around the world.

When the ILWU boycotted cargo from El Salvador and apartheid-ruled South Africa, when we would not work scab grapes from California valleys or cross picket lines in support of the fired Liverpool dockers, these were concrete expressions of our understanding that the interests of working people transcend national and local boundaries, and that labor solidarity truly means that when necessary we will engage in concrete action.

## WTO Foreplay

Although the hand-holding between labor leaders and environmentalists got a lot of media play during WTO week, the alliance was already well forged. In Houston, on May 19, 1999, the Alliance for Sustainable Jobs and the Environment, a collaboration of labor unions, environmental organizations, community leaders, social activists, and political thinkers, presented their "Houston Principles" to Charles Hurwitz, CEO of the Maxxam Corporation, which owns Kaiser Aluminum and Pacific Lumber Company. The Houston Principles acknowledge the common interest of labor and environmentalists in insisting that corporations be held accountable for their actions worldwide.

The Winter 2000 issue of *Earth Island Journal* reported on the Alliance and noted that "by clearcutting ancient redwoods in Northern California and by locking out striking steelworkers in five cities, the Maxaam Corporation has become an icon of corporate irresponsibility."

The Houston Principles bring together labor, the environment, and social issues in recognition of the "tremendous stakes" and the need to "challenge illegitimate corporate authority over our country's and communities' governing decisions."

That is why the ILWU is here today, with all of you—to tell the agents of global capital that we, the workers, those who care about social justice and protecting our rights and our planet, will not sit quietly by while they meet behind closed doors to carve up our world. We know that what they have mind for us is a race to the bottom, dismantling our protective laws wherever they find us weak, that they want to pit workers of one country against the workers of another, to erase our protections and standards in an international corporate feeding frenzy in which workers are not just on the menu—we are the main course. We will not cooperate!

We know our history, our legacy, and our ongoing responsibility. No one can make this statement stronger than longshore workers, who make their living moving international cargo. And what do we want? We demand fair trade—not free trade, not the policies of the WTO that are devastating workers everywhere and the planet that sustains us.

And let us be clear. Let's not allow the free traders to paint us as isolationist anti-traders. We are for trade. Don't ever forget—it is the labor of working people that produces all the wealth. When we say we demand fair trade policies, we mean we demand a world in which trade brings dignity and fair treatment to all workers, with its benefits shared fairly and equally, a world in which the interconnectedness of trade promotes peace and encourages healthy, environmentally sound, and sustainable development, a world that promotes economic justice, social justice, and environmental sanity. The free traders promote economic injustice, social injustice, and environmental insanity.

We are sending the WTO this message loud and clear: We will not sit idly by while you corporate puppets of the WTO plot this economic coup. You will not seize control of our world without a fight.

Are you ready for the fight?

*Damn right!*

The crowd was on its feet. Not long after McWilliams's rousing speech, I joined the huge crowd outside Memorial Stadium waiting for the march to get under way. I hung out near a woman who was one of the hundreds of marshals, except she had a radio and was in contact with other organizers. I overheard some near-desperate conversation. The crowd was so dense that they couldn't get AFL-CIO president John Sweeney up to the head of the line, where he was to lead the marchers on their way. There was a testy struggle between the organizers up front who wanted everyone to wait, and those at the back who were dealing with thousands of unionists who just wanted to get going. The march ended up starting by default. The triumphant front line became the triumphant 50,000. And some of them stayed the course.

## We've Come a Long Way Baby— and Gone Nowhere at All

At the turn of the last century, labor struggles were growing, strikes were multiplying, and people were fighting to the death for workers' rights. The police and the military were brought in to break strikes, and there was a growing divide between rich and poor. Howard Zinn, in his timeless book *A People's History of the United States*, writes, "According to a report of the Commission on Industrial Relations, in 1914, 35,000 workers were killed in industrial accidents and 700,000 injured. That year the income of forty-four families making $1 million or more equaled the total income of 100,000 families earning $500 a year."

In 1911, Helen Keller, who was deaf, blind, and a gifted writer and social activist, wrote to a suffragist in England: "Our democracy is but a name. We vote? What does that mean? It means that we choose between two bodies of real, though not avowed, autocrats. We choose between Tweedledum and Tweedledee. ... What good can votes do when ten-elevenths of the land of Great Britain belongs to 200,000 and only one-eleventh to the rest of the 40,000,000?"

"In the 1980s," writes David Korten in his 1999 book *The Post-Corporate World,* "capitalism triumphed over communism. In the 1990s, it triumphed over democracy and the market economy." (In 1997, Fran Lebowitz said the same thing.) Korten cites the dramatically growing gap "between the very rich and the rest of humanity," and writes, "Our political system is even more beholden to corporate money. Negotiators press ahead to complete new international trade and investment agreements that further strengthen corporate rights at the expense of human rights."

In the first year of this new millennium, the three richest men in the world earn more in one year than the combined incomes of 600 million people in the world's forty-seven poorest countries. What price progress? Ask those who work in the maquiladoras. Or in India. Or in Indonesia. Or in Iowa.

When the ILWU rank and file took to the streets for the march, it was behind a wide banner that read "An injury to one is an injury to all," a longtime Wobbly slogan from way back. And when they finally got all the union muck-a-mucks lined up, they were an impressive bunch: AFL-CIO Vice President Linda Chavez-Thompson, AFL-CIO President John Sweeney, Teamsters President Jim Hoffa, and United Auto Workers President Stephen Yokich were all elbow to elbow. McWilliams strode along with Ron Judd from the King County Labor Council, and somewhere in the crowd was George Becker, international president of the United Steelworkers of America. There were big contingents from Hawaii and Canada and union local chapters from across the country. The West Coast was heavily represented with big union groups from Los Angeles, San Francisco, Portland, and Bellingham. The international contingent included workers from France's La Confédération Générale du Travail (General Workers Confederation) as well as farm leaders from around the world. The march burst out onto the streets with noisy high spirits and global goodwill.

It was the beginning of some novel partnerships—like the student/steelworker alliance that grew teeth after WTO in support of the

## Subject: Action Alert

## Steelworker Picket at Port of Tacoma

I was down at Pier 7 for sixteen hours yesterday, so here's the latest update: The arbitrator ruled that the big-'n'-scary steelworkers present a heath/safety risk to the longshoremen, therefore the longshoremen did not have to unload the ore. So the picket is really established. However, the steelworkers will have to maintain a presence there at each and every shift change in order to maintain that health/safety risk. And late last night, the port agreed to let the steelworkers picket at the inner gate (rather than the street, where we were yesterday)—but steelworkers only. Which is very unfortunate, because it really helps them out, both in terms of numbers and spirits, to have supporters there.

They still need our help, though, to go down to the regular picket at the Kaiser gate and relieve the steelworkers there so they can go to the Pier.

Food and coffee would probably be appreciated too. ➤

strike at Kaiser Aluminum in Tacoma and Spokane. Student Vanessa Lee and her cohorts took up supporting the Teamsters in a big way. All through the early months of 2000, I was getting e-mails about the strike action in the port city of Tacoma, Washington, what was happening when, and who was needed where (see sidebar, Subject: Action Alert). In June, seven months after the WTO labor love-in, the longshore workers honored the steelworkers' picket line as it expanded to include the dock where ore was to be unloaded for delivery to Kaiser. An arbitrator was called in to decide if the longshore workers could indeed refuse to cross the Teamsters picket.

Not only loading and unloading ships, but crewing ships, presents a whole other can of WTO worms. As more and more U.S. shipping companies go transnational and register themselves outside the country, they hire nonunionized foreign crews for much less money and even less workers' rights and benefits. Joanne Calhoun's words about American unions helping workers organize in other countries represent an altruistic sentiment with a potentially practical payoff. And her brother and husband, both involved in the shipping industry, are watching carefully.

---

Things are looking up! Remember, they've been locked out for twenty-one months and their situation is getting desperate. But this small victory yesterday, and the other small victories in the days and weeks to come, may very well add up to the final victory that wins their fair contract. Bottom line: Kaiser will not be able to function without ore.

Oh yeah, and the police were not friendly. Two picketers were arrested—one as a test case (to test the charge that we were trespassing on Port property; we all vacated, but he stayed behind), and one as an intimidation tactic, I guess (the charge was also trespass, because he had set foot across the property line about ten minutes earlier). It took twenty or more fully riot-geared cops with guns to arrest this one man. (Both are out on bail.) Police harassed us periodically throughout the day. *So,* if you go down, don't jaywalk, make sure your tabs are current and your taillights work, and use your turn signal!

*Viva los steelworkers!*

—E-mail from activist Vanessa Lee, June 12, 2000

After the WTO rally on N30, the three joined the march to downtown, which went off without a hitch. None of the thousands gathered at Memorial Stadium knew that police violence had started hours earlier and that the streets downtown were under siege. As the march got under way, there was only a modest police presence controlling traffic at intersections, but they were well clear of the crowds and seemed almost disinterested in what was going on.

## Back to the Future

A hundred years ago, there were more than one million children working in factories, mines, and mills across the country. There were 500 garment factories in New York City alone, where thousands upon thousands of women worked up to eighty hours a week in dark, filthy, cold conditions more suitable to the resident roaches than to human beings. When they went on strike in 1909, it was in November. More than 20,000 walked out and hit the winter streets. There were beatings, arrests, and imprisonment, but the International Ladies Garment Workers Union, the ILGWU, was born. The American Federation of Labor, the AFL half of the AFL-CIO, was already in existence, but it organized only white men with skills—and the union officials catered more to high society than to the legions of low-paid workers across the country.

In Chicago in 1905, the Industrial Workers of the World, the IWW, organized a gathering of anarchists, socialists, and trade unionists from all over the country to "confederate the workers of this country into a working-class movement that shall have for its purpose the emancipation of the working class from the slave bondage of capitalism," according to Big Bill Haywood, who opened the convention, as described by Howard Zinn in A People's History of the United States.

In the early 1900s in Washington State, the IWW, or Wobblies as they were called, took strong steps toward unionization. Joanne Calhoun's grandfather was one of them. In Aberdeen, Chehalis, Spokane, and Everett, people were jailed, beaten, and killed for speaking out for workers' rights. In Everett, the sheriff gathered up 200 armed vigilantes and fired on a boatload of Wobblies, killing 5 and wounding 31. According to Zinn, "Law and military force again and again took the side of the rich."

In Seattle during WTO week, people were clubbed, gassed, and pepper-sprayed by the police for taking a stand for freedom of speech and assembly, human rights, social justice, and environmental integrity. People were thrown in jail arbitrarily, without cause, and held for days. We've come a long way, and gone not far at all.

At the intersection where the route was being diverted, Calhoun got stopped because of the direct action activities. "Those kids had conviction," she said. "They weren't going to move for anybody." Some union members were trying to choreograph a sit-down protest in support. "Here are all these old union guys. They wouldn't sit on the ground if they were shot," said Calhoun. "A couple of them kind of kneeled; we sat down on the curb." She laughed. "Yeah. Right. A sit-down." She laughed harder, "Oops, we forgot to bring our chairs."

The three left the march where it had been stopped and went back to the Pike Place Market, where Calhoun got her first sight of tear gas. She then went off to catch the ferry to Bainbridge Island, where she and Bob would be making another shift in anticipation of their approaching retirement. "We're going to go back to our '60s lifestyle. Eat better, feel better, live on a much smaller budget," she said, starting to laugh. "Simplicity. Only we won't be retiring at thirty-five and living off our millions and buying lots of really fine art." Just heading north to Alaska on April Fools' Day 2001.

# 15 WOMEN TURN OUT—
IN WHICH NIPPLES ARE A TRADE BARRIER

"Reality came forth to her,
since her eyes were cleansed to see it,
not from some strange and far-off and spiritual country,
but gently, from the very heart of things."
—Evelyn Underhill, English poet, novelist,
and mystic (1875–1941)

Because of the doldrums, I'm going to Carolyn Canafax's house in West Seattle. It's a maze to get her house because there's a "gated" community between where she lives and the main arterial. She described a huge redwood tree as a reference point, and it works. I arrive on time. It's early spring, and big droopy tulips are clustered in bright colors at the top of her driveway. She had used the word "doldrums" in a telephone conversation just the night before when I asked her about the overwhelming nature of staying the course with activism.

"Ah, yes," she said. "I first got the doldrums when the Rosenbergs were executed. We tried hard to prevent that. It was tough." Julius and Ethel Rosenberg, charged in 1950 of conspiracy to commit espionage, were found guilty and sentenced to death by the presiding judge. There had been a worldwide campaign protesting their death sentences, including letters from such notables as Albert Einstein and Pablo Picasso, but to no avail. In 1953, they were both put to death in the electric chair. Thus began the McCarthy era in the United States, and the demonization of Communism and Communists. Including Canafax, who lost many a teaching job because of her activism.

Carolyn Canafax is 4 feet 10 inches tall. She's in the prime of her seventies, and her eyes are bright with ageless humor and a wise and canny understanding of everything. I am assessed from the inside out, and then welcomed into her home. Instantly, I am sidetracked by the art, which is everywhere. She gives me a quick tour and then we sit down to chat. Before long, she brings out her box full of WTO materials. "Here," she says. "Have at it."

She'd collected most of the stuff after WTO week. "I felt that I needed to have some perspective," she said. "We're activists in town; we get a piece of the picture, but not the entire piece." Canafax was born and raised in Seattle. She and Leo, her husband of fifty-three years, have been involved in social justice issues their entire marriage. (Leo's union protected his political rights, so he was able to keep his jobs.) Yet for all her years of activism, the extent of the WTO protest was stunning to Canafax. "Unbelievably amazing," she said. "We sat in the stadium just above the sheet-metal workers in their light blue jackets. We were so happy to see them. And the Teamsters were down there, standing the whole time. And the longshoremen closed down the ports, and the cab drivers wouldn't drive." It was the sheet-metal workers who had rallied to Leo's side during the difficult years.

Canafax provided housing and hospitality to three women during WTO week, all members of the Women's International League for Peace and Freedom (WILPF—pronounced "wilf"). One of the women, eighty-three-year-old Madeline Duckles from Oakland, was stopped by the police after the big labor march on N30 and ordered to get out of town by the 7:00 P.M. curfew. But the taxis were on strike and the buses had been shut down. As she was making a phone call in search of help, she was blasted by tear gas. "I was dazed and staggering and in terrible pain," writes Duckles in the WILPF newsletter, *Pacific Vision.* "I leaned against a building, not able to see but trying to orient myself." Duckles was rescued by some young protesters who rinsed out her eyes with water and offered her the use of a cell phone. Because she was unfamiliar with the city, it took her a long time to get back to the Canafax house. But she still had her humor. "Maybe, in a tired eighty-three-year-old, they could still recognize a dangerous woman," she mused.

The world is full of dangerous women, and many of them were on the streets during WTO week. From union leaders to religious leaders, and from every corner of the globe, women organized, showed up, and spoke out. Some even bared their breasts as well as their minds. (And, in response to accusations of public indecency, nipples were covered up with small strips of electrical tape forming Xs over those illegal bits of body.)

Carolyn Canafax didn't bare her breasts on N30, but she was up on stage with the Raging Grannies, a radical street theater group made up of women of a certain age and experience. She started out early in the day, boarding one of the "retirees@wto" buses that arrived at 9:00 A.M.

at the Mercer Arena, a building just a short walk from Memorial Stadium, site of the big labor rally. The Raging Grannies performed for the big crowd of senior citizens. "There were quite a few old rads there," she said with a big grin. The seniors were there with George Kourpias, the president of the National Council of Senior Citizens, who offered a statement on their behalf, beginning with "Seniors are in Seattle today because we are concerned about jobs" and ending with "Seniors will stand strong today and in the future, for a trade policy that is based on fair treatment for workers across the world and for our families in America."

There were a lot of elders in the march on N30, some in wheelchairs, a few in chairs held aloft, others supported arm-in-arm with friends. And as the week progressed and the demonstrations widened in support of the 600 in jail, and in support of the democratic principles of freedom of speech and the freedom to protest, the numbers of elders increased. Thousands of new and different people rallied during the days after N30, when the signs and banners were suddenly blazoned with slogans more often featuring the words "Up with democracy" and "Down with police violence." If the WTO had seemed obscure to some, the

---

## The Curse of Wealth

Many of us still live in what is sometimes referred to as "frontier lands." These are territories that still have substantial natural resources and that transnational corporations and governments can't wait to exploit. Sometimes we wonder if it is a boon or a bane. An Amungme elder from West Papua once asked, "Why are we cursed to have this wealth on our lands?" He was talking about the mineral wealth in their lands that is being exploited by Freeport-McMoran for more than thirty years.

The WTO has paved the way to remove the last remaining controls on the national level so that transnational corporations and the rich governments of the world will easily get their hands on this wealth. From the mountains and coasts of Australia to Papua New Guinea, from the Philippines to India, from the north of Russia and Samiland to Canada and the United States, from Mexico to Colombia, and from South Africa to Nigeria, the world's biggest mining and oil corporations are competing with each other to extract the mineral wealth and oil found mostly in indigenous territories.

—Victoria Tauli-Corpuz, director, Indigenous Peoples' International Centre for Policy Research and Education, Baguio City, Philippines

treatment of peaceful protesters and innocent bystanders was all too clear. And all too ugly.

Carolyn Canafax knows about ugly, but the violence against her over the years happened behind closed doors. When she tells her story, there's a phrase that pops up repeatedly: "And then I got canned." Because of her involvement with the Rosenberg defense, she lost a lot of jobs back in the fifties—as a teacher, a union boilermaker with Todd Shipyards, and as a seaman-paper-carrying cafeteria worker on the ferry *Kalakala* (Seattle's waterborne version of the Airstream trailer).

The anti-Communist hysteria in those years was both emotionally and intellectually rabid. The House Un-American Activities Committee reigned throughout the early fifties with ongoing investigations into the lives of individuals across the country. Many were blacklisted, and they lost jobs, friends, and family because of it. In *A People's History of the United States*, Howard Zinn quotes President Truman's Attorney General: "There are today many Communists in America. They are everywhere—in factories, offices, butcher shops, on street corners, in private business, and each carries in himself the germs of death for society." Even the ACLU, the last bastion of freedom of expression in the United States, expelled one of its own charter members, Elizabeth Gurley Flynn, for being a Communist and refusing to end her involvement with the Rosenberg case.

This was the atmosphere during Canafax's political coming-of-age. Leo, who fought in World War II, was investigated because of his marriage to her. "But he's always been supportive," says Canafax. During the tough years, she and Leo took turns scrambling for jobs to keep their family fed and sheltered. But neither of them lost their passion for speaking out and acting on behalf of justice, peace, and freedom. Canafax, who joined WILPF in the sixties because of its broad-reaching platform, went on to found that organization's newsletter, *Pacific Vision*. "When I was elected to the international officers section of WILPF, somebody from Australia was running against me. It was in The Hague, in Holland, and the Australian woman said, 'Don't forget us.' The whole idea seized me. So I just started compiling stuff—always in the words of the women."

WILPF has a long and auspicious history in world peace, politics, and economic justice. It was founded when the Women's Peace Party, which mobilized in the United States in 1914, joined with a group of European women to convene the International Congress of Women at The Hague on April 28, 1915. World War I was nine months old, and many of the women, who gathered from twelve countries and represented more than 150 organizations, were officially wartime "enemies." Jane Addams from the United States presided. It was a heroic gathering that triumphed over a variety of logistical challenges, ranging from the daunting details of arranging transoceanic voyages during wartime to resisting the concerted interference of governments that wanted to prevent the event.

The women were called foolish, naive, interfering, ill-informed, irresponsibly feminine, and boldly unwomanly—for starters. The Hague congress went on to adopt twenty resolutions that laid the groundwork for the women's peace movement. One of its boldest was the last one, "Envoys to Governments," which called for personal delegations of women to carry the message of the congress to "the rulers of the belligerent and neutral nations of Europe and to the President of the United States." This they did immediately after the congress, and their ensuing report supported the idea of a neutral conference for mediation, which became a worldwide topic of both grassroots and top government discussion. Since its 1915 congress, WILPF has been actively and continuously involved with issues of peace and justice on all levels, and has been a fierce promoter of women at top levels of government.

The WILPF concerns about WTO trade policies are long established and far-reaching. For years, WILPF has been involved with issues that suddenly became "news" when WTO hit Seattle. The piracy of medicinal plants by pharmaceutical companies, the impact of intellectual property rights on the lives and economies of indigenous peoples, and the dangers of biotechnology are all too familiar to WILPF members around the world. The issue of corporate exploitation of culture and resources, and the exhausting indebtedness of developing countries to the World Bank and the IMF, have been on the WILPF agenda for decades. It is not surprising that the streets of Seattle during WTO week were full of WILPF activists, many of them our elders, women who have been active on the streets and in the halls of governments for half a century or more, pushing peace and social justice. It was old hat to them.

But the dramatic coalition-building in Seattle was new. "I was flabbergasted!" said Canafax. "We've been working for this kind of unity. WILPF is dedicated to it. You don't have just a single issue, you've got the works."

Ruth Hunter, a WILPF member from Santa Cruz, California, was part of the linked-arm circle around the convention center on N30. She was tear-gassed, pepper-sprayed, and hit with rubber bullets. The next morning at daybreak, she was back to protest again. This time she was arrested, along with three other women from Santa Cruz: an attorney, a Methodist minister, and a massage therapist. Although Hunter was put in arm and leg chains, deprived of food for more than twelve hours, and allowed no attorney contact, she found the solidarity among all the different causes profoundly moving. At the end of an essay she wrote about her experience, she says: "It has reinforced my deep belief that the voices of people, not global corporations, are our hope for a decent quality of life in the decades ahead."

✿ ✿ ✿ ✿ ✿

WTO week drew many powerful women to its teach-ins, rallies, marches, and demonstrations.

Vandana Shiva, a physicist and philosopher of science, came from India. She is director of the Research Foundation for Science, Technology and Ecology in New Delhi and co-director of the International Forum on Food and Agriculture. Shiva's books include *Monoculture of the Mind; Biotechnology and the Environment;* and *Biopiracy: The Plunder of Nature and Knowledge.*

Helena Norberg-Hodge is Swedish, currently lives in England, and spent thirty years in the Himalayan mountain province of Ladakh, where she helped the people learn about, and resist, the culturally destructive effects of globalization. She founded the International Society for Ecology and Culture and has written several books, including *Ancient Futures: Lessons from Ladakh.*

Susan George, a native of the United States who now lives in France, is recognized internationally as a leading thinker on North-South (hemisphere) power relations. Her books, which have been translated into many languages, include *A Fate Worse Than Debt; The Debt Boomerang; Faith and Credit: The World Bank's Secular Empire;* and *The Lugano Report: On Preserving Capitalism in the Twenty-First Century.*

Victoria Tauli-Corpuz came from the Philippines, where she has been an activist for thirty years fighting the liberalization of mining investments and the corporate appropriation of genetic resources and indigenous knowledge. She is director of the Indigenous Peoples' International Centre for Policy Research and Education.

Sara Larrain came from Chile, where she co-founded the new national political party, the Partido Alternativo de Cambio (Alternative Party for Change). She also founded the Chilean office of Greenpeace International and was formerly a professor and researcher at the Catholic University of Chile.

Agnes Bertrand came from France, where she is the director of ECOROPA-France, which launched the Farmers-Ecologists-Consumers Alliance, the anti-GATT campaign, and the "Fifty Years Is Enough" coalition in France, which targeted the IMF and the World Bank.

Anuradha Mittal, a native of India, is policy director at the Institute for Food and Development Policy in Oakland, California. She's coordinator of a national campaign to combat growing poverty, hunger, and economic insecurity in the United States. Her most recent book is *America Needs Human Rights: Fighting Against Hunger and Poverty in the Richest Nation on Earth.*

Katie Quan, a labor policy specialist from the University of California at Berkeley, was a rank-and-file seamstress and union organizer for more than twenty years. She's a board member of Sweatshop Watch and on the faculty of the labor studies department of City College of San Francisco.

Barbara Shailor of the AFL-CIO came from Washington, D.C., to participate in the teach-in "Labor: Extinguishing the Rights of Labor in a Globalized Economy."

Lori Wallach, the "Guerrilla Warrior of the Trade Debate" and director of Public Citizen's Global Trade Watch, was active behind the scenes throughout the planning of WTO week as well as a prominent speaker during the events. A graduate of Harvard Law School, Wallach recently cowrote *Whose Trade Organization? Corporate Globalization and the Erosion of Democracy.*

One woman who was in Seattle during WTO week, whose contribution against the WTO has been a cornerstone, is Maude Barlow, the so-called "Ralph Nader of Canada" and national volunteer chairperson of the 100,000-member Council of Canadians. In the early 1980s, Barlow was the director of the Office of Equal Opportunity for the city of Ottawa, and was senior advisor on women's issues to former Prime Minister Pierre Trudeau. She's written many books; her latest is *Blue Gold*, a report on the global water crisis. She credited student activists with heroic status for bringing down the WTO talks. "I am so proud of our youth," she said at a follow-up teach-in at the University of Quebec. "This is nothing less than revolution."

For Barlow, the battle is between agriculture and agribusiness. Chemical agriculture and genetic engineering "violate the laws of life" and threaten our "global citizenship," she says. She passionately calls for the development of an international scientific protocol to conduct research that is not shaped by corporate interests. She also calls for the assessment of socioeconomic issues as part of the protocol in order to preserve the local and sustainable culture of agriculture. Barlow speaks of corporate-designed food policies that force farmers to buy genetically modified seeds from giant multinational corporations instead of using their own seeds, which have developed naturally to thrive in their own unique environment. Preserving the natural biodiversity of life on the planet is a sacred mandate to Barlow. "This is globalization without representation. We must have the power to take a stand."

When I listened to Barlow speak about biodiversity on a recent Saturday-afternoon "Alternative Radio" show, she reminded me of Dr. Helen Caldicott, whom I heard on public radio back in 1981. As president of Physicians for Social Responsibility, Caldicott was addressing students at Harvard about the fundamental folly of nuclear weapons. I sent away for a copy of her talk, and it saw me through many a discouraging day during the anti-nuclear years. Barlow has the same combination of credentials and humanity, and the same articulate passion. And, as different as a grain of rice might seem from an atomic bomb, the underlying concern of the two women is the same: human survival.

During WTO week in Seattle, Barlow was one of the hundreds, perhaps thousands, of people who used the downtown First United Methodist Church as a sanctuary. "We'd go there for food and hugs, and then get back out onto the streets," said Barlow.

It was the Reverend Kathlyn James who made the church open and available in support of WTO week. It was used for everything secular, from a dressing room to an international think tank, as well as a place of spiritual solidarity for all religious voices.

Women were everywhere during WTO week. But perhaps it was the *absence* of one Seattle woman that really symbolized the strength of protest in the Northwest. Hazel Wolf, who died two months later on January 19, 2000, at the age of 101, wanted to be at the WTO demonstrations so she could be arrested one more time—but she had a broken hip, so she couldn't make it. Wolf was the grassroots grande dame of conservation politics in the Northwest. Born in Victoria, Canada, she moved to Seattle in 1923, when she was a twenty-five-year-old single mom. During her lifetime, she was a Communist (she liked the idea of unemployment insurance), a Democrat (she didn't like the idea of racism), and a bird-lover (she helped found twenty-two Audubon chapters around the world). When she was ninety years old, she met with a Soviet delegation to plan the first Leningrad Audubon Society. Into her nineties, she was still doing things like going to Nicaragua to "check on the Sandinistas' environmental record." In 1997, Wolf joined the company of Rachel Carson and former President Jimmy Carter when she won the National Audubon Society's Medal of Excellence in Environmental Achievement.

Hazel Wolf, who organized the first Indian Conservationist Conference, held in 1979 in Seattle, had a canny understanding of environmental politics and justice. "The environmental community is almost 100 percent white and middle-class," she said. "But it's the low-income neighborhoods where toxic landfills and incinerators are found." Wolf may not have been on the streets of Seattle during WTO week, but her spirit and her politics were everywhere.

# 16 THE POST-WTO CAFÉ—IN WHICH THERE'S NO LEADER, NO BUDGET, AND NO DONUTS

"The only tyrant I accept in this world
is the 'still small voice' within me."
—Mahatma Gandhi

On a Friday evening in late March 2000, four months after WTO, I joined Fred Miller at the Peace Café for a coalition meeting to organize a protest rally and march against the IMF and the World Bank, to be held in Seattle on April 16, 2000. It was being planned in solidarity with the big event on that same day in Washington, D.C. At the meeting there were thirteen people, ranging in age from early twenties to sixty-something; each person represented a constituency of the WTO protest movement.

I arrived a few minutes late and sat on the edge of the group; nobody paid me much attention. The talk under way was about the police: how to handle them, what to tell them when, who would communicate with them, and, generally, who felt what about them.

The opinions ranged from "Screw them, let's not tell them anything" to "Let's negotiate to get what we can." Bitterness from WTO week was still very strong. More than anyone on the outside realized, there had been a lot of communication with the Seattle Police Department about what would be happening when the WTO was in town. SPD had been informed in detail about many of the protesters' plans—including the planned civil disobedience and the intention of keeping delegates away from the convention center. The demonstrators' feelings of betrayal were poignant, as if a partnership had been violated. The rage was also in full bloom. One woman spoke so aggressively about her hatred that any possibility of her agreeing with anyone else seemed impossible. "I don't want any liaison. None. They are not our buddies."

"But the cops are edgy. We'll be in solidarity with the protesters in D.C.; they'll be in solidarity with the D.C. cops," said one fellow.

"Let's just tell them what we're going to do. This will shut off the possibility of a 'No' and also shut off the excuse that they were surprised," went another suggestion. One young woman, who had family members who were police, was concerned about the shutout. "It might not be so great," she said. "But maybe it's just me or maybe I'm an amateur."

On the other end was a commitment to going through the process, getting a permit and police escort, doing it by the book. The discussion was vehement yet friendly; no one held back, nor held back another. Gaining consensus seemed unlikely. Appearances, too, were contradictory. One fellow—short hair, beard clipped, neatly dressed, who looked like a Microserf on leave—went way beyond radical. His articulate anarchist views were authoritative and intellectual; his speech was not messy with emotion, epithets, or incomplete sentences. He took over when he spoke, was listened to intently, and had his views thoughtfully considered. The fellow with long flowing locks and wearing thrift-shop fashion was the voice of practical reason. And it was reason that eventually prevailed.

After two hours of discussion, it was decided that a permit would be sought for the rally at Westlake Park, a public space downtown; the police would be politely informed about the march route, the city councilmembers in support of the anti-WTO movement would be solicited for support, the mayor's office would be contacted. It would happen no matter what. Being told "No" was not an option. The goal was to get out the information about the IMF and the World Bank and to do it with a positive attitude.

All this took place through a modified consensus process, in which the vote was not a simple "yes" or "no." An issue was presented, and those in favor expressed as much; those with reservations were "stand asides"; the third possibility carried the big stick. If someone had strong moral and ethical reasons for opposing the proposal, they could "block," which would send everybody back into discussion. Even with the dire extremes of opinion, there was no "block" expressed.

The next hour took up details. Who would speak at the rally? What about the march being a guided tour of the most notorious WTO sites— McDonald's, the Gap, Niketown, Starbucks, Bank of America, Fidelity Savings, Sixth and Stewart where the police started the riot on N30? Someone could speak about each site. The map of the march was planned accordingly. Someone suggested that it go the wrong way down a one-way street "to kowtow to our anarchist constituency." The Big Puppet committee was established; music was essential, as were TVs and radios to keep up with what was happening in D.C.; and don't forget the bullhorn.

Someone suggested making a replica of the Pentagon to represent the federal government, with a sign reading "Exploit globally, repress locally."

The next big discussion was how to get the press to discuss the details of the IMF and the World Bank. "If we give the press a chance, nine times out of ten it'll report the wrong story," said someone. There was much frustration about the limited capabilities of reporters when it came to substantive issues. "Why do they focus on us and not the issues?" was the big question.

It was at this meeting that I first watched Vanessa Lee in action. Her mantra was "Okay, this discussion is very important but we have to …" and she'd move it right along with a light and informed touch. She also brought the group up to date about what was going on with the steel-workers' strike against Kaiser Aluminum, and reminded everyone that the overall purpose "is to build a movement for social change," which meant, among other things, using union printing shops—something that people forgot to do in the WTO whirlwind.

I left before the meeting ended, but not before taking note of the slogan on the back of someone's T-shirt: "If not here, where? If not now, when? If not us, who?"

On Sunday, April 16, 2000, this broad-based coalition pulled off the rally and march in Seattle to show support for the World Bank/IMF demonstrations in Washington, D.C. On Monday morning, in a front-page article about the event in the *Seattle Post-Intelligencer*, Vanessa Lee was pictured leading the parade, bullhorn in hand.

✿   ✿   ✿   ✿   ✿

Later, when we met to talk over lunch, I was very surprised to learn Vanessa Lee was a latecomer to the WTO movement. Lee, who graduated from Fairhaven College, an alternative-minded part of Western Washington University in Bellingham, has an interdisciplinary degree in multicultural studies, political science, and narrative.

"I'd heard about N30," she said. "But I was really cynical. I thought it was a whole bunch of hype." The idea of shutting down the WTO had seemed ludicrous to her. So on N30, Lee was at work as usual at her job at North Seattle Community College. She spent most of N30 in the student lounge watching the nonstop coverage of WTO on TV. "I was amazed," she said. "I also knew I wasn't getting the whole story. It was really obvious that there was so much more going on."

WTO week in Seattle was her first exposure to a major political protest, and it was the violence against the protesters that mobilized her.

"Apparently, I needed a catalytic moment," said Lee. "And I got one. I have to thank the police for that. We really do owe them a debt of gratitude because they exposed the real situation, to me and a lot of other people."

It was early Wednesday evening on December 1, after the second day of televised violence, that Lee realized she'd know what was really going on only by checking it out for herself. She set off with her then-boyfriend, Eric. "We got ourselves some bandannas and some bottles of water and went out, prepared to be gassed." The two, who lived on Capitol Hill, went downtown and found a group of about fifty people occupying an intersection. "The police were hovering around, not doing anything but kind of edgy," said Lee. "I remember one person saying, 'Last night they chased us out of here, and we went out running; it was

## Closing the Gates

We are proud of our democratic heritage, but the general public is disenchanted with the heavy hand of wealthy special interests in the electoral process. Voting participation and confidence in elected officials are at historic lows. Much of the decision-making power of our economy has been removed from the government bureaucracy—which at least was in some limited way responsible to the voters—and invested in the powers of corporate bureaucracies, which are answerable to none but their largest shareholders.

The wealthy distance themselves from community with the poor, moving to the suburbs or even to "gated communities" and removing themselves from tax rolls, which would help support inner-city schools and services. Underfunded schools cannot achieve their education mission, and become little more than warehouses for all but the most-motivated children until they are old enough to enter the workforce at its lower levels.

—Jubilee 2000, Episcopal Church, Office of Peace and Justice Ministries

really demoralizing, and we don't want to go through that again. Let's leave of our own accord.'"

Lee watched as the group used a consensus process to agree to sit down in the intersection until curfew, when they would then march up to Broadway and meet up with other groups with whom they were in contact. Lee and her friend sat down with the group.

"Then one police car came along and tried to drive through us," said Lee. "One guy leapt up; he had his fist up as though he was going to hit the car. A lot of people grabbed him and everybody started chanting, 'No violence, no violence,' and everybody just stayed put. The police car backed up and drove away. And I thought, 'Oh wow! This is really working.'"

While the sit-in was under way, one of the protesters negotiated an agreement with the police and told them what route they would be taking. "So we peacefully marched out of there and met up with other groups along the way," said Lee. "We had no trouble. We were marching quite happily, and by the time we got to Seattle Central Community College, there were a few hundred of us."

Seattle Central Community College (coincidentally the site of the old Broadway High School, attended by Carolyn Canafax) is toward the south end of Broadway at Pine, only a few blocks east of Seattle's Interstate 5 freeway overpass, where the police had tear-gassed, pepper-sprayed, and used pushing, shoving, and rubber bullets to get people out of the downtown area the night before.

I'd watched that same encounter on TV and had been utterly amazed. The freeway overpass was a natural barrier to the downtown area, and the freeway itself was the eastern border of the area that was to be closed after curfew. Why the police couldn't just hold that point was bizarre. Instead, they had aggressively bullied the crowd beyond the border and up into residential neighborhoods, where uninvolved bystanders going about their business were inadvertently caught up in the violence. Tear gas went wafting through windows into homes and apartments. Flash-bangs exploded like bombs. The residents of Capitol Hill were outraged. The subsequent protests in that neighborhood had everything to do with police violence; the WTO seemed sometimes secondary, even if it was the cause of Seattle's turning into a police state.

On that Wednesday, December 1, though, after the crowd dissipated, Lee and her friend went off to eat Thai food farther north on Broadway. It was after dinner, when they were on their way home, that they ran into the National Guard lockstepping down Broadway. "It was a terrifying sight," said Lee. "I was in shock." Lee and Eric went back north down Broadway, where they came to a line of police in riot gear blocking Broadway. "Little middle-class, privileged me; I thought, 'Well, I'll just ask the police why the National Guard is here,'" said Lee. When she did, she was pushed away and not answered. Then Lee saw another young woman ask the same policeman what was happening, and he used his stick to push her back really hard. "Why did you do that?" Lee asked him. "She wasn't doing anything." At that point, he came out of the police line, chased her into an alcove, and pepper-sprayed her three times until he was able to get her directly in the face. Eric, who'd asked a police officer for his badge number, was also pepper-sprayed.

The Broadway area is one of Seattle's most socially active neighborhoods. It actually has a sidewalk life—something that is sadly missing in most of the city. It's also lively with the gay and lesbian community, as well as with young people from the community college. There are coffeehouses, ethnic restaurants, movie theaters, and late-night activity. In the sixties, it was home to many anti-war demonstrations, but for the police to pinpoint a WTO connection to this community was a stretch. These days, it's a pretty happy place. There was nothing that would set it apart as a particularly threatening part of town. On Tuesday night, N30, people were forced into the area by the police. Why there was such a police and military presence there on Wednesday night, D1, was bewildering until it was discovered that the DAN warehouse, aka the Convergence Zone, was located just west of Broadway at Denny and Olive.

For Vanessa Lee, the experience was a wake-up call, and her activism began instantly. Every day after work, for the next four days, Lee went to keep vigil at King County Jail in downtown Seattle, where many of the protesters were being held. She was acting out of an independent passion. "I didn't know anybody," said Lee. But she was compelled to be there.

✿　✿　✿　✿　✿

This phenomenon, the politicizing aspect of WTO week in Seattle, was extremely widespread. Many Seattle residents started out wondering what all the WTO fuss was about anyway, but why the WTO demonstrations warranted such a violent response became a question that could not go unanswered. It opened a floodgate of public involvement and concern. The local television stations had been showing hours of live coverage of police aggression and violence. The protesters often appeared desperate, trapped, and terrified; the police appeared armed, well protected, and intent upon first-strike.

People flocked from their homes to show support for those arrested. They starting sitting in peaceful circles around the jail. On Wednesday morning, D1, the steelworkers quickly got another march organized along Seattle's waterfront. Groups like the one that Lee joined sprouted up spontaneously around the city. And it was civil rights, not WTO, that got people up from their TVs and out to demonstrate after N30.

"It was an amazing experience," said Lee. "There were so many people there, all taking care of each other." The vigil was in place until Monday morning when the last person was out of jail. "Just as you got hungry, food would appear out of nowhere. It would start to rain, and within fifteen minutes the tarps were up. And there was always music." This was December in Seattle. It gets light at 8:00 A.M. and dark at 4:00 P.M.

Lee was there on Friday, D3, when lame-duck renegade Republican King County Councilmember Brian Derdowski made the announcement at the jail that the WTO meetings had ended in a shambles and the delegates were all going home. Even those who hadn't been all that concerned about the WTO cheered wildly. The sense that something deeply important had been accomplished was an inarticulate and enlivening presence.

"Ever since I'd graduated, I'd been wanting to get involved with this group or that, but I never got off my lazy butt," said Lee. But N30 changed all that. "The thing that I realized is that we only have our First Amendment rights until we try to use them."

Everyone who had been on the streets on N30 knew that 99 percent of the crowd was peaceful, and intended to be so from the beginning— even those who had been in civil disobedience training for months were determined to be peaceful in their protests. Violence was not on the agenda. Those behind the scenes knew well what any violence would mean: instant discrediting of the protest movement. There was an almost desperate urgency to keep things peaceful at all costs. That the police attacked hundreds of people without provocation was known by too many firsthand observers. Too many ACLU attorneys, senior citizens, journalists, business professionals, and other "reputable" types were witnesses to the aggression. It would not be overlooked. Even if the national and international press did drop the violence as an issue just as quickly as they'd adopted it in the first place, it was not going away in these parts. Too much had been exposed.

After WTO week, Lee went to a lot of meetings trying to find a fit. "I knew this was serious stuff," said Lee. "I knew I was committed." She went to the city council hearings that were being held to address the issue of police violence in the neighborhood of Capitol Hill. "I sat through all eighteen hours," she said. "It was exhausting." Then she got on the list-serve of the student activists at the University of Washington who had originally called themselves "No to WTO," but after WTO week renamed themselves Students for Economic Democracy (SED). There was frenzy of e-mail between all the different organizations. The coalition movement that put WTO week in the history books was not about to lose its momentum. The first big follow-up meeting was at the Catholic Seaman's Hall, and it was attended by hundreds of people from all over the activist spectrum; the second, soon after, was at the Teamsters Union Hall, Local 174.

The commitment was ongoing and across the board. Four months after WTO week, when I first interviewed Vanessa Lee, she told me, "It's pretty much been a meeting every night."

This cross-cultural coalition, which could be coined the "sturtle" movement ("What do you get when you cross a steelworker with a turtle?"), surfaced in support of the steelworkers who were on strike against Kaiser Aluminum; they were on the docks together in successful protest when the freighter loaded with PCBs from U.S. bases in Japan tried to tie up in Seattle. They watchdogged all the city council meetings that were investigating both the police violence and the history of why the WTO was invited to Seattle in the first place. "We've been spending a lot of time together," said Lee.

It's taken some real tenacity for the group to keep track of the city's post-WTO meetings. "At first there were a lot of problems. [The city would] reschedule the meetings without giving notice, or change the room, or cancel them. I don't think all that was unintentional."

I asked her about the April 16, 2000, demonstrations in D.C., and she said the police aggression was expected, but shutting down the convergence space where the protesters were preparing, because of supposed fire hazard, was a real setback. "Why did they wait until Saturday morning, when the lawyers weren't at work?" asked Lee rhetorically. "And why did they arrest the puppets?" She scoffed at the idea of the Molotov cocktail supposedly found on the site. The sign-making and puppet-building going on meant an array of dirty rags, paint thinner, and glass jars and bottles. "It was obviously ridiculous."

Her concern at the time of our interview was more for the prison abuses that she was hearing about. It's the violence behind closed doors, where "national security" can so easily take precedence over the personal security of individuals, that is of deep concern to Lee.

"My mother wants me to call her anytime I go to anything," she said. "She's worried about my safety." But her family fully supports her activities. "I think they are both proud of me," she said of her parents. "I feel very lucky."

# Stalking DAN

Direct Action Network is as indirect an organization as cannot be found. It's like a ghostly umbrella that gets popped up whenever there's a need for "action"—be it fixing food for hungry activists, establishing a language bank for translation needs, providing medical services or legal advice, organizing on-site nonviolent training, coordinating communication, offering quick lessons in effective street theater, getting sound bites to the media, or enhancing the cover pages of daily newspapers. It operates by having fundamental faith in human beings—that wherever there's a need, there's an activist. There's no hierarchy, no membership; nobody belongs and everybody belongs.

"During WTO, many, many people were key in Direct Action Network," said Erica Kay, who's active in CAN (Community Action Network), in whose offices DAN set up its operation while in Seattle.

No one owns the name; nobody makes decisions for anyone else. DAN is rooted in the rhetoric of common sense, community need, and individual action. The faces in the DAN office changed with the needs, and the needs changed with the faces, many of whom never laid eyes on one another. The umbrella was passed around according to the weather.

In Seattle during WTO week, organizations from Washington, D.C., to San Francisco used DAN as an umbrella to stay out of the rain (via housing help) and in the mix (via contacts with other groups). DAN was home away from home for those already involved; it served as a big logistical loop to help people flooding in from out of town to work together as effectively as possible. It provided a map—literal and political— of the city of Seattle so that the hundreds of diverse organizations that descended upon the city could find their way around during WTO week.

DAN was a moving target for the powers-that-be who wanted to nail blame for the WTO protest on one group or individual. But trying to pin down DAN details was like taking a chain saw to your great-aunt's favorite Jell-O salad. The nuts and the marshmallows went everywhere, and the heat turned the whole thing to Jell-O juice.

DAN assumed the mantle of the highest common denominator, and anybody smart enough, committed enough, and courageous enough to take advantage of its shelter was yet another face in the big crowd under the big umbrella. All you had to do was be there.

She then recounted the story of Jeanette, a young, quietly articulate woman who was at the April 16, 2000, planning meeting I attended. She was the police negotiator for the event, and her youthful composure had impressed me. "Her family is a bunch of Texas Republicans," said Lee. "They haven't spoken to her since WTO; they're just so mortified that she'd be involved with something like that."

Lee's father, who is Korean, has a Ph.D. in physics and works with computers. He was influenced as a child by the Korean War and moved to the United States as an adult. "He's not very liberal," said Lee. "He'd like you to think he was superradical like Abbie Hoffman, but he's a good old capitalist, and that's fine."

He grew up in a farming community and both his parents were teachers. Lee's Korean grandmother was a preacher and started the first Christian church in her village. She was also no stranger to civil disobedience. "During the Japanese occupation, she taught Korean history and Korean songs to the children in the village, which was illegal," said Lee. She also grew and distributed the Korean national flower, the rose of Sharon, in her garden, which was also illegal. "She was just basically defiant," said Lee. "So she went to jail." During the war, Lee's grandmother's house was the base for the local field militia that was trying to protect the crops—from both sides. She died before Vanessa Lee was born, but it's not at all difficult to see her legacy hard at work in her granddaughter.

Lee says she sees signs of a big social awareness movement at work in the student community. "But what really gives me so much hope, the thing that makes me say that this is different, is the coalition support." Although she's now in a union, she says she knew nothing about unions until the WTO movement developed. "I grew up middle-class. Blue collar wasn't part of my experience." She then rattled off the initials of about five different unions with which she's been working. "I've met some fantastic steelworkers," she said. "And with that Terminal 18 thing [the PCB embargo], we were working with the longshore workers and the Teamsters." Then she laughed. "I never know what I mean when I say 'we' anymore. It's whoever was there at that particular moment. It's the movement."

She's keenly aware of the skepticism some feel about such unlikely alliances. "I know some people are looking for holes. Take steel, for example. They say steel manufacturing is environmentally destructive, and therefore it's problematic for environmentalists to have a coalition with steelworkers." Lee, however, sees great potential in the partnership.

"This is a movement that has a strength that American social movements haven't really tapped into before.

"Solidarity," she said. "It's a word that I don't think I ever used before five months ago. Now I seem to use it in every other sentence."

I asked her if she could articulate the one thing that everybody was in solidarity about. "Corporate greed," she responded quickly. "Corporate dominance has been the rallying cry. But it seems to me it's more than that. People are realizing the need to take back control of our own lives."

# 17 THE UNIVERSE IN A GRAIN OF RICE— IN WHICH FARMING IS NOT FOREVER

"There is quite as much education and true learning
in the analysis of an ear of corn as in the analysis
of a complex sentence; ability to analyze clover and
alfalfa roots savors of quite as much culture
as does the study of the Latin and Greek roots."
—O. H. Benson, from *Elbert Hubbard's Scrap Book*

big part of the response to the WTO seemed to be the desire to
take back control over one of the most basic aspects of our lives:
what we eat. "It was a life-changing experience for me," wrote
Anne Schwartz in the *Washington Tilth Journal of Organic and
Sustainable Agriculture;* her words caught my attention. "Alone, it
is certainly overwhelming to think that we can slow or stop the corporate
machine. But after being in Seattle, I feel much less overwhelmed. I feel
ready to try; actually, I feel compelled to try." I'd picked up the Tilth journal at the Skagit Valley Co-op in Mount Vernon one day coming home to
San Juan Island from Seattle, and there was a photograph of Schwartz sitting on a WTO panel between Nebraskan corn grower Keith Dietrich and
radical French farmer Jose Bové.

The number of farmers at WTO week was astonishing, and they
came from down the road and around the world. I saw almost as many
farm groups as I did unions, yet in the mainstream media I saw no mention
of the Food and Agriculture Day held on Thursday, December 2, of WTO
week, and not much in the alternative media either. If it hadn't been for
Jose Bové and his proximity to the breaking of the window at McDonald's
(which he tried mightily to prevent), the word "farmer" might have been
excluded altogether.

I wanted to talk to Schwartz, president of Washington Tilth
Producers, about all of this. I'd done the ferry thing and was driving

60 miles east to get to her Blue Heron Farm in Rockport. Driving through the countryside to Rockport, I noticed quite a few small family vegetable gardens in yards along the way. It reminded me of Bové's homeland, where even in densely populated little villages, nearly every home has its tidy, abundant vegetable garden, as well as its neighborhood cheese.

I wondered what kind of farm Schwartz had, so close to the Cascade Mountains. I was prepared for everything but bamboo. Schwartz and her husband, Mike Brondi, farm blueberries, raspberries, vegetables, and bamboo, primarily as nursery stock—which doesn't preclude a tasty bamboo shoot or two along the way. They also have a family garden where they grow food for themselves and the community of interns who are involved with their farm.

When I got there, Schwartz told me that I really should talk to Tom Forster on Orcas Island, because he had about twenty farmers from all over the world at his house for WTO (which suddenly became the acronym for World to Orcas). The San Juan Island archipelago has lots of different islands, only four of which are served by ferries: San Juan (where I live), Lopez, Shaw, and Orcas. So it turned out that when I'd tracked down the Japanese rice farmers who had so dramatically caught my attention during the labor march on N30, I ended up in my own watery backyard. As Schwartz was telling me to turn around and go home, all I could do was nod. But first we talked.

It was lunchtime when I arrived at Blue Heron Farm. Four or five people were fixing food in the spacious kitchen, and there was talk of a big salad for supper because there was a lot of spinach and lettuce ready. In arranging a meeting, Schwartz had suggested a rainy day because otherwise, when it was light, she was outside working. Anne and Mike live on six acres where they farm bamboo and other trees for nurseries throughout the Puget Sound area; they lease about seven other acres close to the Sauk River, where they farm their raspberries and vegetables, which are sold at the Pike Place Market and other markets in the area, including the Skagit Valley Co-op, where I often stop to shop on my way home from Seattle. I asked Anne Schwartz about the meaning of the word "tilth." She told me, "The old definition is 'the cultivation of wisdom.' It's come to mean the quality of cultivated soil." But it's a wisdom hard-won.

Schwartz was worried about her leased land because corporate logging practices in the watershed area had caused the hillsides to tumble into the creeks, which caused the creeks to tumble with their dirt into the river, which could therefore no longer offer safe spawning to the salmon. The upshot is that salmon are now endangered, and all activity within 200 feet of rivers, creeks, and streams, including Anne's berry farming, might be curtailed in order to restore salmon habitat. There is no free tree.

Anne Schwartz is from New Jersey. She ended up in the Skagit Valley in the mid-seventies, when the valley was rich with writers and artists, as well as farmers, and the town of La Conner was a low-rent district. These days it's full of chichi shops, and each spring the valley is full of techies tiptoeing through the tulip festival. In 1979, Schwartz and Brondi moved upriver to Rockport, where the land was affordable and the mountains magnificent. Now it's the corporate chain saw that threatens her livelihood.

The WTO wants global free-logging agreements; Anne Schwartz wants to keep growing organic vegetables on her local leased land. Her livelihood is now threatened on two counts—the logging practices themselves, which have mucked up the watershed and could become even less regulated because of WTO; and now the environmentalists, who want to impose the 200-foot buffer zone between activity and all running water in order to help salmon recover. "I don't own the land, but I've developed an irrigation system, fenced it all, and spent twenty years building it up and loving it," said Schwartz. It's a big circle, no matter where on the planet we take up space.

And it's a big corporate circle. Agribusiness is replacing agriculture. Which says it all: Business is buying out culture. To farmers, farming is a way of life. It doesn't matter if you're a farmer in Kansas or Korea. It's a choice to live in direct relationship with the land, to work long, independent hours outside, to smell the fruits of your labor, to understand the intimacy between the weather, the soil, and the seed. Being a farmer is like being an artist: You choose a lifestyle and you hope you break even. It's a partnership with creativity; it's its own reward. So when farmers lose their lifestyles on the land, they lose the meaning of their lives. And so, in some ways, do we.

✧   ✧   ✧   ✧   ✧

Throughout history, people grew up close to where their food was grown. The peasant farmer had prestige in the community, and the link to seasonal abundance and scarcity was a natural part of everyone's life. This relationship to our food and to those who grew it has all but disappeared. Now we relate to the closest grocery store, and our food, after being picked, processed, and distributed, has often traveled a couple of thousand miles from the hand of the farmer before it lands on our plate.

We have a closer relationship to the person who bags our groceries than we do to the farmer who grew them. And now, with the advent of agribusiness mergers, this distance has expanded dramatically.

The seeds of this separation are now represented by the literal seed itself, from which come the staples of existence: corn, rice, and wheat, among many others. Plans are afoot to own, via patent, the seeds of the foods that have nourished humanity through the ages. These seeds can be engineered not only to grow with their own built-in pesticides, but also to die. Instead of naturally reproducing, they can be artificially infected with a terminator gene, which tells them not to reproduce. Development of this Terminator Technology was well under way by the Monsanto company, but a huge groundswell of resistance from farmers, scientists, and civil society organizations brought it to a stop in late 1999. For the time being.

These new technologies are only just beginning, and they threaten millions of farmers around the world who farm for their daily sustenance. Agribusiness could claim ownership via patent on the seeds that might have been in the farmer's family for thousands of years. And this is why the Japanese rice farmers were on the streets of Seattle during WTO week.

It was Tom Forster on Orcas Island who filled me in on the rice paddy culture that is fighting for its life in Japan. A week after my visit to Blue Heron Farm, we sat out on the steps of his hand-built home in the country on Orcas Island and talked about the complexities of that which is most basic—our food. And it's no small topic. In fact, we talked for two hours, and his language was so full of international food-speak (the alphabet-soup kingdom is alive and well in the world of agriculture, too) that I was dizzied and disconcerted when I left. The next day he was flying off to Copenhagen for an agriculture conference, so he wanted to make sure that there was no seed left unsown.

Forster, who's been engaged as a policy maker in the food fight for years, was at the first Earth Summit in Rio de Janeiro in 1992. Officially, it was the UN Conference on Environment and Development. Out of it came the realization that the environmental crisis cannot be solved without building global economic and social justice. And that started with the food supply.

"The Japanese farmers have been in the front trenches working to uphold multifunctionality in agriculture," said Forster. "Food production is at the heart of their culture." He went on to explain how rice culture is an intrinsic part of group ethics in Japanese life. "They share paddies, irrigation, and work. They are the upholders of culture. And they are being attacked by the United States and other countries for being protectionist of trade. But what they're doing is simply protecting the farmers," he said.

It's similar to the vineyard culture in France. Many different family vineyards can be located together on one hillside. One family might have just a few rows of grapes, but theirs is still a cherished family business that has survived through generations. An entire village can be represented by one hillside. When corporations take over such local businesses, it means a loss of cultural history, family tradition, independent economy, and a lifestyle rooted in meaning, and a victory for the monolithic concerns of money. Family farmers cannot compete with corporate prices, so they are threatened in the marketplace as well as in the boardroom.

It's a vast array of challenges that beset the life of a farmer these days. And the WTO in Seattle was a meeting ground for them all. "What was most striking for me and [my husband] was how we were getting the same message from everyone," said Anne Schwartz. "From Keith Dietrich, a six-foot blond Nebraska corn farmer, to Via Campesina, the peasant farmers from Central America: 'Global trade is killing us.'"

Globalization takes the face off farming, just as it takes the face off everything else. Yet for more than 60 percent of the world's population, farming contributes directly to sustaining a family and a local community. Seeds are as precious as pearls. They are at the heart of survival. When farmers in such places as India, Japan, and South America are unable to own their own seeds, they are unable to own their own lives. When farmers in Kansas have no control over seed, storage, transportation, or distribution, they are at the mercy of the corporations that do. When we, as consumers, aren't informed about genetic modification in the foods that we buy, we are in the hands of corporate-controlled science, not nature.

When Dr. Vandana Shiva addressed the WTO teach-in crowd in Seattle, she looked the audience in their collective eye and in no uncertain terms told everyone what they didn't know. "You have been fooled," she said. "You have been eating genetically modified foods for years, and they didn't tell you. I feel sorry for you."

India is leading the way in agriculture awareness, and Vandana Shiva, a physicist, activist, writer, and director of the Research Foundation for Science, Technology, and Ecology in Dehradun, India, is informing us, vehemently, about our own agricultural technology. Primarily because she knows too well the tragedy of what's happening to farmers in India, where, in the past two years, more than 500 have committed suicide in the Warangal district alone. All because of cotton.

The pressures of an export-based global economy resulted in Indian farmers shifting from traditional food crops to cotton, which was described to them as "white gold." Under corporate pressure, they shifted from open-pollinated seeds, which can be saved, to high-priced hybrids, which have to be purchased each year. But the hybrids require increased use of pesticides. Suddenly the farmers, who understood they would be making a greater profit growing cotton, were having to take out high-interest loans to afford the hybrid seeds and the pesticides. And it was the very same corporations that sold both the seeds and the pesticides that in turn lent the money to the farmers to buy them. The response to this burden of debt was an epidemic of suicides.

## The Forest for the Trees

The tree of life is just that. We need forests for any number of reasons—including keeping the earth in its place. The relationship between indiscriminate logging and our lives at large is comprehensive and complex. Taking down a tree, be it in a rain forest in British Columbia or in a jungle in Brazil, can take any number of life cycles with it, which rends the web of life. Many endangered species, protected by U.S. environmental laws, are now re-endangered by the laws of the WTO.

Deforestation is devastating, and the WTO, in the name of free trade, is bent on eliminating all barriers to trade, which means gutting the integrity of our earthly home. And it's already happening. The WTO—in which the United States is a prime player—is now threatening to eliminate the following environmental U.S. rules and policies: border safeguards to protect forests from insects, disease, and invasive species; support of recycled paper and paper products from sustainably managed forests; eco-labeling that gives us consumers the opportunity to buy wood products that come from sustainable practices; and laws protecting governments from being sued by investors who think that their environmental laws are getting in the way of corporate profits.

But India has suffered in too many other ways as well. Soybeans imported from the United States have decimated the cooking oil industry; corporatization of wheat growing threatens the livelihoods of millions of Indian wheat farmers; large-scale shrimp production factories are destroying coastal agriculture and indigenous small-scale shrimp farming. These assaults on traditional agriculture, combined with the displacement of millions of people due to dam construction, is threatening the very fabric of Indian culture—a culture that has survived in rich complexity for thousands of years.

In an essay in *Views from the South*, published by the International Forum on Globalization, Shiva writes: "Global free trade in food and agriculture is the biggest refugee creation program in the world. ... It is equivalent to the ethnic cleansing of the poor, the peasantry, and small farmers of the Third World."

✿  ✿  ✿  ✿  ✿

Vandana Shiva was on the stage with Anne Schwartz on the Food and Agriculture Day of WTO week in Seattle, as was progressive radio commentator and author Jim Hightower, French farmer Jose Bové, and Public Citizen's Ralph Nader. More than 3,000 people gathered in the First United Methodist Church for the day's events, which started early in the morning with an organic Farmer-to-Farmer Breakfast hosted by Vashon Island Organic Growers. There were workshops on everything from industrialization of agriculture and genetic engineering to food safety and farmworker strategy. The proceedings were instantly translated into four languages—Japanese, Spanish, French, and English—and there were headphones at each seat in the church.

Other speakers included Walden Bello, a Philippine activist, scholar, and writer with a Ph.D. in sociology from Princeton, who until recently was the executive director of the San Francisco–based Institute for Food and Development Policy (Food First); Al Krebs, who wrote *The Corporate Reapers: The Book of Agribusiness* and is director of the Corporate Agribusiness Project in Washington, D.C.; Corky Evans, minister of agriculture from British Columbia; and Anuradha Mittal from Food First. "It was a great educational opportunity for the press," said Schwartz. "And there were a lot of them there. Why wasn't the story told? What's with the media?"

According to Tom Forster, the WTO agriculture issues were on the front pages of papers throughout the rest of the world. "This issue is huge," he said. "Recent trade talks had made it very clear that agriculture is under siege by the WTO. And everyone is concerned about the issue of intellectual property rights [as it relates to plants]."

The issue of intellectual property rights is yet another complexity in the WTO view of the world. For example—and simply put—through genetic identification, a pharmaceutical corporation can patent the active medicinal properties in a plant (including everything from seeds to leaves) in South America. That company can then claim intellectual property rights to the plant, which means the company can reap millions from its "rights," while the indigenous people who have lived with such medicinal plants throughout history no longer have the "right" to use them, let alone profit from them.

The concept of expanding the parameters of intellectual property rights to support trade profits originated within the World Trade Organization as TRIPS: trade-related aspects of intellectual property rights. The possibilities are endless. Jeremy Rifkin, author of *The End of Work* and *The Biotech Century,* and president of the Washington, D.C.–based Foundation on Economic Trends, says, "Now that we are moving into the Biotech Century and shifting our resource base to genes, whoever controls the genes controls the twenty-first century."

But the control is flawed in reality as well as in theory. Corn that has been genetically modified to resist insects has pesticides incorporated into its kernels. Now it's being discovered that this is resulting in stronger and tougher insects. Does this mean we need stronger and stronger pesticides inside our corn? And what's it doing to us? There are also indications that through cross-pollination, plants surrounding the cornfields are encouraging pesticide-resistant pests. And that fragile butterflies are dying. Mother Nature breeds survival tactics that none of us can predict.

Although two-thirds of the world's population is engaged in food growing directly, in the United States there are so few farmers left that the 2000 census didn't include them as a category. Yet nowhere else in the world has such a wide array of foodstuffs been available for purchase. Globalization of agriculture serves the relatively few of us on the planet who are estranged from the land but not from the dollar. The global food export economy enables us to buy many tasty specialties to please our palates, yet billions of people aren't free to grow the food they need for basic sustenance for their own families and communities. What they grow is controlled by corporations or governments that make money from food exports.

Our purchasing power dictates the way we are fed, and we are catered to in the most astonishing fashion. A few years ago, I took a Green Tortoise trip through the Southwest. The Green Tortoise is a '60s-style tour bus that defies description. It was April, and there were only seventeen of us onboard. Fourteen of the travelers were from other countries. We stopped to do our shopping for the ten-day trip at a large grocery outlet east of San Francisco. The foreign travelers who were new to the United States were stunned by the amount and the variety of the food available.

In the United States, corporate agribusiness produces and markets more than 95 percent of the country's food. It's these same corporations that are lobbying for laws, nationally and globally, that protect business at all costs. We might have a lot of brand names on the shelf, but they're likely to be owned by one of only a handful of corporations: Philip Morris, for example, or Tyson Foods, or Monsanto, or Archer Daniels Midland. And it's corporate trade representatives from companies such as these who end up as WTO ministers. The officers from Cargill, the world's largest grain-trading company, have been trade advisors to presidents and helped author trade agreements such as GATT, which gave birth to the WTO.

"When you go into a food co-op, there's barely any independent organic food products made anymore," said Schwartz. "Basically it's all Fortune 500 companies."

Very few of us have a clue where our food comes from, who owns it, and what's in it. Poet, writer, and food activist Wendell Berry said something to the effect that "every bite is an agricultural act." Simply knowing this can broaden our awareness and link us to both our local and our global family. Supporting a local farmers market, asking for local products to be carried in a grocery store, and getting involved with community-supported agriculture (subscription farming) are part of the ripple effect of change.

"Civil society," one of the phrases that Tom Forster uses liberally, is the millions of people worldwide who participate in the thousands of groups or organizations that are working to keep a human face on the future. Civil society is mobilizing around globalization. And because the farmers of the world are faced with the most immediate of consequences, they are on the front lines of civil society. "A rules system dominated by the corporate sector is a death knell to the small farmers of the world," said Forster. "Civil society converged on Seattle to save agriculture."

And, according to Forster, it was a convergence on the WTO that affected many layers of power. "It's like an onion," he said. "In the center are the decision-makers; then you've got the nongovernmental organizations that are accredited to lobby the WTO decision-makers; then there's the knowledgeable outsiders who know about the inside but can only lend support because they're not accredited; then there's the street action; and then there's the general public. They all converged in Seattle, and what most people don't realize is that not only did the protesters keep the delegates from the convention meeting sites, they also kept them from getting to secret meetings in hotel rooms where the deals were to have been made and then carried to the convention center.

"Many of the representatives from Latin America, Africa, and Asia were there to fight for agricultural freedom; they had the same concerns as the protesters," said Forster.

At the end of June 2000, Jose Bové, who defiantly ate his "illegal" Roquefort cheese (and drank a little French wine) with his compatriots in the streets of Seattle during WTO week, finally went on trial in France for attacking the local McDonald's in August 1999. On the eve of the trial, thousands of cheering supporters, including Via Campesina farmers, were flocking to the little French town of Millau on the banks of the Tarn River to support Bové and his buddies. The wall above the town said, "The world is not for sale," and public forums on such globalization issues as privatization, women's rights, and genetically modified food were taking place as Bové went off to court. He called the event "Seattle on the Tarn."

At the end of my afternoon near the banks of the Sauk River at Blue Heron Farm, Anne Schwartz's forester husband, Mike Brondi, took me on a tour of his trees. One grew from an acorn that he found in Sherwood Forest, Robin Hood's backyard. Then we went through the bamboo groves. "More of humanity experienced the Bamboo Age than the Stone Age," he told me, and listed any number of products in which bamboo is used—from eating utensils to water pipes. He cut a few bamboo shoots for me to take home for supper. And they literally are shoots; at just a day or two, they are 6 to 8 inches high. Then I walked through one of the old groves. It was like being in a green cathedral: a gentle swishing of branches in the breeze, a feeling of being surrounded by the gentlest, and hardiest, of life.

# 18 THE NATURE OF LIFE—IN WHICH WEALTH HAS NOTHING TO DO WITH MONEY

"Nature is doing her best each moment to make us well."
—Henry David Thoreau

Over the holidays of the new millennium, Dr. Michael Cohen wrote a book about the vital missing link in the WTO. He wrote it because he was unable to be there in person on N30. And because his partner, Serena, had gone to her family home for Christmas without him, he had time on his holiday hands, so he put them to work. The result was *Einstein's World—Educating and Counseling with Nature: A Scientific Integration of Economics, Nature and Psychology, Peace, Wellness and Spirit.* Cohen is an applied ecopsychologist. His work is rooted in the belief that nature's intelligence is missing from the way we have been taught to think. That we have essentially bitten the hand that feeds us, and if we don't wake up and smell the seaweed, we're done for as a species.

There's lots of growing scientific evidence to support the dire effects of our distorted thinking: Global warming and its devastating consequences have already started. The relentless connectedness of everything and everyone on the planet is evident in just the few degrees of climate change that it will take to forever alter life as we have come to know it. Species are dropping like flies. Our great rain forests, a big source of oxygen on the planet, are losing their lives and, therefore, putting our own lives in jeopardy, let alone all those of the indigenous people throughout the world to whom the forests are truly home. We're messing with the web of life, with the way things work naturally—which has taken only a few billion years to perfect.

Lots of people are telling us these things. Why aren't we listening?

Because, says Cohen, we have learned not to feel and think with all our senses. And not just our five well-worn senses, but our fifty-three (at last count) natural senses, from our sense of time to our sense of play. From our sense of gravity to our sense of an emotional life. From our senses of reason, language, and consciousness to our senses of humility, humidity, and humor. We are awash in sensory experience—most of which we've managed to nip in the bud, so to speak. Cohen, who's somewhere in his seventies and who still sleeps outside at night, has a pretty little plant growing out of his car-door hinge. And he didn't plant it. Life will find its way, indeed. But will human life? That is the question.

> "Climb the mountains and get their good tidings. Nature's peace will flow into you as sunshine flows into trees. The winds will blow their own freshness into you, and the storms their energy, while cares will drop away from you like the leaves of Autumn."
>
> —John Muir

I first met Mike Cohen on a dance floor. Every Tuesday evening on our island, Bob and Barbara Dann, who are both very gracefully occupying their seventy-somethings, have folk dancing at their house, which was built for the occasion. Their living room is 15 feet by 40 feet, and ever since they retired here, the world has been welcomed at their door to dance—as long as you don't track crap in on your shoes. Every Tuesday, we go to the corner table where Bob has listed dances from all over the world on cards and arranged them according to country. We each pick a few for the evening—or not, if we don't feel like it—and for a few hours, we enter into the dancing spirits that come as gifts from around the world.

Mike Cohen knows all the dances and is very light on his feet. He also sings folk songs, too many to count. So I first knew him as a playful spirit, a man who seemed to land lightly wherever he went. His thirty-five years of teaching the psychology of the natural world and our place in it is something I learned about only when I told him at the Danns one night that I was working on this book. "Oh," he said. "I just wrote a book about the WTO," and within a few days I had a copy of *Einstein's World* and one of his earlier books, *Reconnecting with Nature: Finding Wellness Through Restoring Your Bond with the Earth*. The WTO synchronicity strikes again.

*Einstein's World* is an obsessed little book, quickly written, self-published, spiral-bound, passed out free to all takers, an act of love in a time of desperation. Cohen's earlier book, *Reconnecting with Nature*, is the one with blurbs on the back by best-selling author Dr. Larry Dossey and Dr. Robert Muller, winner of the Albert Schweitzer Peace Prize and former assistant secretary-general of the United Nations. Through a distinct, practical process in his book, Cohen brings us to our expanded senses and to the natural law of attraction that is at the very foundation of our existence.

Cohen is a renegade. Although he has founded environmental psychology degree programs with the Lesley College Graduate School, Greenwich University, and the Institute of Global Education (a nongovernmental organization that does consulting for the United Nations Economic and Social Council), he unteaches. Sitting outside in one of his nature-reconnecting classes (called Project NatureConnect) is a study in forgetting what we've learned and getting intimate with what we know. This, he documents, is the way home to sanity on this planet, where we are going completely and self-destructively crazy. And the key is not so simple as stopping to sniff the nearest flower; it's also in learning how to ask permission of the flower to sniff it in the first place. It's in acknowledging the astonishing force of life in all its glory on this planet, and our partnership with it. Which in turn heals the spirit, restores the senses, and brings meaning back to the natural world—where we always belong. So go tell that to the World Bank.

One of Cohen's doctoral students is doing precisely that. Gerry Eitner is introducing Cohen's Natural System Thinking Process (NSTP) into the training programs offered by the World Bank. The goal is to raise awareness of the need for responsible relationships with the earth's people and ecosystems, right in the place where the buck both starts and stops.

> "I am bonded to electrical conveniences, my car, my TV set, the need to have lots of money, the ideas and standards about acceptable body weight, other people's opinions, my identity as an artist, a good student, a Scorpio, et cetera. I could list a million separators that nature knows not, but which I am chained to. When they are threatened, I feel like I'm failing and I get defensive or depressed. Others have their own set of chains and do likewise to protect certainty at the expense of freedom. I have been hypnotized into believing I am 'smaller' and less free than I am."
>
> —Project NatureConnect participant

On the other side of the WTO coin, another doctoral student, Allison Weeks, is bringing Cohen's NSTP to WTO protest organizers and organizations in the Northwest. They, too, get tired and forget to smell the seaweed, forget to get nourished back as they go about the business of encouraging global fair trade and freedom in the human marketplace.

✼　✼　✼　✼　✼

Cohen started his first official outdoor program for youngsters in 1959 in Killington, Vermont, because he wanted to live the outdoor life; it eventually became the National Audubon Society Expedition Institute. Before that, he was director of American Youth Hostels in New York. Before that, he was a camp leader in the progressive camping movement under the tutelage of Josh Lieberman. Cohen's exposure to folk dancing and singing happened through his parents' participation in the Settlement Houses established by Eleanor Roosevelt in the 1920s and 1930s, where people coming to the United States for the first time could go to keep alive "the old-time ways."

Cohen's mother and both his father's parents, who were born in Russia, came to the United States to escape the pogroms. For the most part, Cohen was left alone to decide how to grow up, which to him meant growing up outdoors. For fifty years he has taught people how to connect to the natural world, and feel naturally connected. His theory, in an acorn shell, is that if we feel connected to nature, and our intimate partnership with it, we will not need a garage full of stuff to feel connected to our lives. Power will prevail, but it will be the power of natural attraction: a state of inherent

"I began telling the natural things here what I liked about them. That was easy, there were so many things that attracted me, the spring, the trees, the wind, the sun, the grass ... so many things. I probably spent thirty minutes telling things what I liked about them. As I did so, I felt an easing in my solar plexus. It began to relax and open up. Then my heart opened and I began to feel the love that was everywhere. Next my throat opened and I was feeling generally wonderful. I felt welcomed and a part of the place by the time I was done."

—Project NatureConnect participant

grace, in which we fit into the web of life and keep our inherent sensory awareness well tuned for the occasion.

It's this awareness of attraction that Cohen tries to get people to recognize. The very first thing he teaches is, "Go out and find something in nature that attracts you, obtain permission to be there, and find out what it has to tell you." Pretty unusual stuff. Even the Ph.D. students who have worked with his concepts for years have to struggle through their reliance on the intellect before they can allow a more sensory receptivity to take over. "No matter how often I've done it before, it's always a challenge," said Larry Gray, who comes from northern Canada to take Cohen's workshops. "And it always works."

In *Einstein's World*, which—surprise, surprise—quotes copiously from Albert Einstein, we are led down the path of science and economics at play, where if we could just get the WTO to put "webstrings" on its agenda, we could all get back to work on the real

## The Wordless Lesson

As I walked alone along a forest path asking permission from nature to learn from it about wealth, I waited for something to attract me. Everything looked beautiful, but nothing in particular held my attention. I began to realize that this time, my attraction was not the vibrant color of a flower, the beautiful song of a bird, the strength of a massive tree, or the softness of the moss on a rock. It was the forest in its entirety. My attraction to the forest held firm, so I sat on a small boulder to "listen" as the wordless lesson began.

As I watched, the diverse and teeming life before me became apparent: the insect attracted by the nectar of the flower, gaining sustenance from it as it helped the flower pollinate; the plant reaching for the life-giving energy of the sun and sharing it with the caterpillar; roots attracted to the damp, moist earth while holding the earth in place; "dead" leaves and trees transforming into new earth for new life. As I became increasingly aware of the exquisite interconnectedness of the forest, my consciousness shifted and I stopped seeing separate entities. Instead, the physical reality before me became a beautiful, continuous flow of Life.

"Ah," said my rational brain, never too happy to be wordless for long. "This is the lesson about wealth you are seeking."

—Allison Weeks, Project NatureConnect participant

stuff of our lives—enjoying the ride. The being here. Together.

"Webstrings" is the word Cohen has coined to describe the far-reaching effect of our connections to one another, to place, to planet, to planetary possibilities, and on out there forever. To recognize webstrings is to think with nature: "the unseen intelligence that loved us into being" (Elbert Hubbard). This does not endear him to the scientific community, most of whom are working to isolate, not integrate. Most of whom are suspect of such off-the-grid goals as recognizing our attraction to the motion of grasses in the wind, seeking permission to be there, and then sitting quietly to receive the wisdom waving around in the breeze. The mind, of course, goes quickly to metaphor: the vulnerability, strength,

"I arrive at the stream's edge and listen with my eyes shut. I smell skunk and wood burning and thank these senses. On opening my eyes I see a bright patch of green moss exposed by the movement of snow under my boot. The green glow of life is striking and I lean down to touch it in thanks with my ungloved hand."

—Project NatureConnect participant

and flexibility of the grasses; the power of being rooted to the earth but open to the brilliant changes of each moment; the wonder of wind—where does it come from? The sky wide, the wide mind, the moment that it's all in this together. That we're all in this together. Tell that to the scientists fighting with each other about mapping the human genome.

But Cohen is making headway. The United Nations recognizes his work, and his courses are officially and unofficially on traditional campuses via the Internet or trained instructors. In 1985, when he founded the Gaia Conference titled "Is the Earth a Living Organism?" he was called a maverick genius. In 1996, he was awarded the UN's Distinguished World Citizen Award.

I was invited to sit in on one of Cohen's graduate seminars. He does lots of his teaching via the Internet, but a couple of times a year, his students come to—unbelievably, my own backyard yet again—San Juan Island for five days of deep nature study. This particular session was held in a big log cabin at Lakedale, a middle-of-the-island rustic retreat and lakeside resort. He introduced me around, told them about this WTO book, and asked me if I was willing to participate in a nature activity. "Sure," I said, not really wanting to at all.

Throughout my life, I have cultivated a profound sense of nature snobbery. I like my nature to myself. I've considered it a private matter, a nonverbal experience that cannot be shared. A sacred place where I feel better. I have gone to great lengths to preserve my solitary experiences in nature. Now I was being asked to get communal about it all, and I felt a huge resistance. But Cohen had yet another question. "What are you here for? What do you want from us?"

I had been thinking about David Korten's talk at St. Mark's Cathedral back in September 1999, when he spoke about the difference between being rich and being wealthy. His ideas were familiar, yet the two positions seemed so incompatible as to be irreconcilable. "What is wealth?" I blurted out to Cohen. He shrugged. "Okay, what is wealth?" he asked everybody. And sent us off with an activity in the natural surroundings to find out.

About twenty minutes later, we gathered back together to share our findings. There were twelve people in the room, from all parts of the United States and Canada, all with professional backgrounds, all linked together through their work with Project NatureConnect. Wealth, it turned out, was a lot of things: the feeling of a cedar branch against the face; a small tree planted by hand that needs attention to survive; the flow of connection that, when we stop it up with greed, is replaced with all our addictions; knowing the right to exist in the network of sentient beings; waking up to my own experience and knowing that "no one can tell me I didn't have it"; when I come to this place I feel wealth supporting me; the courage to stand alone; getting into deep water; the berry that is ripe enough to just drop by itself into my waiting hand, then I know it is meant just for me; a large, mossy, mother rock; forgetting myself.

> "The other day, I was in a neurophysiology class and the teacher said something very interesting. He said when men invented the engine, they had the knowledge that carbonic gas was toxic to humans and animals, and that by having too many cars together, it would create some form of pollution. But because cars were such a good financial prospect, they gave in to greed and avidity and left aside the death and disease warrant. What else can I say about men? What can I say about myself?"
>
> —Project NatureConnect participant

One woman was quiet, and spoke last. "I've been sitting here for twenty minutes mulling over what I got," she said, in tears. "I went to the water, to a tree, to a slug, to the earth, and I'm not getting it right now." What she got was grief from being disconnected. "The wealth," she said, "is the answers you get from nature. Even when they hurt."

Somebody also had a realization about being rich. "I followed the sound of a bird as it went from place to place in the woods, but I couldn't quite catch up. It was like going after money. Pretty soon I didn't even watch where I was going."

The reductive challenge we face every day in contemporary life to describe, weigh, and measure the secrets of our lives means that they lose their power, their numinous nature, their stature. "The most beautiful thing we can experience is the mysterious. It is the source of all true art and science," says Albert Einstein. There is nothing mysterious about money, but try sitting with a cedar tree for ten minutes and listening to what it has to tell you.

The truth is that nature is always restoring. Always attracting, recovering, healing. It feeds our biological and psychological ability to regenerate. And when we connect to the natural world with our reasoning, consciousness, and language, together with all our other senses, we are opened up to real power that transcends the dollar.

"The more alive we are," said Michael Cohen, "the more rewarded we are by the wisdom of earth and nature, the less dependent we are on the power of money and prestige, and the less damage we do to one another and to the planet. When are we going to learn this in contemporary society?"

# 19 FROM BOOKS TO BOOKED— IN WHICH ALL THINGS ARE ARRESTING

"In any gathering, in any chance meeting on the street, there is a shine, an elegance rising up."
—Rumi, from *The Illuminated Rumi*, translated by Coleman Barks, illustrated by Michael Green

One day in early April 2000, sometime in the middle of researching and interviewing people for this book, I realized the need for an orderly overview, a perspective that understood the soul of Seattle beyond its new-millennium fascination with nouveau money and the twists and turns of technology. So I went to the Elliott Bay Book Company in search of Rick Simonson. When I lived on Bainbridge Island back in the '70s and '80s, this place was like a home on the Seattle side of the bay. Simonson, the man responsible for the literary heart of the bookstore, was my friend. In recent years, because I was living on a different island much farther away, our paths rarely crossed. But he is a beacon in my life, so I hoped for a glimpse of him. When I was at the Jubilee 2000 circle of debt forgiveness, I had seen him walk by, so I knew WTO was in his blood, too.

It was late in the afternoon when I parked on South Jackson Street, just around the corner from the bookstore. I fumbled around for parking change, got out of the car, and there was Rick, right in front of me, as if conjured. He had only a few moments, but it was enough time for us to shake our heads at WTO week, and yes, he said, he'd be happy to talk to me. "But you should talk to Michael, one of our managers," he also said. "He was on the front lines of WTO, got arrested, and now is really into it." Rick and I agreed to talk the following week, and off I went to meet Michael.

He was working behind the front counter. This is an art form. The front counter at Elliott Bay Books is on a platform upon which any number of people are working nonstop at once. Even if you're at the back of a crowd of customers and getting ready for a long wait, it's usually only seconds until a counter person catches your eye across the crowd and deftly manages the transaction. It's a bit of theater: Everyone knows their role, their lines, and their limit. This flair with customers at the back of the crowd might be a Seattle tradition. At the Pike Place Market, they fling salmon at you; at Ivar's Acres of Clams, they snatch your order from the back of the crowd, turn it into an undecipherable code and fling it to the cook, and it materializes into clams and chips when you get to the front of the line. At Elliott Bay, they fling books.

When I asked for Michael, found him, and asked if we could meet, he looked at me and said, "Certainly not now." We arranged to meet early the following morning in the bookstore's café. So I went off for a browse and a raspberry Swedish cream (try getting one of those on-line at Amazon.com).

Michael Mossberg has worked at Elliott Bay Books for five years, and before that he worked at the "U" Bookstore—"U" as in University of Washington. He's thirty-six years old, and spent his growing-up years in Illinois and Michigan. After high school, he did a six-year stint in the Air Force, and in the mid-'80s he spent some time at the Strategic Air Command (SAC) headquarters. "It was the height of the Reagan era," said Mossberg. "'Let's spend it into the ground.'" He slept within sight of a "megatonnage of nuclear weapons," and in case of emergency, they practiced fallout exercises. "At ground zero," he said. "Right."

In the middle of his Air Force stint, his mother got a job at the Unitarian Universalist summer assembly at Lake Geneva, Wisconsin. He took some leave and joined her there. The assembly of about 800 people, many of whom have grown up together, gathers over the Fourth of July weekend every year. That first visit had a big impact on Mossberg. "The people I met there helped me ground my values and get me through the military," said Mossberg. "It's an incredibly intimate gathering."

Since he first attended the assembly in 1985, Mossberg has gone every year but one—the summer he started at Elliott Bay Books. And quite possibly he would miss the 2000 gathering because he was spending his vacation funds to go to the April 16 World Bank/IMF demonstrations in Washington, D.C. That's why we were meeting in such a hurry: He was scheduled to fly out that evening.

Mossberg first heard about the WTO coming to town in February 1999, and it immediately caught his attention, but not for long. "As is my wont, I got all excited about it, but it didn't last." Then his brother, Jesse, who also works at the bookstore, told him about the general strike that was being called for on N30 and asked him if he was going to participate. At first Mike said no. "Then I felt this deep pain. It was one of those things I knew I should do, but because of fear and my attachments to everyday life, I usually ended up not doing them." So he changed his mind. Mossberg knew why he wanted to participate. "The WTO, the IMF, the World Bank are symptoms of a larger problem," he said. "Our society is totally centered around money. What was originally a convenient medium for exchange has become the end-all and be-all of existence."

To be involved, he didn't have far to go because the bookstore was already heavily involved with WTO events. Mossberg was scheduled to help sell books at the International Forum on Globalization teach-in at Benaroya Hall on the Friday and Saturday before N30. The bookstore did a lot of business, and Mossberg was so busy selling books that he had little time to listen to the speeches, which were being broadcast out in the lobby because the teach-ins were sold out and had to turn away more people than got in. It was his first taste of the scope and scale of what WTO week would be like.

The IFG teach-ins at Benaroya Hall astounded many, who'd vastly underestimated how many people would be there. "Tickets were sold out more than three weeks ahead of time," said Jerry Mander, president of IFG and one if its founding members (see sidebar, The Big Thinkers). There was no room for latecomers to the 2,500-seat symphony hall.

The IFG participants stayed at the Alexis Hotel on First Avenue, just far enough south in downtown to be clear of the tear gas. "But five of our staff were arrested," said Mander. "Three of them were in jail for five nights." Victor Menotti, who heads up the IFG committee on the environment, was pounced upon and arrested as he came out of a hotel where he'd just had a meeting with U.S. Trade Representative Charlene Barshefsky about a logging agreement. "He was arrested for doing nothing," said Mander. "He's filed a lawsuit."

When we talked, Mander was pleased with the recent results of another lawsuit filed by Earthjustice Legal Defense Fund attorney Patti Goldman on behalf of the Northwestern Ecosystem Alliance, the Pacific Environment and Resources Center, Defenders of Wildlife, the Sierra Club, the Buckeye Forest Council, and the International Forum on Globalization against the U.S. trade representative and the Department of Commerce for not including environmentalists on committees that advise WTO negotiators on forest and logging policies. Forest- and paper-products industry representatives were invited to join, but not environmentalists. This was found to be illegal by U.S. District Court Judge Barbara Rothstein. In her ruling she stated: "The highly charged nature and the stakes at issue in the free-trade environment debate over timber sales are well documented. Matters affecting the wood and paper products sector are dramatically and inextricably intertwined with the environmental health and protection of this nation. ...The composition of forest product ISAC's [Industry Sector Advisory Committees], thus, violates FACA's [Federal Advisory Council Act] requirement to be fairly balanced in terms of viewpoints to be represented." "The law mandates that environmentalists be included," said Mander. "We appointed Victor [Menotti] but he was rejected.

"I was elated at the success in Seattle," said Mander. "But I'm concerned that the opposition to WTO is not as clearly focused as it needs to be. It's a multifaceted and multi-armed problem that needs attention in a lot of different ways. If people don't understand it, it's not their fault. And the media doesn't help. They're very irresponsible. It's a cesspool of stupid media hype."

During WTO week, Mander was in his hotel room organizing for much of the time, but he did get to the reception at Elliott Bay Books that *YES! A Journal of Positive Futures* had arranged for its subscribers. Michael Mossberg helped to set it up, and other anti-WTO notables were there, including Vandana Shiva of the Research Foundation for Science, Technology and Ecology; Fran Korten, publisher of *YES!*; and executive editor Sarah Ruth van Gelder. Author David Korten was unable to get back home from the East Coast, where he was temporarily hospitalized with a recurring nose bleed. Korten's book on corporate rule and its devastating consequences was first published in 1995; Mossberg had introduced Korten at Elliott Bay when he read from his most recent book, *The Post-Corporate World*. In many ways this was Korten's week, even though he was unable to be present in Seattle.

Unknowingly, Korten helped reassure Mossberg about the new owner of the much-revered Elliott Bay Book Company. Ron Sher, who bought the institution from Walter Carr in 1998, showed up when Korten read from *The Post-Corporate World*. Sher subsequently went on a Korten-led retreat, which gave hope to Mossberg that perhaps they shared the same general mind-set. For two decades, the bookstore had been bringing literary life to Seattle; the change in ownership had sent shock waves through the hearts of word lovers of the Northwest.

A corner bookstore is the cultural reflection of a vital community. It's like buying local lettuce—everybody in the community gets fed well, including the (book)worm. These small independent businesses are often taken for granted—they've always been there, and most book lovers don't know that even apparently thriving bookstores such as Elliott Bay Book

Company are threatened by chain megabookstores and the cyber-secret world of Amazon.com. The discounts and immediate gratification that Amazon.com offers are sweet seduction indeed but, as with other megacorporate intrusions, the big company undercuts the little neighborhood-friendly ones until you have nowhere to go *but* the megabookseller. For me, the smell of a small local bookstore is the smell of freedom—and I can't smell Amazon.com, even if it does give great research.

On the eve of N30 at the Elliott Bay Book Company, Michael Mossberg was introducing another man of the movement, Paul Hawken, who wrote *The Ecology of Commerce* and *Natural Capitalism.* Little did they know that before the next day was over, they would be living parallel lives and would be gassed in the streets of Seattle. Hawken's outraged and eloquent article about his experience, "N30—Skeleton Woman in Seattle," was one of the first in-depth pieces to be circulated on the Web, and it also came out in *YES! A Journal of Positive Futures, Orion,* and *The Amicus Journal.* Hawken was on the receiving end of police brutality big-time, and at one point was helped in the streets by Anita Roddick, founder of The Body Shop. But on Monday evening at Elliott Bay Books, Hawken roused the crowd who had come to hear him. And before his talk was over, the audience had grown to include lots of wet people who'd been out in the storm circling the Kingdome for debt relief. It was very late by the time Mossberg got home and went to bed.

✦　✦　✦　✦　✦

On N30, Mossberg slept in and didn't make it to the 7:00 A.M. direct action gathering at Victor Steinbrueck Park in the Pike Place Market. "Didn't get up in time," said Mossberg. He also decided to expand his daylong strike to include the conveniences of Western civilization, which meant walking downtown from his home in Magnolia, about 5 or 6 miles northwest of downtown.

"I left the house just a few minutes before dawn," he said. "It was raining, and I thought, 'What does it say about what God thinks of our cause, that it's raining this hard on this day?'" The last part of his walk took him through Myrtle Edwards Park, which extends along the shores of Puget Sound. "It was very peaceful—and weird to watch the unmarked black helicopter that was in the sky all day fly over a couple of times." By the time he got downtown, the rain had stopped.

Mossberg ended up at the labor rally at Memorial Stadium, where he stayed for the whole thing. "They had a lot of powerful speakers there," he said, "particularly people from the Third World. They moved me the

most. They were basically saying, 'We can't be there. Please be our voice.'"
Somehow, among the tens of thousands of people, his brother Jesse recognized Michael's hat in the crowd and tracked him down. They walked together in the big march. Just before they reached the human barricade intended to turn the march away from the convention center, there were people walking along the edge of the march asking people to ignore the change in route and to just continue toward the demonstrators at the convention center. "They've been waiting all day to see you" was the mantra. It was at this point that Michael and his brother were separated.

Mossberg was inspired by the words of one of the labor rally speakers—"Always forward, never back"—and this was what he was shouting as he made his way through the line of union marshals and along the originally planned route. "I just kept walking south on Fourth and got to the blockade of people, and wove my way to the front. On Fourth Avenue there is—and I'll always remember it—a seam in the concrete between Wendy's and the luggage store across the street, where the King County sheriffs were holding the line." He had stayed the course, and it led right to a police line.

This revision in the labor march route roused lots of reaction, but Mossberg wasn't one of the critics. "My friend Anne was in that march," he said. "She was nine months pregnant and asthmatic; I'm really glad she didn't break the line, even though she wanted to." His perspective was that even the direct action organizers didn't want the union supporters to get caught up in the street action. It was no place for the unprepared.

Mossberg himself had arrived on the scene unprepared. He had not received any training from Direct Action Network and was following his conscience minute by minute as it rose to the occasion. Now he was on the front line in a face-off with the police. "Other than holding real estate, they weren't doing anything specific. They weren't directly defending the convention center, which made their perceived job that much harder." The police had set up plastic water-filled barricades, and the protesters had pushed them back until they were directly in front of the police line. There were a lot of epithets being tossed at them, but Mossberg was trying to connect in a human way with the officer directly in front of him. "I could tell he didn't want to be there. He looked tired and was in a gas mask. I had been in the Air Force and had had to wear those things; just a half hour or forty-five minutes in one is a bad experience. And if you have to wear one all day, it's really miserable. I said, 'It must suck being in that mask.' He just closed his eyes and nodded."

Then a group of protesters tried to push their way through one end of the line, and that broke the tenuous peace. The truncheons went into action, and one officer who seemed to be in charge went along the line and systematically pepper-sprayed everyone. "I sat down and covered my eyes," said Mossberg. "I can only remember two times when I got mad that week, and that was one of them." He asked the officer if that was the best he could do, and the fellow came at him with the canister again. Mossberg used his hat to protect his face, and then they let loose with the tear gas. "They fired it over my head at the retreating crowd, and a wave of gas came sweeping back." At that point, all Mossberg wanted to do was get arrested.

While we were talking, he pulled out a copy of the December 9, 1999, issue of the University of Washington *Daily* (the student newspaper). There he was, identified by his landmark hat, up against the barricade with the police and tear gas bearing down on him. It was a dramatic photograph, and the image in front of me of Mossberg as a likely aggressor was a world away from the earnest man with whom I was talking.

Mossberg had started off alone that morning, had been inspired by the speeches at the labor rally, had marched with the unionists, and stayed

## The Big Thinkers

The International Forum on Globalization has been active on the front lines in fighting corporate globalization since 1994. After NAFTA passed, about thirty international activist leaders in trade and globalization issues got together for an ad hoc meeting sponsored by the Foundation for Deep Ecology. "We knew there was something new at large, and it went beyond trade agreements," said Jerry Mander, president of IFG. "Internationally, all these people were working on different issues, but they didn't know each other." In spite of their different stories and opinions, it became very clear that trade was rapidly going global and something needed to be done. "It was a juggernaut," said Mander. "We knew we needed to work together and educate each other, quickly."

Some of the other founding members at that first meeting included Maude Barlow, "the Ralph Nader of Canada"; Walden Bello, writer, scholar, and activist from the Philippines; John Cavanagh, writer, activist, and director of the Institute for Policy Studies in Washington, D.C.; Tony Clarke, theologian and social movement activist from the Polaris Institute in Canada; Martin Khor, president of the Third World Network; David Korten, author, scholar, and activist from Bainbridge Island; Helena Norberg-Hodge, Swedish philosopher now living in England; Mark Ritchie, president of the Institute for Agriculture and Trade Policy; Lori Wallach from Public Citizen; and Vandana Shiva, physicist and philosopher of science from India.

THE BATTLE IN SEATTLE

on course to support the protesters. It was the tear gas that wrenched him from his place and sent him running for the sidewalk. "The gas got in my lungs, I got disoriented, I couldn't take a breath." It took about an hour for him to regain mobility. People came and helped him wash out his eyes, which was no simple task because he was wearing contact lenses. In wandering the area after he'd recovered, Mossberg came across a completely different scene just a block from where he'd been gassed. A line of seated protesters were up against a line of sheriffs officers who had their masks off. The atmosphere was borderline friendly. The protesters were offering drinks and food, and although the officers were declining, there was conversation going on. "It was an amazing contrast," said Mossberg. "The person in charge of the sheriff line even let someone through to talk to the protesters about the curfew that had been insti-tuted." Mossberg sat down and joined them for a while.

This friendly scene was interrupted by the sounds of concussion grenades, exploding confusion in the streets, and waves of tear gas

After their first meeting, the group was excited enough by the possibility of interna-tional activism that another meeting was held about six months later. This time more than forty people showed up representing every continent and about sixteen countries. "By this time, GATT had passed and we realized that the WTO had come out of it," said Mander. "We knew we needed to educate the public." It was at this meeting that the group came up with their name, International Forum on Globalization. "We're a potpourri of progressive groups," said Mander. "We do publishing and public events designed to educate the public about the complexity of globalization. But right away, the media summarized us as protectionists against free trade. It was hard to get the issues attended to."

In Seattle, IFG organized more than the teach-ins at Benaroya Hall. The coalition put on a debate with Ralph Nader, Vandana Shiva, and John Cavanagh versus U.S. Undersecretary of Commerce David Aaron (now resigned), Scott Miller, chairman of the U.S. Alliance for Trade Expansion, and Jagdish Bhagwati, professor at Columbia University and economic policy advisor to GATT. IFG also sponsored the Food and Agriculture Day and the Corporation Day. Their informational booklets offer detailed understanding of one issue at a time.

"We like to get there before the protesters," said Mander. "That way we can educate them on the issues as well."

pouring down from the convention center where, according to Mossberg, the Seattle police had decided "enough was enough" and were clearing the streets using all weapons at their disposal. Mossberg tried to find his way out of the downtown area to go home, and repeatedly encountered barriers of police. By about 6:00 P.M., he'd made his way to a distant bus stop and waited with about thirty others for a bus. "Onboard it was a very congenial atmosphere, with people chatting about their day," said Mossberg. "One woman even had everyone sign in her sketchbook." Back home, Mossberg decided to skip the live-action TV reports of the battle on Capitol Hill and went to bed. "It was all so upsetting. I'd had enough excitement for the day. I didn't want any more."

The next day, Mossberg was scheduled to work at 2:00 P.M., so he set out early once again, before dawn, planning to be on hand to show support for those who were persevering for the cause. When he arrived downtown at about 8:00 A.M., he joined a march of about 300 people. Once again, police and pepper spray were at large, so the group decided to do a peaceful sit-in at Westlake Park, the public plaza a few blocks west of the convention center. Once there, they were immediately surrounded by police. The consensus process was instigated, and those willing to be arrested clustered together on the ground. The arrests started and Mossberg was politely asked by an officer if he would go willingly or if he would need to be carried. He went willingly, and was handcuffed and put on the bus—not before, however, educating a couple of press people about the violation of his right to speak and assemble peacefully. As he boarded the bus, he asked the driver if it was "pay as you enter" or "pay as you leave." "It got a smile," he said. He was in jail from 9:00 A.M. Wednesday morning until 11:00 A.M. Sunday. All charges were later dropped.

As our conversation in the café downstairs in the bookstore wound down, Mossberg gestured and said, "This is my job, but what I did at the WTO and what I'll be doing in Washington, D.C., is my work." We arranged to meet again when he got back from the IMF/World Bank protests in D.C.

❖    ❖    ❖    ❖    ❖

While Mossberg was back East, I got a chance to sit down with Rick Simonson, once again in the bookstore café. Rick and I go back a long way. He is a man of great decency, and he has more books stacked in vertical piles in his house than anyone I have ever met. Rick has been in the midst of the art and letters scene in Seattle for twenty-five years. His involvement with the thousands of writers who've passed through town in the twenty years he's been arranging readings means that he knows some of the more important things in life. I was counting on him for some WTO insights.

Elliott Bay Books is a meeting place of the highest order, and Simonson's first story was about bumping into California State Senator Tom Hayden in the café on the evening of N30 as he was getting food to take back to his hotel. Hayden had been a guest at the People's Gala the night before, and when Simonson saw him on Tuesday evening, Hayden's big concern was the growing confrontation between residents and police. "No one has an exit strategy," he told Simonson. "There is no graceful way to get out of it." The police were way outside the curfew zone and way inside people's neighborhoods. The tear gas was wafting into kids' bedrooms, and folks out for an evening stroll were getting ambushed by the police.

The irony of all this happening close to Christmas was not lost on Simonson, even if he is in the book biz. Besides, the weekend book sales were hot at the teach-ins at Benaroya Hall. "It was so energizing to be around a group of people with such heart, intensity, and urgency at a time of year when all we hear is the hollow societal messages to go shop," he said.

He told me about the British activist and writer who spoke about the excesses of the WTO in clipped upper-crust tones. Suddenly from out of the audience came a passionate, "Go on, girl." The audience cheered. The woman, unsure of what that meant exactly, got rather flustered. Perhaps it meant she was supposed to get off the stage. A typical bit of WTO class action and cultural comedy.

Actor Danny Glover, who now lives in Portland, also showed up at the teach-in during WTO week. "He's working with David Korten on some things," said Simonson. "There was quite the array of people in town."

Simonson's WTO week experience was a combination of professional duty and personal participation. On Monday evening, N29, he ducked out of the store to go to the Jubilee 2000 event, which was right in the bookstore's backyard. Then he ducked back in for the Paul Hawken reading, which had originally been scheduled as a dialogue with David Korten, the guru of globalization who was stuck on the East Coast. "But Hawken is quick on his feet," said Simonson. Hawken went on to pinch-hit for the ailing Korten throughout WTO week.

The activist scene in Seattle seemingly knows no bounds, yet as Simonson said when we talked, "We're light on our feet here." The co-op movements, from food to REI; the collectives, from art to politics; and even Microsoft and Starbucks—all started out small, with very little fanfare. We're the Northwest, where for many years it was Emmett Watson's underground Lesser Seattle movement, a citywide conspiracy, that we relied on to keep out the hordes. The *Seattle Times* columnist was always quick to write about rainfall statistics and traffic mayhem as well as all the pitfalls of personality and place that would discourage a visitor from becoming a resident.

"There was a time when Nordstrom's didn't have any competition," said Simonson. "Now so much of what goes on in the world involves Seattle. It makes for some deep conflicts in the city."

✿　✿　✿　✿　✿

Those of us who were here before the Highway 520 floating bridge over Lake Washington and the freeway through Seattle remember a different city, one tucked into the heart of nature. Now it's a town tucked into the back pockets of various cyber-billionaires, such as Bill Gates, Paul Allen, and Amazon.com's Jeff Bezos. Nice guys maybe, but they can't compete with the view of Mount Rainier on a nice day. We should have seen it coming when Seattle's garage-sale grunge took over the fashion and music scenes.

But in many ways, it's still a small town. While Simonson was walking in the labor march, he heard a chant come from out of the crowd: "Down with Barnes & Noble." He was pretty startled, and turned to see where it was coming from. There was a sympathetic book lover grinning at him. "It was just for me," he said. "There really was a vestige of everybody's cause."

Simonson also reminded me of the independence of this town. In 1991, after the Gulf War victory, Seattle wouldn't allow tanks in the parade, so the military said that if their troops couldn't bring their guns, there would be no parade. "Seattle was the largest U.S. city not to have a victory parade," said Simonson. The city was all for honoring the troops; it just didn't want to honor the tanks. It was also a city in which 40,000 people were out in the streets protesting the war the night before it started. "An event that didn't make the national news because it was nighttime, it was the West Coast, and it was against the war," said Simonson.

A few years later, he had cause to discuss this with Indian writer Gita Mehta, who was in town to do a reading and later told him that when she shared this information with her Iraqi friends, they already knew and said to her, "Only knowing about places like Seattle gives us any faith in the United States."

Simonson was quick to bring the WTO home. He reminisced about Earth Day, which had recently celebrated its thirtieth anniversary to much radio fanfare. "Remember when fuel efficiency was an issue?" he asked me. "And is it now? Now we have people driving SUVs and complaining about the price of gas. Totally oblivious. The WTO is us in so many ways."

He was also quick to point out the stress that is accompanying the so-called economic boom. "How many people are really at ease with how it's better? Work is at work and at home. The whole notion of time is so compressed now. The time to be in love, or not in love, or to grieve, is a different kind of time. People are trying to find out what that kind of time is."

Simonson says he's heartened by the intense participation by the very different groups in Seattle that are battling the policies of the WTO. "This movement doesn't act as if it just made itself up," he said. "It's good when you get the discipline and gung-ho of the labor unions along with the students and the church-based groups, and they all realize that there's so much more at stake and that their differences pale in comparison."

Then he went on to strike at the cyberspace heart of the Northwest. "All these dot-com companies are less concerned about what they can do and more concerned about how fast they can make money out of it." A few months later, his words were echoed by another Northwest native radical, Matt Groening, creator of *The Simpsons,* as he addressed the 2000 graduating class at the Evergreen State College in Olympia, his alma mater. He recounted the story of one of his teachers, who told him that he was pretty good at what he did, and now all he had to do was figure out if it was worth doing. Welcome back to the Northwest.

At the end of WTO week, Mayor Paul Schell showed up at Elliott Bay Books in an effort to restore happy capitalism on the streets by passing out T-shirts saying something about what a great town Seattle was and that it really was a place for everybody to shop and have fun. One of the managers told the mayor, "Oh, good; we'll save one for our assistant manager, who is in jail."

# 20 IN TREATIES WE TRUST— IN WHICH IT'S NOT A WHITE WORLD AFTER ALL

> "You see the sky now but the earth is lost in it
> and there are no horizons.
> It is all a single breath."
> —Leslie Marmon Silko, *Storyteller*

hief Seattle was twelve years old in 1792 when British explorer George Vancouver arrived in Puget Sound. It is said that Seattle was impressed with the friendliness of the first white men he had ever seen. He grew up to become a peaceful warrior, which was revolutionary at the time. He was also tall of stature, a skilled orator, and a leader of great dignity and strength. Seattle was described in the history books as "the greatest Indian friend white settlers ever had."

In the 1830s, after the arrival of Catholic missionaries, Chief Seattle converted to Christianity and took the name Noah. But he never lost touch with the heart of his spirituality and the ways of his people. His grave site in Suquamish, across Puget Sound from the city of Seattle, honors both traditions, as did he.

In 1852, white settlers around Puget Sound were so impressed with Seattle's generosity that they changed the name of their small settlement, originally called New York Alki, to Seattle in his honor.

In 1855, he was the first signer of the Port Elliott Treaty, which placed Washington tribes on reservations. Seattle was saddened yet resigned at the turn of events, and honorable. "Whatever I say, the Great Chief at Washington can rely on," said Seattle. "Our people once covered the land as waves of a wind-ruffled sea cover its shell-paved floor, but now my people are few. Let him be just and deal kindly with my people."

Indian people in the United States have since struggled for freedom, equity, and respect for 150 years. And now the WTO is another of the things that threaten their sovereignty. During WTO week in

Seattle, Native American leaders came from across the country—and around the world—to lay claim to their own land in the face of the growing power of the World Trade Organization.

Chris Peters, executive director of the Seventh Generation Fund, began his talk by saying, "The World Trade Organization is a symptom. It is a symptom of an illness, a very significant illness. A cancer that eats its host." He addressed the heart of the issue for all indigenous people around the world: "It is a symptom that started 5,000 years ago with a particular kind of thought. A thought that separated human species from the world, from all other species, from our Mother Earth. It is a thought process that is mechanistic, that was created primarily to advance a single thinking process in the world. And it has been successful.

"It exists at the demise of an ecological thought process that looks at the earth as alive, a living species. It exists to the detriment of indigenous peoples from around the world, who still adhere to that philosophy, that belief system. That we have certain responsibilities here on earth to take care of it, to honor it, to give reverence to it. That we exist on the earth in a system of reciprocity, with ceremonies. We have a belief system that is founded upon natural law that says if we care for the earth, the earth will care for us."

Peters went on to speak out for protection of the millions of acres of forests under indigenous control that are threatened by the global free-logging agreement under consideration by the WTO. Such sacred, sovereign lands around the world are being targeted as "trade barriers." With such global greed, there will be no land left on the planet to speak for itself. And no homeland for those whose life histories depend upon it.

"We believe that there has to be systemic change, systemic change at all levels of education, of social existence," said Peters. "Systemic change in economics. Systemic change in spiritual understanding. We need to look at a new narrative if we are to survive into the next millennium. That new narrative has to be founded upon principles that the whole earth is sacred, all life is sacred. That we can only survive if we have a sustainable life system. That we change how we behave."

And it's not just the lands of indigenous peoples that are threatened. Through biopiracy, the very DNA of indigenous peoples is being harvested for research, even patented for corporate ownership. Debra Harry, a Northern Paiute from the Indigenous Peoples Council on Biocolonialism, said in her presentation during WTO week, "It's very, very serious because what we are talking about is a violation of the integrity of life itself. Biotechnology can alter what it means to be human."

## The Treaties Will Protect Us

My name is Esther Nahgahnub. The bear is my totem. When I left Minnesota and flew here to Seattle, I thought I knew a little something. Maybe just a little bit. I thought I knew something about NAFTA. I thought I knew something about GATT. And just a little bit about the WTO. I found out I didn't know anything. But the Old Ones at home say, "The more you learn, the more you know you don't know anything." What I learned here is that there is layer upon layer upon layer of information that I never knew about. There are even layers under the layers of things that I knew about.

When I was a child, when my grandfather said, "The treaties will always protect us," it didn't matter what happened; the treaties would protect us.

In the beginning, I was told, all things were sovereign. The winged ones, the two-legged, the four-legged. Everything was sovereign. And that was the beginning. In the beginning, when the newcomers came to this Turtle Island, all they wanted was religious freedom. That was then, this is now.

In the Great Lakes, I feel that we are under attack. More than once we have been asked to share the water of Lake Superior with far-off communities. Once, we were asked to send it clear to Arizona. Other times they tried to take our water from another lake and send it down to cool a nuclear reactor. But I could hear my grandfather say, "The treaties will protect us."

I didn't listen to things like GATT and NAFTA, even when my friend Walt Bresette would call and say, "Esther, I'm really worried about this." I could hear my grandfather say, and would repeat it to Walt, "Walt, the treaties will protect us." But did my grandfather know? Did he know?

In Lake Superior, we have mercury coming in from all over. We have the St. Louis River flowing into it with toxics. And now they've found something new; it's called a flatworm. It's threatening the lake. They're finding many, many, many ducks that are bleeding intestinally. They couldn't figure out why. When they finally found out, it was a little flatworm. They didn't know where it came from. And it turns out this flatworm comes from the Danube River. Now how did a little flatworm from the Danube River get into Lake Superior? ➤

I heard my grandfather say, "The treaties will protect us."

The water in Lake Superior right now is at least 12 inches low. There are islands popping up all over Lake Superior. The Department of Natural Resources says the islands are coming up so quick they don't have time to name them all. But the people are not saying, "Why is this happening?" They are saying, "That island belongs to me."

So Canada decided that it could sell water from Lake Superior. And they loaded the tanker and headed it toward Asia. America found out and it wasn't happy. So the two countries decided, after a little argument, to make what they call the International Joint Commission to study this.

The International Joint Commission went around and around the Great Lakes states. They listened to us. The next year they came back and they asked the same questions. And the same people answered those questions, and the IJC went away. And they came back, and the IJC asked the same questions. And the people answered in the same way. I got a little upset, and I asked them, to quote a cliché, "What part of 'no' don't you understand?" And I asked them, "What about the treaties? Our treaties border this land. What about them?" They looked at me like I was some kind of child who had asked some rude question. And they didn't want to answer.

So a woman stood up and said, "As long as we are talking about treaties, what about the WTO?" And all of a sudden things began to get a little tense. So I stood up again because nobody was talking. I said, "Are you going to tell me that the indigenous treaties of this country, which are in the Constitution, which are the supreme law of the land—are you going to tell me that the WTO is going to supersede them?" The man from the IJC said, "I don't know. We haven't made our decision yet."

Now it's time. It's time to ask them to hold up their end of the bargain. They have become fat and rich on this Turtle Island of ours, and it is time for them to hold up their end of the bargain and honor the treaties. We can make them do that with concerted effort. And this is what I would ask you to think about. To talk about the treaties. Talk about them protecting the land. Because my grandfather said: "The treaties will protect us."

—Esther Nahgahnub, in an address to the Indigenous Forum during WTO week in Seattle, December 1999; also printed in *On Indian Land—Support for Native Sovereignty,* Winter 1999–2000

The planet's genetic diversity of food, plants, animals, and humans is clustered around the equator and throughout the southern hemisphere, and this is where scientists are gathering material for research, which then leads to patenting of DNA. The medicinal components of native plants, used throughout history by indigenous people, are already being patented by pharmaceutical companies that go on to reap huge profits in the marketplace. And, once again, it's the interests of corporations that are protected by the WTO, not the interests of the indigenous people who have used these plants for thousands of years.

With the explosion into human genome research, blood has become a commodity of choice. According to Debra Harry, there are now several hundred research projects studying the genetic variations in the DNA of indigenous peoples. "Human protection standards such as basic informed consent do not apply in many cases when researchers are out in the field with one goal in mind, and that is to get blood," she said. "If unique qualities are 'discovered' in these genetic samples, researchers may apply for patents on the DNA. This will allow them to commercialize the DNA in new pharmaceutical products, or in other genetic research, allowing them to make a profit from their so-called discovery."

Another aspect of DNA research is transgenic experimentation, which involves genetic engineering that crosses species barriers, such as mixing human DNA with plant and animal DNA. "Some of the work that is going on is to try to get animals, such as sheep, to produce pharmaceuticals through their milk," said Harry. "This is called 'pharming.'"

The scientific complexity of all this research is about as accessible as the workings of the WTO. "The problem with all this is that scientists are their own gatekeepers," said Harry. Which is the same problem with WTO. It lays claim to all the knowledge, power, and wisdom that it deems "necessary for free trade." But necessity is in the eye of the beholder. Fair-trade proponents have their own vision of reality.

Tom Goldtooth of the Indigenous Environmental Network closed the Indigenous Forum at the WTO with a passionate talk about the threat of neocolonialism and the importance of waking up to corporate exploitation. "Many nonindigenous people we meet are beginning to understand and to identify their own relationship with the land. Because an indoctrination over thousands of years has been the issue of who controls the land, controls the people. It was a control issue years ago. It is a control issue now—from controlling and mining of the land, mining our bodies, mining our minds, mining life itself."

# 21 GETTING IT TOGETHER—IN WHICH WE ALL GET WHAT WE WANT AND NEED WHAT WE GET

"The heart that goes out of itself gets large and full of joy.
This is the great secret of the inner life.
We do ourselves the most good
by doing something for others."
—Horace Mann, American educator (1796–1859)

WTO sea turtle activist Ben White was with Students for a Democratic Society in the sixties until it split up, when he chose not to join the more anarchist Weather Underground Organization (Weathermen). "I decided then that that isn't the way," he said. "We're not going to bomb or force or fire people into submission. Change is not going to come that way. And if it does, I don't want any part of it."

The discussion among the activist community about the impact of those who broke windows at Starbucks, Niketown, and the Gap has had a long half-life. "I was pissed," said White. "But ask me about it now, a couple of months later, and I do know that there's still attention being paid to WTO in Seattle. But I personally think that the power of nonviolence is so much greater than the power of violence. Violence is easily dismissed because we're used to it, we know it. It's where we live as a society. It's powerful, tenacious nonviolence that's truly revolutionary. Violence is the same old shit."

And perhaps it's because violence is "where we live as a society" that it was the violence that commandeered the attention. "Look who *60 Minutes* interviewed," said White. "They went to find the Eugene anarchists, to find out who they are and what they think. Nobody came and talked to me."

White, whose activism includes teaching nonviolent action, uses three film clips to illustrate the power of nonviolence to his students. The first is the famous salt-gathering scene in the film *Gandhi,* when row after row of individual men went peacefully to gather the salt that was rightfully theirs and got beaten one after the other by the British military until they dropped; not even the British could stomach such obvious suppression. "That was when the British Empire died in India," said White.

The second is the scene in *Beyond Rangoon,* the film version of the fight for democracy in Burma. Aung San Suu Kyi, who is still under house arrest in that country (now renamed Myanmar), was shown calmly breaking through a line of military police. "She looks at a soldier with such love, such incredible love, that he just starts shaking," said White. "And she walks right by him. Right past his gun. It breaks the back of the rigidity, of everything he's holding back."

The third clip isn't a fictionalized account of the truth, it's a documented real-time event. When White fought the cutting of trees that were part of the Rockybrook timber sale in the Dosewallips watershed, about 50 miles west of Seattle in the Olympic National Forest, he was arrested three times: for blockading the road, for climbing up a tree and staying there for three days and three nights, and for leading a demonstration of 200 people over a "crime scene, do not cross" line. He was prosecuted under the forest closure law that enabled lumber companies to close a large area of the surrounding forests whenever they were logging. White, who was taken to federal prison south of Tacoma, claimed in his defense that the law violated his constitutional right to speak, assemble, and worship in a place he considered sacred. The judge agreed. "We knocked down the forest closure law with that challenge," said White. "Afterward I did some research and realized that the strongest protection we have in this country to dissent is based on freedom of religion."

On January 1, 1997, White incorporated the Church of the Earth in the state of Washington. The sacrament of the church was to use direct action in defense of wild life and wild places. White, who was one of the founders of the Cetacean Freedom Network, an anti-captivity group in San Francisco, organized a Church of the Earth direct action at the gates of Marine World Africa in Vallejo, California, where orca whales and dolphins were held in captivity. Ten members of the network, representing four countries, went inside as a church group. "They couldn't figure out how to deny us admission," said White. "We even got a discount on our tickets.

"We went to the front row, to make contact with the whales and to pray for them. Our premise was that church groups go to the bedside of their sick parishioners; we were going to the poolside of our imprisoned parishioners." One of the whales, Yaka, was one of the last surviving Northwest orcas; she'd been taken from the waters around the north end of Vancouver Island in the mid-seventies. Her partner was an Icelandic whale called Vigga.

"As soon as we went in, cops came out from everywhere," said White. "We had no banners, no signs, no T-shirts, but they knew something was going on." When the whales' performance started, the ten people stood up, held hands, and began to pray together. "About halfway through the show, the whales came right over to us. Especially Yaka; she wouldn't take her eyes off us." The trainers banged on their buckets, trying to get the whales to respond, but they ignored them. "It was by far and away the most emotional, the toughest demonstration I've ever been part of," said White. "I'm used to doing something, hanging a banner, doing *something*. But we just stayed there praying. Finally they just closed the show, got everyone else out, and we stood there, crying our eyes out."

One of the women in the group started singing "Amazing Grace," and White reminded me of the origins of this gospel song. It was written in the eighteenth century by John Newton, a captain of a slave ship who experienced an epiphany en route to America, turned his ship around, and returned his captives to freedom in Africa. "It's a classic evocative song," said White. "I always thought we screwed up in the anti-war movement, the anti-nuke movement, and the environmental movement by not using more music as our anthems, as was done during civil rights times. It evokes the spirit and spirituality of the people and taps into that power."

White, who has a broad intellectual understanding of the issues, had his own epiphany at Marine World. "I realized with that action that even most animal advocates don't really think the animals know what we're doing. We still have this built-in anthropocentrism, but those whales knew. When I tried—and I had to try—to empathetically relate with them, I was overwhelmed with sadness. It's like looking into the mind of someone who's really suffering. What you get is profound grief. And that's what we felt." It's an excerpt from this action that White includes in his trio of film clips demonstrating the power of nonviolence.

His own life, however, has been less than peaceful. "I've been warned and threatened for so many years. My phone's been tapped. And almost every night I have dreams of pursuit and evasion. That's where I live." The underground, and its investigative elements looking under the skirts and stones of global activism, are as prevalent now as they were during the civil rights and anti-war movements of the sixties and seventies.

I mentioned to him the story I had heard about a major environmental group being bought off to not participate in WTO protests because free trade was so important to the Northwest economy. "Most people I work with would die first," he said. White, who has himself been accused of infiltrating the movement, was visibly distressed by the suggestion. "Having been there myself, I'm leery of such accusations."

✿   ✿   ✿   ✿   ✿   ✿

Democracy is messy, divisive, opinion-driven, and, in the best of its tradition, utterly open. The WTO protests were all of the above. "If this what democracy looks like, it looks pretty good," said some momentarily enlightened pundit. And even with the successful shutdown of the WTO, divisiveness is still alive and thriving in the ranks.

For instance, West Coast activist Ben White thinks that East Coast organization Public Citizen is a bit afflicted with noblesse oblige and is too busy jockeying for position within the system. "Too smart, by half," he said. "If they're not careful, they'll lose the guts of it. But they helped keep us all together. And that's huge, and it's to their eternal credit."

The strength of the movement is in its diversity—not only of interests but also of strategies. Public Citizen, the labor unions, the Humane Society, the Jubilee movement, and many other groups don't go anywhere near civil disobedience. Ruckus Society, Art and Revolution, Direct Action Network, the intrepid turtles, and the student activist movement did their historical homework, pushed the innovative envelope, and got courageously in the way of the WTO. And many spontaneously inspired individuals who saw the police brutality, and their friends' and neighbors' civil rights shredded in their democratic backyards, got up from in front of their televisions and hit the streets saying, "No, this is wrong." The Kingdome was circled with prayer, the jail was circled with vigils, the city was circled with uprising, the world was circled with hope.

"I really do see a new paradigm emerging, and it is populist versus corporatist," said White. "It's the beginning of a global populist revolution. We had a far greater effect than any of us had any idea we would. It was like setting off a little bomb on the acupressure point of the world economy."

"I've tried really hard to get inside the mind of the pro-WTOers. I understand it, I think; I understand the seductive concept that you don't really have to pay attention to poverty in your country. All you've got to do is go upscale, globalize, tie your lead into the values of the world's elite, and it will float everybody's boat. Well, it doesn't work that way. And it hasn't. But it's easy to think that it will."

The WTO protests in Seattle have been called a middle-class uprising, spoiled kids who had nothing better to do, old hippies crawling out of the techno-suburbs for a hit of nostalgia, tree-hugging crazies, and whining unionists. Life is good, we are told, and getting better. So what's the big fuss all about?

"I've traveled enough to know that the whole world wants to live like Americans," said White. But the wealth of the times is concentrated in fewer and fewer American pockets, and the media's glorification of growing money for money's sake casts a peculiar shadow over the national character. We are less and less connected to those "without," to those struggling simply to survive.

In the eighties, real-life Americans took control of the Cold War thaw. They went to Russia as regular citizens and said, "Here we are. Here's a quilt from our town to yours; here's our theater group, let's see yours; send us your choirs, your artists, your countrymen." It was a trade of goodwill among civil society, and a lot of it went on in the Northwest. On Bainbridge Island, now home to David Korten and *Yes! A Journal of Positive Futures*, there was a wonderful grassroots movement to break the face of the perceived Russian "enemy" through an exchange of theater culture with real Russian people. Perhaps it's time to do something similar to break the face of free trade, to exchange our personal visions of *free people and fair trade.*

The student–turtle–Teamster–policy wonk–civil society–tree-hugger partnership is not about to become some mushy, unidentifiable soup. "If the people lead, the leaders will follow" is an ancient Taoist saying. There are a lot of people leading, and they're going in a lot of different directions. The other WTO, the one that was won, was when the World Turned Out in Seattle. The faces, the reasons, the cultures were many, but the underlying passion for global economic and environmental justice was pervasive. The people in the streets of Seattle during WTO week represented the collective force of justice at large. It is a force bigger than we are as individuals—bigger, indeed, than our collective economic riches, which can ultimately render us unjust, unnatural in the natural world.

"We finally got our targets right," said White, "and it's taken a long time. We've all figured out that we have the same enemy: the same thing that oppresses women, destroys families, destroys the land, keeps people poor, rips off the animals. The triad of the WTO, the IMF, and the World Bank is the heart of darkness. The policies they're putting out are what's keeping the world poor and keeping the corporations on top. But the force of the people will be insurmountable.

"My own belief is that consciousness doesn't reside in the individual. We pick up on it like you do a radio wave. It changes because of who we are, but I think it's in every molecule, including the rocks. And there are two basic rules of consciousness. Rule number one is that life will out, no matter what. And rule number two is the main rule governing human society: Everyone wants freedom. And they will eventually get it. No matter what."

✡   ✡   ✡   ✡   ✡

It's this yearning for freedom that was the great equalizer on the streets of Seattle. But what is freedom? And where does it come from? Historically, the opposite of human freedom is slavery, when one person is physically owned by another. But what about slavery in which the ownership is less direct, involving, perhaps, a fictional entity, a power with all the rights of a person yet without the human attributes? Then the ownership is more subtle, but in some ways it can be more pervasive. If someone owns us and we are "let go," we walk out into freedom. But what if we are owned by a culture and a value system that we are expected to participate in but not expected to help shape, afloat in a river of information in which we are always being washed downstream and never allowed to get to shore? How can we see the waters, feel the values, and examine the culture to see if it is reflecting who we really are?

The people in this book are a vital part of our culture, but where are they reflected? As Peace Action's Fred Miller said, many of the two-income, well-off people he talks to wish they were doing the work he does. His personal culture, his world, reflects him, as the personal, faith-based cultures of Pete Strimer and Bishop Warner reflect them. Hannah Petros, Vanessa Lee, and Carolyn Canafax move within cultures that reflect their activist values and commitments. Brian Moss works in a healing culture that values spiritually based psychotherapy. Anne Schwartz and her husband, Mike Brondi, live, as do millions of other farmers around the world, in intimate relationship to the earth and its bounty. Their culture reflects them.

Ben White lives in a world that values the patience of a turtle and the passion of radical activism. Sarah Joy Staude is realizing a world that is confusing, disappointing, and frightening. She is not alone. Sally Soriano lives inside the up-close-and-personal politics of the day, the place where our worldly leaders come from. The place where there's always room for one more. Rick Simonson lives with books and their makers, those who write them and those who read them. His culture is knowledge. Michael Mossberg is leaving books for Los Angeles, where he will enter more deeply into the culture of the WTO protest movement. Joanne Calhoun, until she heads north to Alaska, is one of billions of workers in the world who make things happen and keep things going. These are all real worlds, real cultures, real people.

But the one overriding culture we *all* share, whether we like it or not, whether it reflects us or not, is the culture of greed. A culture in which to have new and better *stuff* is the only measure of man, woman, and child. It's almost as though character these days is defined by acquisition. As though, if we don't have the means to acquire, we don't count.

This leads, of course, down a path of no return. The planet cannot be replaced. Its wealth is limited, its resources finite, its wild beauty vulnerable. We are eating our earth alive. The very future of our humanity, literally and otherwise, is at stake. The culture of greed is overcoming even our need to survive.

Why is this? Is it because it is an artificial culture, the culture of a fictional entity that has neither face nor future? Does it exist simply to ensure that we are held hostage by the present, this moment of possibility in which anything can be had and should be had? Have *we* been had? Are we enslaved by a culture that reflects neither our collective humanity nor our individual hearts?

It was the collective heart of humanity that took to the streets during WTO week in Seattle. Many were there for specific reasons; they knew what was at stake. Many of us were there as ordinary people with a yearning for something we could neither articulate nor understand. And we were drawn together into a culture of longing and belonging.

Yet after it was all over, what the media reflected back to us was a culture of hatred and stupidity in which none of us could recognize ourselves. Those who knew why they were there had their own cultures to return to. Those of us who weren't sure why we were drawn to go looked to the media for reflection of the answer. And what a shock. "We all remember the images of Martin Luther King, of Selma, Alabama, and all the images of the civil rights struggle where we were at least honored by having the pictures of the nonviolence," said Bishop Warner. "But here we became an icon for violence."

This sense of betrayal might be the most powerful thing that happened on the streets of Seattle. We wanted to know that we were there, to know why we were there, why others were there, and what it really meant. The answers all came down to a televised continuous cartoon loop of property damage. A broken window became more profound, more telling, more compelling, more valuable than all of us put together.

❁   ❁   ❁   ❁   ❁

The aftermath has been as sobering. It was reported that Seattle Mayor Paul Schell wanted to use fire hoses on the demonstrators, but the fire department refused to do so because it would have been too harmful and besides, firefighters aren't law enforcement. All the talk has been about how the police could have done things differently to control the "protesters," not about how justice can reign in the streets at home and abroad. The newspapers have been full of concern about who is to blame and who is going to pay the bills from the WTO "debacle." The only prominent journalists in town who stayed with the issues and the implications were Knute Berger, thoughtful editor of *Seattle Weekly*, and impassioned *Weekly* writer Geov Parrish. They both stayed the course with persistent and provocative articles about what really happened and why.

Nationally, the arrogance and ignorance of the press was summed up by an unlikely columnist, Marianne Means. In a syndicated column about the World Bank and IMF protests in Washington, D.C., she wrote: "At least I am smart enough to blame the leaders of poor countries for their own problems, not the international institutions that are striving to help them." The scope of this ignorance cannot be measured. Nor can the danger. The same column is a diatribe against those who would demonstrate at the national conventions. "Stupid and self-indulgent," "motley collection of grubby radicals," "bored teenagers trying to mimic the folks of the old days," "childish theater of the absurd"—this is the reality for Marianne Means, whose information source was likely what she saw on TV. Why do such simplistic observations as Means's have to be syndicated reality? If you weren't on the streets in Seattle during WTO week, this is likely the reality you have absorbed through TV and writing such as hers. It's a perceived "reality" that could fuel police mayhem at demonstrations in the future—where people like Michael Mossberg, Vanessa Lee, Sarah Joy Staude, and Bishop Warner might be on the streets, driven there by conscience, values, and faith.

The police, too, are victimized by such irresponsible and inflammatory reporting. In Seattle, the police were told to expect the worst. They were told they would be killed. Who planned so poorly that the police suffered from hunger because they weren't given food or time to eat it? How much of the police violence was a result of cops being too long on the street without breaks, bathroom or otherwise? "WTO protesters were better prepared," shouted the headlines. This is true. They had support teams with sandwiches, people around to wipe the sweat from their brows, and diapers on for emergencies.

The police were equipped with expensive, high-tech protective gear, fear, and few choices. How many were thinking that the person they were looking at was the "protester" they had been warned about who was carrying weapons, biological and otherwise, and was out to kill them? In reality, the person might have had something for them to eat in their backpack. Sarah Joy Staude and her friends offered food to the police, who politely declined. Perhaps because of fear of botulism, perhaps because of protocol. It doesn't much matter. What matters is that there was a gesture of civility. And if civil society is to overcome corporate rule, civility is its most powerful weapon. Good manners go a long way. And in spite of the culture we are in, which falsely reflects who we really are, we will prevail. We know who we are.

"I think the media is always looking for the tension," said Bishop Warner. "But the truth comes out no matter what. And this truth is coming out with the people and it's happening all over the world."

Ethiopian American Hannah Petros was characteristically upfront. "I don't read mainstream media," she said. "You will die if that's the only thing you get in this life."

But the cultures of longing know how to keep one another alive. The network of magazines, newsletters, websites, and e-mail list-serves keeps us informed and inspired. And the network is growing daily. Just this morning I got news of a new environmental watchdog e-mail list-serve developing on San Juan Island, where the orca whales are suffering in our waters from PCBs in their bodies and our land is struggling under the weight of wealth-based development.

❂   ❂   ❂   ❂   ❂

Locally and globally, the problems seem insurmountable. When I asked Petros how she survives wave after wave of despair and desolation that continues to come out of Africa, she looked me over for a long moment and said, "I pray." Then she looked at me again. "But nobody likes to talk about spirituality in this country."

Toward the end of my meeting with Bishop Warner, I told him how odd it was that the church had brought me back to politics. "But they're the same thing," he said. "I have felt that over the years the church has become introspective and has lost its prophetic voice and its passion for the marginalized and the dispossessed. This was an opportunity to speak out. For people of all different traditions of faiths, which is the only way to go. To have Hindus and Muslims and Christians and Jews and people who are not part of any religious tradition all saying this has got to be dealt with.

"More and more over the years, I've struggled with the issues of power and authority, and what I saw [N29] was the overwhelming power of compassion and unity and care, a real sense of loving those who are strangers. And the other power that I saw felt like a police state. It's as if the WTO itself represented a corporate power, a top-down power, a coercive power that was diametrically opposed to the people who were trying to stand with the powerless."

The Battle in Seattle was a spiritual battle. The people who were out in the streets want to live in a world in which the spirit of justice prevails. They're calling for an ethics-based economic system that exploits neither people nor place nor any living thing. A system that bridges the great divide and puts us all in touch, with each other and with the grace of nature into which we are born.

"Those of us in the march were transformed in a way," said Bishop Warner. "We became more and more connected to each other, and that connection helped us to connect to the larger world. It created a passion in us. At least it did in me. This is what it's really all about. This is what ministry is about."

When Ben White was in an audience listening to the Dalai Lama a few years ago, he got a chance to ask him a question. "What can we do about the spiritual impoverishment of our leaders?" he asked. The Dalai Lama responded, "Just remember that they are human beings," he said.

"I thought that was a pretty good answer," said White. It was Vice President Al Gore who came up to White afterward and thanked him for asking the question.

Recently, Ben White lost his home and everything in it to a fire. But he didn't start over; he simply carried on, in spite of the complexity of his loss. He went on planning a tour of colleges with his WTO show, being the dad that he is, living out the lesson that our possessions are but a dream. The deep nature of his life did not get destroyed, even if all his precious books, the book he was writing, the photos of his kids, the cardboard turtle on his wall, were all lost in the inferno. "But life will out," White had said, months before the fire happened. Maybe that's why the Smithsonian Institution is seriously considering adding a WTO turtle to its collection.

The Dalai Lama also said, "The deeper we comprehend suffering, the closer we come to our goal, the release from suffering." And there's no one who can laugh more exuberantly than the Dalai Lama.

It takes a broken, open heart and a big sense of humor to face the reality of these times. To live with grief, and without remorse, enables us to see the truth, to be grateful for all the gifts in our lives, and to feel our way to becoming involved without becoming immobilized and useless. "You can't learn passion," said Hannah Petros. "It's a feeling. And then you do something."

The issues are as close as the buttons on our clothes, and as distant as the despair in Africa. We can do what we are able to do. All we have to do is care.

# AFTERWORD

The photograph that kept me inspired and consoled during the eight months of writing and researching this book is titled "Democracy Keepers." It was taken by Gloria Marohl on Friday, December 3, 1999 (D3), the day the WTO decided they could not meet their objectives, could not come to agreement with their members, and could not set a new round of global trade talks. The photograph is of a line of women, including several Raging Grannies, and the turtle walking stick, rainbow umbrella, and one brightly eye-shadowed brow of Dee Dee Rainbow, Seattle's favorite white woman of color. Two raging grannies are wearing shades of purple, have flowers in their hats and have faces aged with a startling and youthful faith. Another stands tall and looks as though she'd take Michael Moore (WTO Mike) over her knee, spank him and send him to his room. And there is an Asian woman, whose glance says simply, "Take this." The banner, flying high behind them, reads "Democracy, Here We Come."

If Tuesday, N30 was the day of infamy, Friday, D3 was the day of democracy. Throughout WTO week, the people of Seattle responded with heart, mind, and soul to the mistreatment by the police, the press, and the politicians, of the people in their city. People poured out onto the streets to march, demonstrate, and be present for the democratic constitutional rights that were being violated. Many didn't know much about the WTO. What they did know was that something was wrong and something had to be done. So they showed up, organized rallies, surrounded the jail with support for those arrested, and in grand style illustrated the old saying, "When the people lead, the leaders will follow."

There was one common cause: violence. What, exactly, is it? When does it count? The main distinction that's made by everyone from Episcopal priest Pete Strimer to radical activist Ben White is the difference between violence against property and violence against people. In the 1970s, when Jim Douglass poured blood on military files, he was protesting nuclear violence against the human race. When the "anarchists"—be they serious proponents of anarchy or spur-of-the-moment troublemakers—broke windows in Seattle, they were protesting today's economic violence against much of humanity. When the police wielded tear gas, pepper spray, rubber bullets, and physical force against the people on the streets of Seattle, they were acting against civil rights, freedom of speech, and the citizens themselves.

Photographer Greg Redfox, who wrote an account of being assaulted on the streets of Seattle in the newspaper *On Indian Land*, made a chilling observation: "It was very odd to feel like we were back in 1939 Germany and see these officers coming. Rigid, stiff, and obviously doing their job, goose-stepping down the street. I thought, 'This is a group of modern-day Nazi storm troopers.' That was the impression."

And it wasn't only his impression. It was a terrifying show of force, as the police attacked protesters and bystanders alike, and invaded the neighborhood of Capitol Hill—well outside the downtown restricted area. There was tear gas in kids' bedrooms, and retirees were taking rubber bullets in the back.

One group that quickly rallied was the Quakers, the American Friends Service Committee, who had about eighty participants on the streets during WTO week. Quakers Ruth Yarrow, who works for Physicians for Social Responsibility, and her husband, Mike, a retired professor specializing in the sociology of work, were disturbed enough to organize an unscheduled visit to Mayor Paul Schell on Thursday, D2. Along with Anne Hall, the minister at University Baptist Church, and representatives from the Buddhist community, they went off to see the mayor.

For days, Paul Schell had been besieged by pressures. Everyone from President Clinton and Secretary of State Madeleine Albright to downtown business owners and the WTO delegates were after him to get control of the streets. "He was very tired, very worn, and afraid," said Ruth Yarrow. They beseeched him to tone down the violent comportment of the police. Schell's response was, "Do you realize that Washington, D.C., is furious?" They continued to urge him to rein in the troops. "The mayor was scared because he was getting pressure from the federal government, state government, and big business downtown," said Ruth. "What he wasn't listening to were his citizens here in the city and the extent to which we were concerned about the issues of the WTO."

When Schell asked them what they thought he should do, the group had some useful answers. Police should wear visible identification, they told him. And demonstrators should be warned when they were risking arrest. Medics should be allowed to help those injured, and the police should be working to de-escalate the situation. Mayor Schell thanked them, and as they were leaving, some of his staff expressed great relief at their visit. They'd been trying to get him to cool down the police, but he had not been sympathetic.

As the week progressed, the crowds on the streets increased. The rallying cry became: "This is what democracy looks like." On Friday, D3, outside the King County Labor Temple, leaders of unions and faith-based communities led the march calling for justice. The joint statement ended with: "Let us honor protest as an act of love and compassion. Let us celebrate everyone here who has moved us forward this week. The struggle to repair our world, to improve the condition of human beings, to care for all life will continue and grow."

This outpouring of citizen activism spurred extensive investigations, reports, lawsuits, and unrelenting citizen testimony. In July 2000, settlements were starting to be made with people who were brutalized, whose rights were violated, and who were wrongfully detained. In August, the American Civil Liberties Union (ACLU) published its report, which closely examined the civil liberties violations that occurred during WTO week.

"With proper planning, the City could have protected the rights both of delegates and of demonstrators," said ACLU-WA executive director Kathleen Taylor. "Yet the City's failure to plan did not excuse violations of civil liberties during the conference. While the WTO protests were noisy and disruptive, they did not constitute a riot. Police repeatedly used force—especially chemical weapons—in ways that were more aggressive and heavy-handed that the situation warranted." (The ACLU's WTO report in its entirety can be read online at www.aclu-wa.org.)

In September, the film *This Is What Democracy Looks Like* premiered at the Seattle Art Museum. It was produced through Seattle's Independent Media Center, first organized specifically to offer accuracy in reporting during WTO week and now being used all around the world as a model for mainstreaming "alternative" media. The film, which was drawn from the work of more than 100 filmmakers who documented the activity during WTO week, splendidly captures the police tactics at-large, as well as the solidarity of Seattle's citizens and the stunning courage of the young adults who held ground because their lives, and the lives of millions around the world, depended on it.

The stories in this book are but a scratch on the surface of the commitment, valor and vision that rocked Seattle during WTO week.

And it's a story without end. After it was all over, activist Sally Soriano received from a friend in low places, a copy of a printout of her November 17, 1999, driving infraction (defective headlight while en route to Seattle from Bellingham). Dated November 29, 1999, it read:

> A Washington State Patrol Trooper stopped a vehicle for a defective headlight and observed demonstration materials in the vehicle. The driver was asked if she was going to be one of the violent protesters and she said "Not me, but some of my people will be throwing bricks." The driver was Sally Soriano. NCIC and FBI indices checked. Other related information is maintained in Rapid Start Control Form Notebook.

Before the 2000 Republican National Convention started, John Sellers, executive director of the Ruckus Society, was arrested in Philadelphia and held on $1 million bail, later reduced to $100,000. Michael Mossberg, ex-bookseller, was arrested during the Democratic National Convention in Los Angeles.

Suspicions of conspiracy and terrorism seem to be swelling the ranks of policedom. Individuals are being watched, targeted, arrested preemptively, and held up as potential co-conspirators with terrorist inclinations. In September 2000, it was announced that the FBI is establishing an anti-terrorism task force in Western Washington that will involve local, state, and federal law enforcement agencies. Who knows what this means? Paranoia creates a reality all its own.

If there was a conspiracy during WTO week, it was a conspiracy of collective decency. A conspiracy in which faith in the future was the weapon and trust was the terrorist's tool. Trust that we can put people before profits, the planet before greed, and life before annihilation.

Stay tuned.

# RESOURCES

## INFORMED SOURCES

There are thousands of organizations working for peace and justice around the world. This list is just a beginning. Many of the websites listed have terrific links to other organizations, so work the net, the information is out there. For a continually updated list of life-minded resources, and to add your own suggestions online, go to www.battleinseattlebook.com.

### ALTERNATIVE MEDIA

Alternative Radio
P.O. Box 551
Boulder, CO 80306
Tel: 800-444-1977
www.alternativeradio.org

Fairness and Accuracy in
Reporting (FAIR)
130 West 25th Street
New York, NY 10001
Tel: 212-633-6700
www.fair.org

Independent Media Center
(excellent website with
links to many international
centers)
1415 Third Avenue
Seattle, WA 98101
Tel: 206-262-0721
www.indymedia.org

Hightower Radio
Pacifica Network News
RadioNation
www.webactive.com

Institute for Public
Accuracy
65 Ninth Street, Suite 3
San Francisco, CA 94103
Tel: 415-552-5378
www.accuracy.org

Media Island
816 Adams Street
Olympia, WA 98501
Tel: 360-352-8526
www.mediaisland.org

New Dimensions Radio
P.O. Box 569
Ukiah, CA 95482
Tel: 707-468-5215
www.newdimensions.org

Public Media Center
466 Green Street
San Francisco, CA 94133
Tel: 415-434-1403
www.public-media-center.org

Rachel's Environment
& Health Weekly
www.rachel.org
Seattle Community
Network
www.scn.org

### FILMS AND VIDEO

Bullfrog Films
(including *Affluenza* and
*Escape from Affluenza*)
372 Dautrich Road
Reading, PA 19606
Tel: 800-543-3764
www.bullfrogfilms.com

Labor Video Project
*Labor Battles the WTO*
P.O. Box 425584
San Francisco, CA 94142
Tel: 415-282-1908
www.igc.apc.org/lvpsf

People's Video
(Dr. Michael Parenti's
materials)
P.O. Box 99514
Seattle, WA 98199
Tel: 206-789-5371
www.michaelparenti.org

Whispered Media
*Showdown in Seattle: Five
Days that Shook the WTO*
P.O. Box 40130
San Francisco, CA 94140
Tel: 415-789-8484
www.videoactivism.org

Wright Angle Media
*Trade Off*
*(The WTO in Seattle)*
Tel: 206-230-0294
www.wrightanglemedia.com

## MAGAZINES AND NEWSLETTERS

Adbusters
1243 West 7th Avenue
Vancouver, BC
V6H 1B7 Canada
Tel: 604-736-9401
www.adbusters.org

Amicus Journal
Natural Resources
Defense Council
40 West 20th Street
New York, NY 10011
Tel: 212-727-2700
www.nrdc.org/amicus

Corporate Watch
P.O. Box 29344 ➤

San Francisco, CA 94129
Tel: 415-561-6568
www.corpwatch.org

Green Business Letter
Tilden Press Inc.
6 Hillwood Place
Oakland, CA 94610
Tel: 800-954-7336
www.greenbiz.com

The Green Guide
Mothers & Others for a
Livable Planet
40 West 20th Street
New York, NY 10011
Tel: 212-242-0010
www.mothers.org/green
guide

HOPE Publishing
P.O. Box 160
Naskeag Road
Brooklin, ME 04616
Tel: 800-273-7447
www.hopemag.com

In These Times
2040 North Milwaukee
    Avenue
Chicago, IL 60647
Tel: 800-827-0270
www.inthesetimes.com

Mother Jones
P.O. Box 469024
Escondido, CA 92046
Tel: 800-438-6656
www.motherjones.com

Ms. Magazine
20 Exchange Place,
22nd Floor
New York, NY 10005
Tel: 212-509-2095
www.msmagazine.com

Multinational Monitor
P.O. Box 19405
Washington, DC 20036 ➤

Tel: 202-387-8030
www.essential.org/monitor

The Nation
33 Irving Place
New York, NY 10003
Tel: 212-209-5400
www.thenation.com

The New Internationalist
P.O. Box 1143
Lewiston, NY 14092
Tel: 905-946-0407
www.oneworld.org/ni

New Labor Forum
23 West 23rd Street,
19th Floor
New York, NY 10036
Tel: 212-827-0200
www.gc.edu/newlabor
forum

On Indian Land—Support
for Native Sovereignty
P.O. Box 2104
Seattle, WA 98111
Tel: 206-525-5096
(no website available)

Orion Magazine
The Orion Society
195 Main Street
Great Barrington, MA
    01230
Tel: 413-528-4422
www.orionsociety.org

The Progressive
409 East Main Street
Madison, WI 53703
Tel: 608-257-4626
www.progressive.org

Satya Magazine
P.O. Box 138
Prince Street Station
New York, NY 10012
Tel: 212-674-0952
www.stealthtechnologies
.com/satya

Shambhala Sun
1345 Spruce Street
Boulder, CO 80302
Tel: 902-422-8404
www.shambhalasun.com

The Simple Living Journal
Simple Living
4509 Interlake Ave. North,
Box 149
Seattle, WA 98103
Tel: 206-464-4800
www.simpleliving.org

The Sun—
A Magazine of Ideas
104 North Roberson Street
Chapel Hill, NC 27516
Tel: 919-942-5282
www.thesunmagazine.org

This Magazine
401 Richmond St. West,
Suite 396, Toronto, ON
M5V 3A8 Canada
Tel: 416-979-9429
www.thismag.org

TIKKUN
2107 Van Ness Avenue,
Suite 302
San Francisco, CA 94109
Tel: 800-395-7753
www.tikkun.org

TRICYCLE—
The Buddhist Review
92 Vandam Street
New York, NY 10013
Tel: 212-645-1143
Subscriptions:
205 West Center Street
Marion, OH 43302
Tel: 800-873-9871
www.tricycle.com

Utne Reader
P.O. Box 7460
Red Oak, IA 51591
Tel: 800-736-UTNE
www.utne.com

Whole Earth Magazine
Subscriptions:
P.O. Box 3000
Denville, NJ 07834
Tel: 888-732-6739
www.wholeearthmag.com

YES! A Journal of
Positive Futures
P.O. Box 10818
Bainbridge Island, WA
 98110
Tel: 206-842-0216
www.futurenet.org

Z Magazine
18 Millfield Street
Woods Hole, MA 02543
(no phone number listed)
www.lbbs.org

ORGANIZATIONS
IN SUPPORT OF
A CIVIL SOCIETY

ACORN (Association of
Community Organizations
for Reform Now)
88 Third Avenue, 3rd Floor
Brooklyn, NY 11217
Tel: 718-246-7900
www.acorn.org

Alliance for Democracy
681 Main Street
Waltham, ME 02451
Tel: 888-466-8233
www.afd-online.org

American Friends Service
Committee
1501 Cherry Street
Philadelphia, PA 19102
Tel: 215-241-7000
www.afsc.org

Art and Revolution
www.agitprop.org/art
andrevolution

Bank Information Center
2025 I Street NW,
Suite 522
Washington, DC 20006
Tel: 202-466-8191
www.bicusa.org

Collective Heritage
Institute
Bioneers Conference
Visionary and Practical
Solutions for Restoring
the Earth
901 West San Mateo
 Road, Suite L
Santa Fe, NM 87505
Tel: 505-986-0366
www.bioneers.org

The Council of Canadians
502-151 Slater Street
Ottawa, ON
K1P 5H3 Canada
Tel: 613-233-2773
www.canadians.org

Data Center
1904 Franklin Street,
Suite 900
Oakland, CA 94612
Tel: 510-835-4692
www.igc.org/datacenter

David Suzuki
Environmental Foundation
2211 West 4th Avenue,
Suite 219
Vancouver, BC
V6K 4S2 Canada
Tel: 604-732-4228
www.davidsuzuki.org

Democracy Unlimited
of Humboldt County
761 Eighth Street
Arcata, CA 95518
Tel: 707-822-2242
www.monitor.net/democ
racyunlimited

Economic Policy Institute
1660 L Street NW,
Suite 1200
Washington, DC 20036
Tel: 202-775-8810
www.epinet.org

Environmental Research
Foundation
P.O. Box 5036
Annapolis, MD 21403
Tel: 888-272-2435
www.rachel.org

Focus on the Global South
c/o CUSRI, Wisit
Prachuabmoh Building
Chulalongkorn University,
Phayathai Road
Bangkok, 10330 Thailand
Tel: 66-2-2187363-5
www.focusweb.org

Foundation for Community
Encouragement
P.O. Box 17210
Seattle, WA 98107
Tel: 888-784-9001
www.fce-community.org

Habitat for Humanity
121 Habitat Street
Americus, GA 31709
Tel: 800-422-4828
www.habitat.org

Infact (corporate
accountability)
46 Plympton Street
Boston, MA 02118
Tel: 617-695-2525
www.infact.org

Institute for Local
Self-Reliance
2425 Eighteenth Street NW
Washington, DC 20009
Tel: 202-232-4108
www.ilsr.org

Institute for Policy Studies
733 Fifteenth Street NW,
Suite 1020
Washington, DC 20005
Tel: 202-234-9382
www.ips-dc.org

International Center for
Technology Assessment
310 D Street NE
Washington, DC 20002
Tel: 202-547-9359
www.fas.org/pub/gen/cta

International Forum on
Globalization
1062 Fort Cronkhite
Sausalito, CA 94965
Tel: 415-229-9350
www.ifg.org

International Law Project
for Human, Economic
and Environmental
Defense (HEED)
Corporate Charter
Revocation
National Lawyers Guild,
Los Angeles
8124 West 3rd Street,
Suite 201
Los Angeles, CA 90048
Tel: 213-736-1094
www.heed.net

League of Women Voters
1730 M Street NW,
Suite 1000
Washington, DC 20036
Tel: 202-429-1965
www.lwv.org

Natural Capital Institute
P.O. Box 2938
Sausalito, CA 94966
Tel: 415-334-6990
(no website available)

People Link, Institute for
Mass Communications
423 Fifty-fourth Street ➤

Brooklyn, NY 11220
Tel: 718-238-8883
www.people-link.com

Polaris Institute
4 Jeffrey Avenue
Ottawa, ON
K1K-0E2 Canada
Tel: 613-746-8374
www.polarisinstitute.org

Project Underground
1916A Martin Luther King
Jr. Way
Berkeley, CA 94704
Tel: 510-705-8981
www.moles.org

Protect the Local, Globally
11 Park House Gardens
East Twickenham,
Middlesex
TWI 2DF UK
Tel: 44-181-892-5051
www.ifg.org (link)

Public Citizen
1600 Twentieth Street NW
Washington, DC 20009
Tel: 800-289-3787
www.citizen.org

Public Interest Research
Groups (PIRGs)
218 D Street SE
Washington, DC 20003
Tel: 202-546-9707
www.pirg.org/uspirg

Reclaim Democracy!
P.O. Box 532
Boulder, CO 80306
Tel: 303-402-0105
www.reclaimdemocracy.org

Right-to-Know Network
1742 Connecticut
Avenue NW
Washington, DC 20009
Tel: 202-234-8494
www.rtk.net

Rocky Mountain Institute
1739 Snowmass Creek
  Road
Snowmass, CO 81654
Tel: 970-927-3851
www.rmi.org

Servenet, Youth Service
America
1101 Fifteenth Street,
Suite 200
Washington, DC 20005
Tel: 202-296-2992
www.servenet.org

Third World Network
228 Macalister Road
10440 Penang, Malaysia
Tel: 60-4-2266728
www.twnside.org.sg

Turning Point Project
666 Pennsylvania Avenue
  SE, Suite 302
Washington, DC 20003
Tel: 800-249-8712
www.turnpoint.org

Volunteermatch
ImpactOnline, Inc.
385 Grove Street
San Francisco, CA 94102
Tel: 415-214-6868
www.volunteermatch.org

Working Assets
Tel: 877-255-9253
www.workingforchange.com

## EDUCATION

Center for Commercial-
Free Public Education
1714 Franklin Street,
Suite 100-306
Oakland, CA 94612
Tel: 510-268-1100
www.commercialfree.org

Parents for Public Schools
1520 North State Street
Jackson, MS 39202
Tel: 800-880-1222
www.parents4public
schools.com

Project NatureConnect
Box 1605
Friday Harbor, WA 98259
Tel: 360-378-6313
www.ecopsych.com

## FOOD, FARMING, AND HEALTH

Acres, USA
P.O. Box 91299
Austin, TX 78709
Tel: 512-892-4400
www.acresusa.com

American Community
Gardening Association
100 North 20th Street,
5th Floor
Philadelphia, PA 19103
Tel: 215-988-8785
www.communitygarden.org

American Farmland Trust
1200 Eighteenth Street
  NW, Suite 800
Washington, DC 20036
Tel: 202-331-7300
www.farmland.org

Center for Rural Affairs
101 South Tallman
P.O. Box 406
Walthill, NE 68067
Tel: 402-846-5428
www.cfra.org

Council for
Responsible Genetics
5 Upland Road, Suite 3
Cambridge, MA 02140
Tel: 617-868-0870
www.gene-watch.org

E. F. Schumacher Society
140 Jug End Road
Great Barrington, MA
  01230
Tel: 413-528-1737
www.schumachersociety.org

GeneWatch UK
The Mill House
Manchester Road,
Tideswell
Buxton, Derbyshire
SK17 8LN UK
Tel: 44-129-887-1898
www.genewatch.org

Institute for Agriculture
and Trade Policy
1313 Fifth Street, Suite 303
Minneapolis, MN 55414
Tel: 612-379-5980
www.ifg.org/ifa

Institute for Food and
Development Policy
(Food First)
398 Sixtieth Street
Oakland, CA 94608
Tel: 510-654-4400
www.foodfirst.org

Institute for Local
Self-Reliance
1313 Fifth Street SE
Minneapolis, MN 55414
Tel: 612-379-3815
www.ilsr.org

Kerr Center for
Sustainable Agriculture
P.O. Box 588
Poteau, OK 74953
Tel: 918-647-9123
www.kerrcenter.com

Organic Consumers
Association
6114 Highway 61
Little Marais, MN 55614
Tel: 218-226-4164
www.purefood.org

Organic Farmers
Marketing Association
8364 South SR 39
Clayton, IN 46118
(no phone number given)
www.iquest.net/ofma

Pesticide Action Network
North America
49 Powell Street, Suite 500
San Francisco, CA 94102
Tel: 415-981-1771
www.panna.org

Plant a Row for
the Hungry
10210 Leatherleaf Court
Manassas, VA 20111
Tel: 877-492-2727
www.gwaa.org

Redefining Progress
1904 Franklin Street,
6th Floor
Oakland, CA 94612
Tel: 510-444-3041
www.rprogress.org

Rural Advancement
Foundation International
(RAFI)
110 Osborne Street,
Suite 202
Winnipeg, MB
R3L 1Y5 Canada
Tel: 204-453-5259
www.rafi.org

Washington Tilth Journal
Tilth Producers
P.O. Box 85056
Seattle, WA 98145
Tel: 206-442-7620
(no website available)

We The People
200 Harrison Street
Oakland, CA 94607
Tel: 510-836-3272
www.wtp.org

Western Sustainable
Agriculture Working
Group
3040 Belvidere Avenue SW
Seattle, WA 98126
Tel: 206-935-8738
www.ecobio.com/wsawg

WHY—Innovative
Solutions to Hunger
and Poverty
505 Eighth Avenue,
21st Floor
New York, NY 10018
Tel: 212-629-8850
www.worldhungeryear.org

Women, Food, and
Agriculture Network
59624 Chicago Road
Atlantic, IA 50022
Tel: 712-243-3264
(no website available)

## ANIMAL RIGHTS

Animal Welfare Institute
P.O. Box 3650
Washington, DC 20007
Tel: 202-337-2332
www.animalwelfare.com

The Humane Society of
the United States
2100 L Street NW
Washington, DC 20037
Tel: 202-452-1100
www.hsus.org

National Wildlife
Federation
8925 Leesburg Pike
Vienna, VA 22184
Tel: 703-790-4000
www.nwf.org

People for the Ethical
Treatment of Animals
501 Front Street
Norfolk, VA 23510 ➤

Tel: 757-622-7382
www.peta-online.org

Sea Turtle Restoration
Project,
P.O. Box 400
Forest Knolls, CA 94933
Tel: 415-488-0370
www.seaturtles.org

World Wildlife Fund
1250 Twenty-fourth Street NW
Washington, DC 20037
Tel: 202-293-4800
www.panda.org

## ENVIRONMENTAL ISSUES

Center for Energy
Efficiency and Renewable
Technology
1100 Eleventh Street,
Suite 311
Sacramento, CA 95814
Tel: 916-442-7785
www.ceert.org

Earth Island Institute
300 Broadway
San Francisco, CA 94133
Tel: 415-788-3666
www.earthisland.org

Earthjustice Legal
Defense Fund
203 Hoge Building
705 Second Avenue
Seattle, WA 98104
Tel: 206-343-7340
www.earthjustice.org

Environmental
Defense Fund
257 Park Avenue South
New York, NY 10010
Tel: 800-684-3322
www.edf.org

Environmental
Working Group
Washington State Office
Nickerson Marina Building
1080 West Ewing Place,
Suite 301
Seattle, WA 09119
Tel: 206-286-1235
www.ewg.org

Friends of the Earth
1025 Vermont Avenue NW,
3rd Floor
Washington, DC 20005
Tel: 202-783-7400
www.foe.org

Global Ecovillage Network
Western Hemisphere:
560 Farm Road
P.O. Box 90
Summertown, TN 38483
Tel: 931-964-3992
www.gaia.org

Greenpeace
1436 U Street NW
Washington, DC 20009
Tel: 202-462-1177
www.greenpeace.org

Honor the Earth
2801 Twenty-first
  Avenue South
Minneapolis, MN 55407
Tel: 800-327-8407
www.honorearth.com

Indigenous Environmental
Network
P.O. Box 485
Bemidji, MN 56601
Tel: 218-751-4967
www.alphacdc.com/ien

International Council for
Local Environmental
Initiatives
15 Shattuck Square,
Suite 215
Berkeley, CA 94704 ➤

Tel: 510-540-8843
www.iclei.org

International Rivers
Network
1847 Berkeley Way
Berkeley, CA 94703
Tel: 510-848-1155
www.irn.org

International Society for
Ecology and Culture
P.O. Box 9475
Berkeley, CA 94709
Tel: 510-527-3873
www.isec.org

League of
Conservation Voters
1707 L Street NW,
Suite 750
Washington, DC 20036
Tel: 202-785-8683
www.lcv.org

National Association of
Physicians for the
Environment
1643 Prince Street
Alexandria, VA 22314
(no phone number listed)
www.napenet.org

Natural Resources
Defense Council
40 West 20th Street
New York, NY 10011
Tel: 212-727-2700
www.nrdc.org

Northwest Ecosystem
Alliance
1421 Cornwall Avenue,
Suite 201
Bellingham, WA 98225
Tel: 360-671-9950
www.ecosystem.org

Northwest
Environment Watch
1402 Third Avenue, ➤

Suite 500
Seattle, WA 98101
Tel: 206-447-1880
www.northwestwatch.org

Rainforest Action Network
221 Pine Street, Suite 500
San Francisco, CA 94104
Tel: 415-398-4404
www.ran.org

Sierra Club
85 Second Street,
2nd Floor
San Francisco, CA 94105
Tel: 415-977-5500
www.sierraclub.org

Sierra Club Global
Warming Web Site
www.toowarm.org

Smart Wood
Program/Rainforest
Alliance
Goodwin-Baker Building
Richmond, VT 05477
Tel: 802-434-5491
www.smartwood.org

Student Environmental
Action Coalition
P.O. Box 31909
Philadelphia, PA 19104
Tel: 215-222-4711
www.seac.org

Sustainable Northwest
620 SW Main Street,
Suite 112
Portland, OR 97205
Tel: 503-221-6911
www.sustainablenorth
west.org

Union of Concerned
Scientists
2 Brattle Square
Cambridge, MA 02238
Tel: 617-547-5552
www.ucsusa.org

West Coast
Environmental Law
1001-207 West Hastings
Street
Vancouver, BC
V6B 1H7 Canada
Tel: 800-330-9235
www.wcel.org

Worldwatch Institute
1776 Massachusetts
Avenue NW
Washington, DC 20036
Tel: 202-452-1999
www.worldwatch.org

## LABOR RIGHTS, CIVIL RIGHTS, AND HUMAN RIGHTS

AFL-CIO
815 Sixteenth Street NW
Washington, DC 20006
Tel: 202-639-5000
www.aflcio.org

American Civil
Liberties Union
125 Broad Street,
18th Floor
New York, NY 10004
Tel: 212-344-3005
www.aclu.org

American Civil Liberties
Union of Washington
705 Second Avenue,
Suite 300
Seattle, WA 98104
Tel: 206-624-2184
www.aclu-wa.org (for
updated information about
the ACLU WTO Report)

Amnesty International
500 Sansome Street,
Suite 615
San Francisco, CA 94111
Tel: 415-291-9233 ➤

www.aiusa.org
www.amnesty.org

Center for Campus
Organizing
165 Friend Street, #1
Boston, MA 02114
Tel: 617-725-2886
www.cco.org

Center for Study of
Responsive Law
P.O. Box 19367
Washington, DC 20036
Tel: 202-234-5176
www.csrl.org

En'owchin Center
257 Brunswick Street
Penticton, BC
V2A 5P9 Canada
Tel: 604-493-7181
(no website available)

Foundation on
Economic Trends
1660 L Street NW,
Suite 216
Washington, DC 20036
Tel: 202-466-2823
www.biotechcentury.org

Free Burma Coalition
www.freeburma.org

Global Exchange
2017 Mission Street, #303
San Francisco, CA 94110
Tel: 415-255-7296
www.globalexchange.org

Human Rights in China
350 Fifth Avenue,
Suite 3309
New York, NY 10118
Tel: 212-239-4495
www.hrichina.org

Human Rights Watch
350 Fifth Avenue,
34th Floor ➤

New York, NY 10118
Tel: 212-290-4700
www.hrw.org

Indigenous Peoples
Council on Biocolonialism
P.O. Box 818
Wadsworth, NV 89424
Tel: 775-835-6932
www.ipcb.org

International Labor
Rights Fund
733 Fifteenth Street NW,
Suite 920
Washington, DC 20005
Tel: 202-347-4100
www.laborrights.org

Jobs with Justice
501 Third Street NW
Washington, DC 20001
Tel: 202-434-1106
www.jwj.org

National Labor Committee
15 Union Square West
New York, NY 10003
Tel: 212-242-0700
www.nlcnet.org

National Organization
for Women
735 Fifteenth Street NW,
2nd Floor
Washington, DC 20005
Tel: 202-628-8669
www.now.org

Observatoire de la
Globalisation Economique
14 Grande Rue
Sauve, 30610
France
Tel: 33-046-677-0704
www.ifg.org (go to link:
IFG Associates)

People's Assembly
Sentenaryo Ng Bayan
4501 Fifteenth Avenue,
Suite 101
Seattle, WA 98108
Tel: 206-763-9611
(no website available)

People's Decade for
Human Rights Education
Headquarters:
Eurolink Business Centre,
Suite 13
49 Effra Road, London
SW2 1BZ UK
Tel: 44-171-924-0169
Grassroots Outreach
Office:
526 West 111th Street,
Suite 4E
New York, NY 10025
Tel: 212-749-3156
www.pdhre.org

Program on Corporations,
Law, and Democracy
P.O. Box 246
South Yarmouth, MA 02664
Tel: 508-398-1145
www.poclad.org

Public Citizen's Global
Trade Watch
215 Pennsylvania
 Avenue SE
Washington, DC 20003
Tel: 202-546-4996
www.tradewatch.org

Reclaim Democracy
P.O. Box 532
Boulder, CO 80306
Tel: 303-402-0105
www.reclaimdemocracy.org

Southwest Network for
Environmental and
Economic Justice
211 Tenth Street
Albuquerque, NM 87102 ➤

Tel: 505-527-3873
(no website available)

Sweatshop Watch
310 Eighth Street,
Suite 309
Oakland, CA 94607
(no phone number listed)
www.sweatshopwatch.org

Tibet Information
Network
USA:
P.O. Box 2270
Jackson, WY 83001
Tel: 307-733-4670
England:
City Cloisters
188-196 Old Street, London
EC1V 9FR UK
Tel: 44-207-814-9011
www.tibetinfo.net

The Transnational Institute
Paulus Potterstraat 20
1071 DA Amsterdam
The Netherlands
Tel: 011-31-20-662-6608
www.tri.org

United for a Fair
Economy/Share the
Wealth
27 Temple Place, 2nd Floor
Boston, MA 02111
Tel: 617-423-2148
www.stw.org

USTAWI (economic justice
in Africa)
7500 Greenwood Avenue
 North, Suite 414
Seattle, WA 98103
Tel: 206-297-0311
www.ustawi.org

Women's Environment and
Development Organization
(WEDO)
355 Lexington Avenue
New York, NY 10017 ➤

Tel: 212-973-0325
www.wedo.org

WTO History Project
Center for Labor Studies
University of Washington
Box 353530
Seattle, WA 98195
Tel: 206-543-7946
www.depts.washington.ed
u/pcls

## DISARMAMENT AND NONVIOLENCE

20/20 Vision
1828 Jefferson Place NW
Washington, DC 20036
Tel: 800-669-1782
www.2020vision.org

Alliance for Nuclear
Accountability
Washington, DC:
1801 Eighteenth Street NW
Washington, DC 20009
Tel: 202-833-4668
Seattle:
1914 North 34th Street,
Suite 407
Seattle, WA 98103
Tel: 206-547-3175
www.ananuclear.org

Coalition to Stop
Gun Violence
1000 Sixteenth Street NW,
Suite 600
Washington, DC 20036
Tel: 202-530-5888
www.csgv.org
www.endhandgunvio
lence.org

Community Action
Network
P.O. Box 95113
Seattle, WA 98145
Tel: 206-632-1656
www.seattlecan.org

End the Arms Race
405-825 Granville Street
Vancouver, BC
V6Z 1K9 Canada
Tel: 604-687-3223
www.peacewire.org

Ground Zero Center for
Nonviolent Action
16159 Clear Creek Road
Poulsbo, WA 98370
Tel: 360-377-2586
www.gzcenter.org

International Campaign to
Ban Landmines
110 Maryland Avenue NE
Washington, DC 20002
Tel: 202-547-2667
www.icbl.org

International Network on
Disarmament and
Globalization
405-825 Granville Street
Vancouver, BC
V6Z 1K9 Canada
Tel: 604-687-3223
www.indg.org

The Nonviolence Web
P.O. Box 30947
Philadelphia, PA 19104
Tel: 215-382-4876
www.nonviolence.org

Northwest Disarmament
Coalition
c/o Washington
Physicians for Social
Responsibility
4554 Twelfth Avenue NE
Seattle, WA 98105
Tel: 206-547-2630
www.wpsr.org

Peace Action
1819 H Street NW,
Suite 420
Washington, DC 20006 ➤

Tel: 202-862-9740
www.peace-action.org

Peace Action of
Washington
5828 Roosevelt Way NE
Seattle, WA 98105
Tel: 206-527-8050
www.peaceaction.gen.
wa.us

Women's International
League for Peace and
Freedom
1213 Race Street
Philadelphia, PA 19107
Tel: 215-563-7110
www.wilpf.org

## KEEP THE FAITH

Alternatives for
Simple Living
P.O. Box 2787
Sioux City, IA 51106
Tel: 800-821-6153
www.simpleliving.org

Bread for the World
50 F Street NW, Suite 500
Washington, DC 20001
Tel: 800-822-7323
www.bread.org

Buddhist Peace
Fellowship
P.O. Box 46560
Berkeley, CA 94704
Tel: 510-525-8596
www.bpf.com

Canadian Ecumenical
Jubilee Initiative
P.O. Box 772, Station "F"
Toronto, ON
M4Y 2N6 Canada
Tel: 416-927-0234
www.web.net/~jubilee

Catholic Worker
36 East First Street
New York, NY 10003
Tel: 212-777-9617
www.catholicworker.org

Diocese of Olympia
1551 Tenth Avenue East
Seattle, WA 98102
Tel: 206-325-4200
www.olympia.anglican.org

Earth Ministry
1305 NE 47th Street
Seattle, WA 98105
Tel: 206-632-2426
www.earthministry.org

Episcopal Office of Peace
and Justice
815 Second Avenue
New York, NY 10017
Tel: 212-867-8400
www.ecusa.anglican.org

Fellowship of Reconciliation
P.O. Box 271
Nyack, NY 10960
Tel: 914-358-4601
www.forusa.org

Jewish Peace Fellowship
P.O. Box 271
Nyack, NY 10960
Tel: 914-358-4601
www.jewishpeacefellow
ship.org

Jubilee 2000/USA
Campaign
222 East Capitol Street
Washington, DC 20003
Tel: 202-783-3566
www.j2000usa.org

Lutheran Peace
Fellowship
1710 Eleventh Avenue
Seattle, WA 98122
Tel: 206-720-0313
www.lutheranpeace.org

The Naropa Institute
2130 Arapahoe Avenue
Boulder, CO 80302
Tel: 800-772-6951
www.naropa.edu

Pax Christi
532 West 8th Street
Erie, PA 16502
Tel: 814-453-4955
www.nonviolence.org

Peace Action Group
Plymouth Congregational
Church
1217 Sixth Avenue
Seattle, WA 98101
Tel: 206-622-4865
(no website available)

Sojourners
2401 Fifteenth Street NW
Washington, DC 20009 ➤

Tel: 202-328-8842
www.sojourners.com

Unitarian Universalist
Peace Committee
6556 Thirty-fifth Avenue NE
Seattle, WA 98115
Tel: 206-525-8400
(no website available)

# SOME SUGGESTED READING

This is an abbreviated list, eclectic with information and inspiration. I could not begin to offer a comprehensive selection of reading material regarding such widespread issues. So this list is drawn from the books that informed this writing journey, books that were suggested by friends, by those in-the-know and by respected authors, magazines and newsletters. The word is out and the books are out there.

Ausubel, Kenny. *Restoring the Earth: Visionary Solutions from the Bioneers.* Tiberon, CA: H. J. Kramer, 1997.

Bagdikian, Ben. *The Media Monopoly,* 5th ed. Boston: Beacon Press, 1997.

Barks, Coleman, and Michael Green. *The Illuminated Rumi.* New York: Broadway Books, 1997.

Berry, Wendell. *Life Is a Miracle.* Washington, DC: Counterpoint Press, 2000.

———. *The Unsettling of America: Culture and Agriculture.* San Francisco: Sierra Club Books, 1977.

Borg, Marcus J., ed., *Jesus at 2000.* Boulder, CO: Westview Press, 1998.

Brill, Hal, Jack Brill, and Cliff Feigenbaum. *Investing with Your Values: Making Money and Making a Difference.* Princeton, NJ: Bloomberg Press, 1999.

Carson, Rachel. *The Edge of the Sea.* Boston: Houghton Mifflin, 1955.

Chomsky, Noam. *Profit Over People: Neoliberalism and Global Order.* New York: Seven Stories Press, 1999.

Chossudovsky, Michel. *The Globalization of Poverty.* London: Zed Books, 1997.

Cohen, Michael J. *Reconnecting with Nature: Finding Wellness Through Restoring Your Bond With the Earth.* Corvalis, OR: Ecopress, 1997.

*also home study psychology-and-nature courses through Project NatureConnect, Tel: 360-378-6313; www.ecopsych.com

Cutler, Howard, and His Holiness the Dalai Lama. *The Art of Happiness.* New York: Riverhead Books, 1998.

Dyer, Joel. *Harvest of Rage: Why Rural America Has Declared War.* New York: Westview Press, 1997.

French, Hilary. *Vanishing Borders: Protecting the Planet in the Age of Globalization.* New York: W. W. Norton 2000.

Fukuoka, Masanobu. *The One-Straw Revolution.* Emmaus, PA: Rodale Press, 1978.

George, Susan, and Fabrizio Sabelli. *Faith and Credit: The World Bank's Secular Empire.* Boulder, CO: Westview Press, 1994.

Goodall, Jane. *Reason for Hope: A Spiritual Journey.* New York: Warner Books, 1999.

Hartmann, Thom. *The Last Hours of Ancient Sunlight: Waking Up to Personal and Global Transformation.* New York: Harmony Books, 1999.

Hawken, Paul, Amory Lovins, and L. Hunter Lovins. *Natural Capitalism: Creating the Next Industrial Revolution.* Boston: Little, Brown, 1999.

Henderson, Hazel. *Building a Win-Win World: Life Beyond Global Economic Warfare.* San Francisco: Berrett-Koehler, 1996.

Hogan, Linda. *Dwellings: A Spiritual History of the Living World.* New York: W. W. Norton & Co., 1995.

*Housmans Peace Diary: With World Peace Directory.* London: New Society Publishers, 2000.

Khor, Martin et al. "Views from the South: The Effects of Globalization and the WTO on Third World Countries." International Forum on Globalization, Sausalito, CA, 1999, soft-cover book.
*available at www.ifg.org

Klein, Naomi. *No Logo: Taking Aim at the Brand Bullies.* New York: Picador USA, 1999.

Korten, David C. *Globalizing Civil Society.* New York: Seven Stories Press, 1998.

———. *The Post-Corporate World.* San Francisco: Hartford, CT: Kumarian Press, Inc.; San Francisco: Berrett-Koehler Publishers, Inc., 1999.

———. *When Corporations Rule the World.* West Hartford, CT: Kumarian Press, Inc.; San Francisco: Berrett-Koehler Publishers, Inc., 1995.

Krebs, A. V. *The Corporate Reapers: The Book of Agribusiness.* Washington, DC: Essential Books, 1992.

LaDuke, Winona. *All Our Relations: Native Struggle for Land and Life.* Cambridge, MA: South End Press, 1999.

MacArthur, John R. *The Selling of Free Trade: NAFTA, Washington and the Subversion of American Democracy.* New York: Hill and Wang, 2000.

Macy, Joanna. *World As Lover, World As Self.* Berkeley, CA: Parallax Press, 1991.

Mander, Jerry. *In the Absence of the Sacred: The Failure of Technology and the Survival of the Indian Nations.* San Francisco: Sierra Club Books, 1991.

Mander, Jerry, and Edward Goldsmith, eds. *The Case Against the Global Economy: And for a Turn Toward the Local.* San Francisco: Sierra Club Books, 1996.

Miller, Kenneth R. *Finding Darwin's God.* New York: Cliff Street Books, 1999.

Mitchell, Stephen. *Tao Te Ching.* San Francisco: Harper & Row, 1998.

Mokhiber, Russell, and Robert Weissman. *Corporate Predators: The Hunt for Mega-Profits and the Attack on Democracy.* Monroe, ME: Common Courage Press, 1999.

Moore, Thomas. *The Re-Enchantment of Everyday Life.* New York: HarperCollins, 1996.

Nhat Hanh, Thich. *Living Buddha, Living Christ.* New York: Riverhead Books, 1995.

Norberg-Hodge, Helena. *Ancient Futures: Learning from Ladakh.* San Francisco: Sierra Club Books, 1991.

Oliver, Mary. *New and Selected Poems.* Boston: Beacon Press, 1993.

Parenti, Michael. *History As Mystery.* San Francisco: City Lights Books, 1999.

Rifkin, Jeremy. *The Biotech Century: Harnessing the Gene and Remaking the World.* New York: Jeremy P. Tarcher/Putnam, 1998.

————. *The Decline of Work: The Decline of the Global Labor Force and the Dawn of the Post-Market Era.* New York: G.P. Putnam's Sons, 1995.

Roy, Arundhati. *The Cost of Living.* New York: Modern Library Paperback, 1999.

Schiller, Herbert. *Information Inequality: The Deepening Social Crisis in America.* New York: Routledge, 1996.

Sewall, Laura. *Sight and Sensibility: The Ecopsychology of Perception.* New York: Jeremy P. Tarcher/Putnam, 1999.

Shiva, Vandana. *Monocultures of the Mind: Perspectives on Biodiversity and Biotechnology.* London: Zed Press, 1993.

Shrybman, Steven. *The World Trade Organization: A Citizen's Guide.* Canada: James Lorimer and Co. Ltd., 1999.

Shuman, Michael. *Going Local: Creating Self-Reliant Communities in a Global Age.* New York: Free Press, 1998.

Snyder, Gary. *Turtle Island.* New York: New Directions, 1974.

Stout, Linda. *Bridging the Class Divide and Other Lessons for Grassroots Organizing.* Boston: Beacon Press, 1996.

Trungpa, Chogyam. *Shambhala: The Sacred Path of the Warrior.* Boulder, CO: Shambhala, 1984.

Wallach, Lori, and Michelle Sforza. *Whose Trade Organization: Corporate Globalization and the Erosion of Democracy.* Washington, DC: Public Citizen, 1999.

# ACKNOWLEDGMENTS

Writing this book broke my heart. I went to the WTO demonstrations in Seattle for my own idiosyncratic reasons, but it was only when I started working on this book that I discovered the real reasons why I should have been there. The extent of poverty and hardship on the planet is directly related to the extent of wealth we enjoy. This is a truth that's hard to accept, and accepting it is the only way to begin to make a difference. I acknowledge the billions of people to whom the basics of food, shelter, healthcare, and education are but a distant dream. I wish it were different.

Thank you to all those who grow the food and make the things in my life. I am grateful, and acknowledge that I am lucky: however, very little of what I pay for both staples and luxuries goes to the person who made them or grew them. This isn't right and I wish it were different.

Thank you to everyone who is working, in one way or another, for justice on the planet. As I researched, interviewed, and read the work of such writers as Maude Barlow, David Korten, Jerry Mander, Russell Mokhiber, Michael Parenti, Vandana Shiva, Steven Shrybman, and Robert Weissman, and encountered the hundreds of organizations committed to bringing about social justice, I was stunned by how much is going on out there. We just don't hear about it from the mainstream media. I wish it were different.

Thank you to everyone who shared their story in this book: Joanne Calhoun, Carolyn Canafax, Michael Cohen, Tom Forster, Vanessa Lee, Fred Miller, Michael Mossberg, Hannah Petros, Anne Schwartz, Rick Simonson, Sally Soriano, Pete Strimer, Sarah Joy Staude, Bishop Vincent Warner, Ben White, who risks everything, and Brian Moss who taught me that risk is everything. They brought this book to life. And to all whose names surfaced in the telling of this story, thank you for all you are doing. To all First Peoples, sacred sovereignty. May we somehow make amends.

My faith communities—Episcopal and Buddhist alike—have taught me more about tolerance than I will ever know. Thank you in particular to Rev. West and Sue Davis, Emma Eden, and Kandace Loewen for helping me come out of the closet as a Christian—laughing much of the way. Deep gratitude to my Buddhist teachers who helped me come out, period. And thanks to the work of Larry Dossey who taught me that prayer is everywhere; to Michael Cohen who taught me that nature works, even when I don't; to Rev. Lauren Artress who led me to the labyrinth. And to the Tibetan Buddhist monks who cast the colored sands from their mandala into the waters off Jackson Beach, a bow of gratitude. I go there every day.

I have a magnificent family of friends in Seattle and on Bainbridge Island who gave me ongoing support, information, contacts, places to sleep, things to eat, to read, and to be glad about as this book got written. Thanks everlasting to Martha Brice, Martha Brouwer, Annie Duggan, Bruce Dearborn, John Pappenheimer, Martha Scott, Bob Smith, Barb Vose, and Bonnie and David Snedeker. And on San Juan Island, big thanks to Roy and Nancy Cope, Bob and Barbara Dann, Nancy DeVaux, Thrinley DiMarco, Louise and John Dustrude, Kitty Farmer, Joyce and Byron Harrell, Marietta and George Koch, Nancy Larsen, Christine Miller, Craig and Krispi Staude, Agi Vadas and the canasta queens, Susan Vernon, Susan Campbell-Dick and Janet Wright, my island book group, my folkdancing friends at the Dann's, to everyone with whom I ever played soccer, to Robert Bates who keeps my head on straight, to Dynne Mercer, my bi-coastal buddy who keeps me housed, and, of course, to Lee and Tal Sturdivant, who, as usual, keep me on course. Many others generously offered information and support. Thank you; you know who you are.

Images are everything. Thanks to photographers Debi Abelson, Todd Kowalski, and Gloria Marohl for eye and interest; to Dana Schuerholz whose cover photograph says it all; to designer Kate Thompson who created an elegant design almost overnight; and to designer Constance Bollen for her work on the book's formatting. Thanks to filmmaker Shaya Mercer, and to Jeremy Simer and Seattle's Independent Media Center who know what democracy looks like. To Bill Clifford, who knows what anarchy looks like, and to sculptor Dutch Schultz, who knows what courage (and the Spanish Civil War) looks like. My Seminarian friends met without me, but thanks to Philip and Rachel Levine for keeping me in the loop and Tom Jay for inspiration. Thanks to Richard Neill who's still there, and to Erika Goldstein and Len Hudson whose compassion—political and otherwise—has not been forgotten.

And to Elizabeth Wales and Alice Acheson, thank you for wordly, and worldly, advice.

There are special people in the world who rise up from the ashes and know that true power has no name. Sandy Bishop. I love you. And Rhea Miller, too.

On N30, RA Haynie gave me a bus pass; Frederick Bindel offered me five bucks for lunch; Susan Wilson said, "go"; Steve Ludwig gave me a lift and bought me a "No to WTO" sign; Martha Brouwer picked me up afterward.

During the months behind closed doors, my wonderful son, Colin Casabelos, brought me food and helped when all else failed. Alli and Davin Highley gave me courage and were patient as I disappeared so often from view. Bob Lemon took me up Mount Constitution and introduced me to my own. May we always walk on the wild side.

Fulcrum Publishing is an up-close-and-personal company and no writer could have received better support. A terrific editorial team corrected everything from punctuation to politics; thanks to Kris Fulsaas, Sherri Schultz, Erin Lawson, Amy Timms, and Daniel Forrest-Bank.

Fulcrum publisher Bob Baron supported this book all the way with a single-minded vision rare in this mega-merger world. Independence is as independents do. Thank you. We need you. And to editor-in-chief, Marlene Blessing, who said this book must be written, and then made sure that it was, I owe the greatest of gratitude. Writing it introduced me to my global family and my life will never be the same.

# INDEX